USING YOUR SUPPLY CHAIN AS A COMPETITIVE WEAPON

USING YOUR SUPPLY CHAIN AS A COMPETITIVE WEAPON

A Practitioner's Guide to Supply Chain Management

DR. TONY VERCILLO

USING YOUR SUPPLY CHAIN AS A COMPETITIVE WEAPON
A PRACTITIONER'S GUIDE TO SUPPLY CHAIN MANAGEMENT

Copyright © 2014 Dr. Tony Vercillo.

All rights reserved. No part of this book may be used or reproduced by any means, graphic, electronic, or mechanical, including photocopying, recording, taping or by any information storage retrieval system without the written permission of the publisher except in the case of brief quotations embodied in critical articles and reviews.

Because of the dynamic nature of the Internet, any web addresses or links contained in this book may have changed since publication and may no longer be valid. The views expressed in this work are solely those of the author and do not necessarily reflect the views of the publisher, and the publisher hereby disclaims any responsibility for them.

Any people depicted in stock imagery provided by Thinkstock are models, and such images are being used for illustrative purposes only.
Certain stock imagery © Thinkstock.

eBook ISBN: 979-8-8691-6556-5
Paperback ISBN: 978-1-0881-5846-3
Hardcover ISBN: 979-8-8691-6555-8

Library of Congress Control Number: 2014918553

Print information available on the last page.

CONTENTS

About the Author..vii
Preface...ix
Acknowledgments..xi
Introduction..xiii
CHAPTER 1　The Evolution of Supply Chain Management...................1
CHAPTER 2　Prescription for Success..14
CHAPTER 3　Supply Management: The Need for a Global Outlook....25
CHAPTER 4　Outsourcing...57
CHAPTER 5　Order Processing and Customer Service.......................76
CHAPTER 6　Forecasting and Demand Planning................................93
CHAPTER 7　Inventory Management and Control............................113
CHAPTER 8　Logistics and Distribution Management.....................141
CHAPTER 9　Warehousing and Material Handling..........................180
CHAPTER 10　Supply Chain Metrics and Monitoring........................224
CHAPTER 11　The Application of Technology within the
　　　　　　　Supply-Chain...240
CHAPTER 12　Supply-Chain Network Design and Optimization........256
Epilogue...291
Subject Index...295
Recommended Reading..299

ABOUT THE AUTHOR

Dr. Tony Vercillo is a 25-year veteran in the Supply Chain industry. He has a Doctorate in Marketing Management, with special emphasis in Global Supply Chain Theory (summa cum laude). He also received his MBA in Leadership and Human Behavior. Dr. Vercillo is a highly sought-after public speaker known for his "infectious-enthusiasm. " Dr. Vercillo has been a global marketing and supply chain consultant for the past twenty years, performing more than 350 projects in more than twenty countries. He also served as a senior-level Manager and Vice President for PepsiCo and a third-party supply chain firm. Dr. Vercillo also teaches Global Marketing and Supply Chain Theory in the Cal State University system. His passion in life is teaching and coaching and has spent the last fifteen years fulfilling that dream. He resides in Southern California and has three children.

You can contact Dr. Vercillo at:
www. ifmcinc. com
http://www. linkedin. com/in/tonyvercillo
www. Facebook. com/Tony. Vercillo

Follow Dr. Vercillo on Twitter - @DrTVercillo

PREFACE

The impetus behind the writing of *Using your Supply Chain as a Competitive Weapon* was clearly my clients and students. I owe a great deal to both of these groups. Many of my customers and Master's students encouraged me to articulate my thoughts, citing my real-world, visa-vi just academic, experience as the main reason to document my approach. Although many of my colleagues have written excellent works in the field of Supply Chain and Logistics, I'd like to think that the true point of difference for this book is the blending of academic theory with a practitioner's added viewpoint. Simply stated, I practice what I preach.

Using your Supply Chain as a Competitive Weapon is a mix of academic theories, real-world cases studies from actual clients, some consulting methodologies, and a little bit of street-smarts. The primary focus of this work is to provide you with both the theoretical foundation and industry body-of-knowledge along with some practical initiatives that will truly make a difference. By writing this book, I have tried to bring to life many of the actual supply chain initiatives I often recommend to my clients. After implementing many of these tried-and-true approaches to Supply Chain Theory, infrastructure costs at client companies have been reduced by millions of dollars. I can only hope that you experience the same level of success.

The rationale for writing this book is simple. I wanted to answer the question, *"What is supply chain management and why should*

I care about it?" I also wanted to provide my clients and students with a supply chain management template that works. If you follow the prescriptions for success I have provided you in this work, I sincerely believe you will reduce your overall supply chain costs considerably.

I decided to write the book in a way that it would be accepted both as a trade work and a quasi-textbook so it can be used academically and in industry. The case studies I used for this work are actual client projects that worked; meaning, the project was successful and saved the client in most cases millions of dollars.

Note: I intentionally cloaked the company names in all of the case studies to protect the proprietary nature of the consulting engagements.

ACKNOWLEDGMENTS

I found this section to be one of the most difficult to write. I owe thanks to so many people who have encouraged me, kept me on the straight-and-narrow path, and praised me when I shined yet scolded me softly when I messed up. Here goes.

To start, I owe a lot of "who" I became to two people, both coincidentally named John. To John Ledwith, my original Mentor, who took a risk on a young 16-year year old Brooklyn boy and taught him (me) the ropes. He forced me to be accountable for my actions, and used patience to teach me about business. I think about him often.

To John Thyne, my boss at PepsiCo, who groomed me, kicked my butt when I deserved it, and taught me about people...you shaped my character and I owe you a great deal for pushing me toward success.

To Dr. Irene Lange and Pat Lussier at Cal State Fullerton, who both saw something in me and "gifted" me with the pleasure of teaching. Thanks for believing in me.

To my three children, Anthony, Darien, and Nicolas, who are my reason for living...thanks for understanding when I missed that occasional soccer game, party, or other event because I was traveling.

Please know that my heart was always with you no matter what part of the globe I may have been at the time.

To my students who have blessed me with years of enjoyment...many of you have touched my heart and I just hope I have given back a little in return. You make all the late nights of evening classes worth it for me and I feel truly honored to have crossed your paths.

INTRODUCTION

Using your Supply Chain as a Competitive Weapon is an attempt to provide you with some tools that, when applied, will make your supply chain a force to be reckoned with. The primary focus of this work is simple; to reveal some implementable strategies and tactics that will reduce overall supply chain costs while increasing service. When formulating the outline for this book, I struggled to document my personal definition of supply chain management. After considerable thought, I arrived at this explanation:

> "Supply Chain Management is a philosophy, attitude, and approach that uses quantitative and qualitative methods to minimize infrastructure, process, and delivery costs while maintaining service levels."

It is this definition that drove me to think about the hundreds of projects I have been involved in that either improved process or reduced costs. Supply chain management, particularly in the global economy we now enjoy, has become a way to level the playing field against the competition and create a sustainable advantage in the marketplace. What we have learned over the past decade is that supply chain theory can be applied to any business and make a real difference in the area of profitability. We have also finally figured out that 80% of all supply chains are identical regardless of the product being delivered. While this may sound hard to believe it is less doubtful when you consider that all supply chains have orders, processing, customer service, payables, and delivery or pickup of some kind, etc. If you take a leap of faith with me that most supply chains act in a similar manner, then you can further conclude that most sound supply chain tactics can be applied across a countless number of businesses.

The purpose of this book is to provide you with a playbook and a set of guiding principles that, when applied, will positively *tweak* a business in order to reduce costs or improve process control. The objectives of this work are:

1. To reveal the best practices and methodologies that work each and every time.

2. To give you real-world implementation strategies that will make a difference.

3. To show you case studies where we used the strategies outlined in this book in practice.

4. To document my 25 years as a supply chain strategist.

The best way to use this book is to use it as you would a school textbook. Highlight the critical concepts you find interesting and lift the templates and documents I've provided to use at your company. You may also want to carefully review each summary and answer the questions at the end of each chapter to ensure your comprehension. In addition, you should assign some of the questions or application exercises to your staff as a fun way to gain buy-in. One more thing... although all the cases studies are taken from real clients, I disguised the company names as most of the work is considered proprietary.

Let's rock.

1 THE EVOLUTION OF SUPPLY CHAIN MANAGEMENT

"If automobiles had followed the same development cycle as the computer, a Rolls-Royce would today cost $100, get a million miles per gallon, and explode once a year, killing everyone inside."

Robert Cringely

It's not your Father's Buick was an advertising campaign used by General Motors to signify that the Buick automobile had evolved into something trendier and more appealing to the younger generation. GM even hired Tiger Woods in an attempt to make the Buick more *hip*. This ad campaign attempted to show how the Buick had evolved over time from an old-man's car to a younger person's ride. The same can be said for supply chain management.

What was once solely a logistics function has now evolved into a multi-faceted and all-encompassing functional area that spans the entire enterprise. Essentially, the word logistics was replaced with the word distribution, which later got replaced with the phrase supply chain.

The evolution is shown in the following tables:

Exhibit 1.1 - Corporate Supply Chain Vernacular and Responsibility Evolution

Functional Area Name	Years Used	Roles and Responsibilities
Fleet Management	1970-1980	Private Fleet Management
Transportation	1980-1990	Freight, Traffic, Fleet
Distribution	1990-2000	Inbound & Outbound Distribution
Logistics	1995-2005	Distribution, Warehousing, Supply
Supply Chain	2000 & Beyond	Distribution, Warehousing, Inventory, Order Processing, Material Handling, Supply, Customer Service, Reverse Logistics.

Exhibit 1.2 - Supply Chain Management Orientation and Evolution

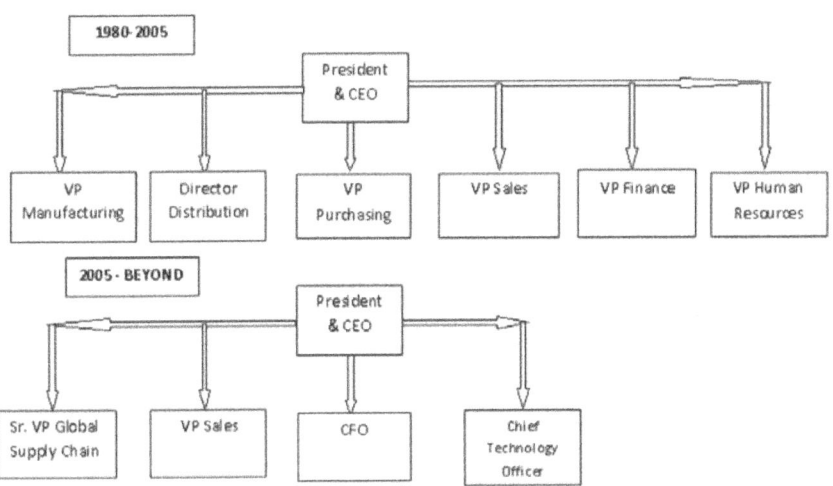

Exhibit 1.3 - World Class Supply Chain Progression

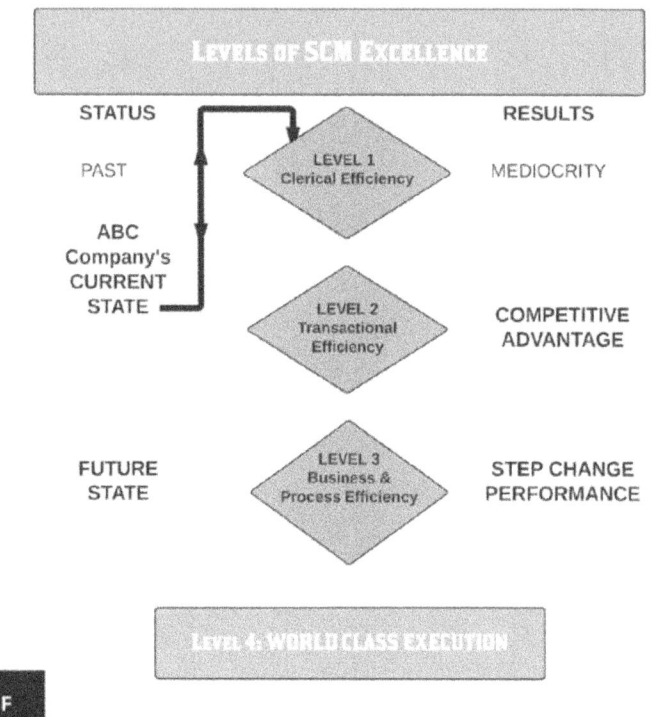

As seen in the accompanying chart, corporate supply chains typically operate at a certain level of efficiency, categorized by their behavior. These stages of supply chain prowess help to rate the level of effectiveness evidenced by the supply chain's ability to efficiently move goods and materials along the chain. There are four (4) stages of supply chain effectiveness:

Level 1: Clerical Stage
Level 2: Transactional Stage
Level 3: Process Efficiency Stage
Level 4: World Class Stage

It is important to note that most company supply chains tend to operate in between two stages. For example, even the most inefficient supply chain operating primarily in the clerical stage may be good at transactions, albeit manually performed.

Level I – Clerical Stage

Signs that your Supply Chain is in the Clerical Stage:
- Spreadsheets "R" Us
- Paperwork Abounds
- Data Integrity Issues
- Manually Intensive Efforts
- Lack of Technology
- Lack of Key Metrics
- Lack of Process Control
- Working *in* the Business, not *on* the Business

Level II – Transactional Stage

Signs that your Supply Chain is in the Transactional Stage:
- Focused on Order Completion
- Reacting to Events
- Data available but located in four functional areas
- Manual efforts still obvious
- Some Technology
- Low Level Reporting of Key Indicators
- Starting to pay attention to Process Control
- Working on developing a Strategic Plan

Level III – Process Efficiency Stage

Signs that your Supply Chain is in the Process Efficiency Stage:
- Focused on Process Control
- Formal Quality Control Program in Place
- Data located in one main source
- Less Manual Efforts
- Technology in place but too many systems not 'talking' to each other
- Reporting of Key Indicators

- Emphasis on Cost, Quality, and Time
- Coordinated Efforts
- Strategic Plan in Place

Level IV – World Class Execution Stage

Signs that your Supply Chain is in the World Class Execution Stage:
- Strategic & Global Sourcing in Place
- Six Sigma or Equivalent Utilized for Quality Control
- Systems are Integrated across the Enterprise
- Practically no Manual Efforts
- Information drives the business, not the other way around
- Executive Information Summary (EIS) of Key Metrics
- Emphasis on compressing order cycle time and tightening on-time delivery
- Time and Place driven
- Understands and measures the true cost of customer service
- Functional Harmony due to common reward system
- Strategic Plan driving management behavior

Exhibit 1.4 - Logistics Costs as a % of Revenue

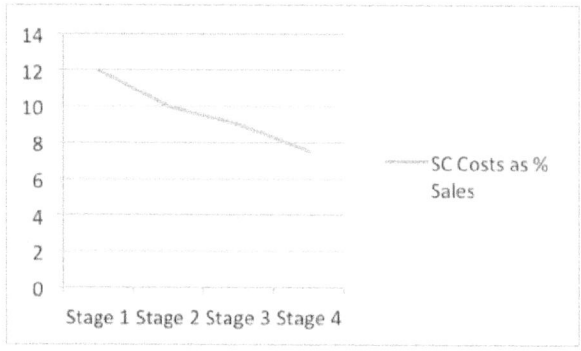

The evolution of supply chain management is evidenced by four (4) dynamics:
1. A change in vernacular and industry terms/names.
2. A flattening of organizational management structure.
3. A progression toward world class supply chain execution.
4. A reduction in Supply Chain costs as a % of Sales (Exhibit 1.4).

Over the past twenty years, as industries started to consolidate and contract, many companies reacted by collapsing departments and flattening organizational structure. The days of old-school logistics and fleet management are gone. Most progressive and world-class organizations have eliminated functional disharmony by folding most operational activities under a senior supply chain executive. At the same time, the vernacular of old was replaced by words such as supply chain, global supply, and distribution instead of transportation.

This normal evolutionary cycle has forced organizations to become introspective; that is, to assess their supply chain effectiveness against the competition. This can be seen in Exhibit 1.3 which reveals the four stages of supply chain execution. As sad as this may sound, even in an era where technology has exploded and computer speed has caused the cost per bit of information to be drastically reduced, I would venture a guess that 70% of our client companies were operating in Stage 1 or Stage 2. Only in the past decade or so has supply chain execution become paramount or a means of gaining a sustainable competitive edge. Exhibit 1.4 shows how the progression to Stage 4 supply chain execution impacts overall infrastructure costs. The best run companies that have embraced supply chain theory as a means of gaining competitive ground have realized a significant reduction in costs.

Companies that operate in Stage IV have figured out that having too many vice presidents causes functional disharmony, conflicting priorities and reward systems, and plain old organizational chaos. By flattening the organization and placing all supply chain activities under one roof the corresponding effect is a smoother run organization focused on sales and operational excellence. A world-class supply chain places a great deal of emphasis on *time* and *place*.

The Definition of Supply Chain Management

As mentioned in the introduction, my definition of supply chain management (SCM) is:

"SCM is a philosophy, attitude, and approach, that uses quantitative and qualitative methods to minimize infrastructure, process, and delivery costs while maintaining service levels."

Supply chain management is now the new logistics, which has historically been defined as the flow and delivery of goods and services to the right place, at the right time, in the right quantity, at the lowest cost.

Supply chain management is the only function within an organization that touches each and every other department within an enterprise. Co-dependencies exist between sales, manufacturing, finance, distribution, customer service, etc. and the supply chain. These co-dependencies create the need for a synergistic relationship that fosters common goals and priorities. The evolution to supply chain management has also forced many firms to re-evaluate the reward systems they have in place to create synergy, common goals and priorities, and metrics that foster functional cooperation. In reality, most large companies finally figured out that they needed to insist senior executives learn to play well together in the sandbox without all the finger-pointing, back-stabbing, and the every-person-for-themselves mentality.

Exhibit 1.5 - Supply Chain Activities

Supply chain management has become quite complex as shown in the activities chart below:

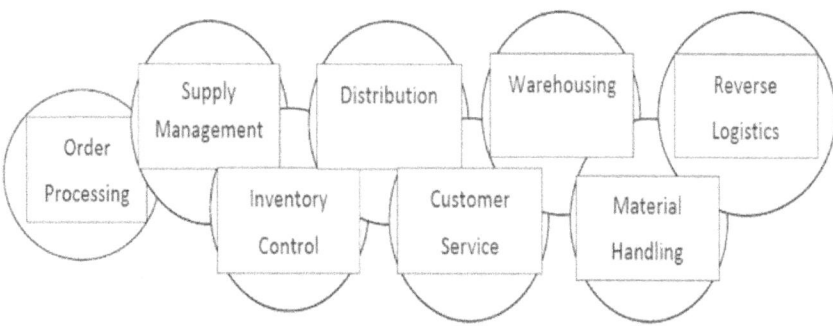

The number of activities and tasks that have been added to supply chain management has increased three-fold over the past decade.

The supply chain team now manages most non-sales activities and is responsible for overall operational execution. In essence, the supply chain manager is the operational general manager who controls the flow of goods and information.

Exhibit 1.6 - The Importance of Supply Chain Management

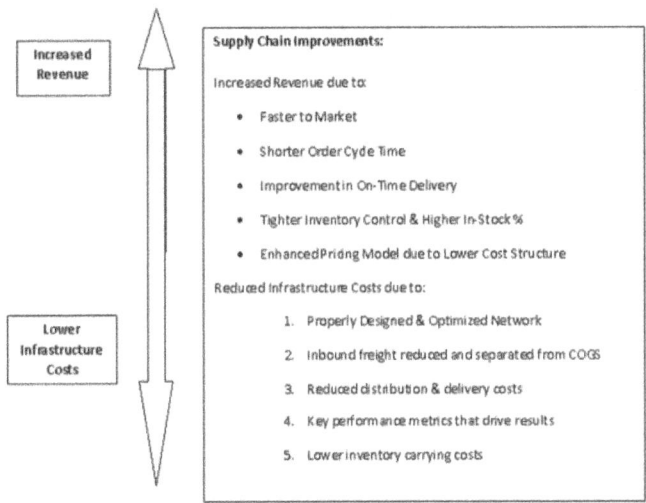

Source: Adapted from World Class Supply Management. Dobler.

As shown in Exhibit 1.6, proper Supply Chain Management can have a dramatic impact on profitability, productivity, and even sales. The appropriate application of supply chain theory will work wonders in the areas of tighter inventory control, lower freight and delivery costs, improvements in customer satisfaction, and yes, even increased sales. In fact, after a two-year revamping of one company's supply chain strategy, a customer actually went to the trouble of writing a letter praising the firm for its operational excellence. That's when you know you have made it; when customers are continuing to come back due to your supply chain superiority.

In later chapters, we will explore how supply chain management positively impacts each area within the enterprise. We shall also delve into the specific tactics to use to create the ultimate supply chain.

Flexibility by no Other Name

As seen in the accompanying exhibits, supply chain management (in particular logistics costs) have dropped in recent years driven primarily by the economic downturn the United States experienced in 2007/2008. As the economic crisis continued to squeeze American businesses, many companies reacted by hunkering-down and reducing capital expenditures while tightening their belts by reducing excess inventory. Inventory carrying costs at the same time dropped dramatically as the government lowered interest rates to stimulate the economy. The drop in logistics costs as a percent of GDP and corresponding reduction in overall logistics costs (Exhibits 1.7 and Exhibit 1.8) as reported by the Council of Supply Chain Management Professionals is the most significant decrease we have seen in twenty years.

Exhibit 1.7 - Logistics as a % of GDP

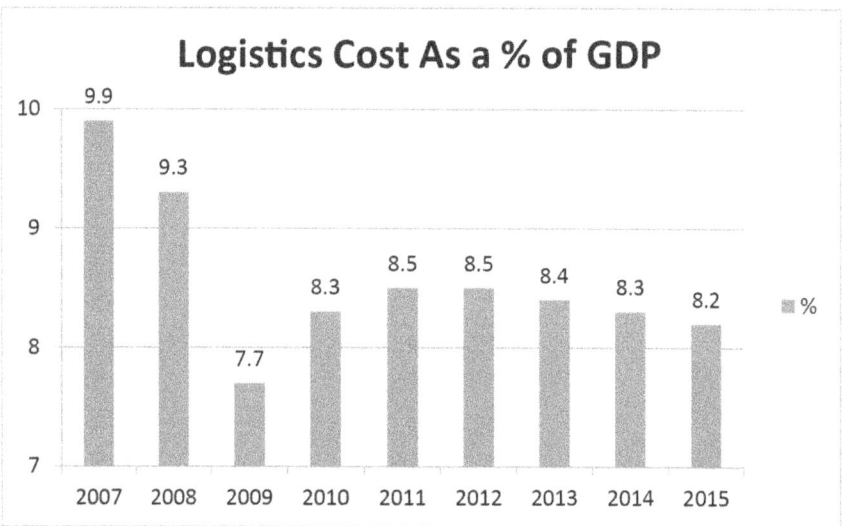

Source: 2007-2012 Council of Supply Chain Management Professionals. 2013-2015 estimate – IFMC, Inc.

Exhibit 1.8 - U. S. Business Logistics Costs Graph

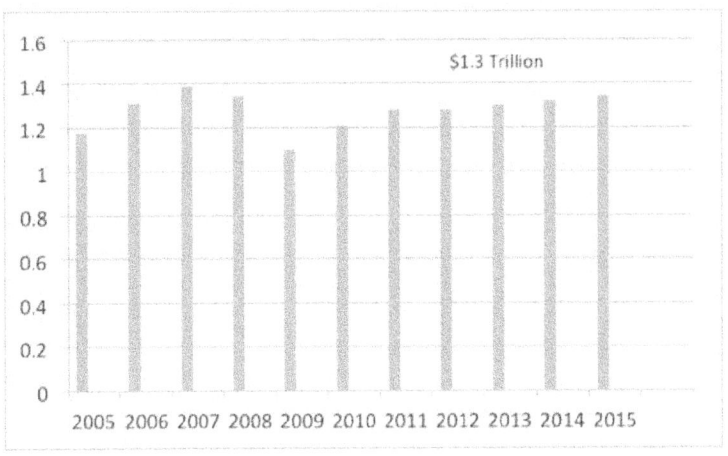

Source: 2005-2012 Council of Supply Chain Management Professionals. 2013-2015F IFMC, Inc.

The good news here is that these charts can be viewed as somewhat empirical evidence that supply chain flexibility is a powerful way to assist companies in bad times. World class supply chain firms have been able to weather the storm the past few years through continued emphasis on time and place; that is, applying non-stop pressure on the organization to improve in-stock %, on-time delivery, perfect orders, and inventory control.

Conclusion

The evolution of supply chain management was driven by a few forces, namely, globalization, the speed of information (technology) and finally, a forced efficiency placed upon U. S. -based firms as industry collapsed and consolidated over time. The globalization of the world economy has created a significant need for alternative sourcing methods as we try to compete on a global landscape. In addition, computer speed and the explosion of the Internet and social media have made business communication more instantaneous and global in reach.

The real question that must be asked here is what is the next generation of supply chain management? Will their eventually be a more formal supply chain certification that is akin to a CPA designation? Will supply chain extend its reach outside of operations or continue to focus on efficiency and effectiveness of infrastructure? An argument can clearly be made that other than sales & marketing, supply chain strategists may take on a broader role in American business. Only time will tell. On a personal note, I believe supply chain managers should be elevated within the organizational structure on par with all other executives.

Chapter Summary

- Supply chain evolution has been driven by globalization and technology.

- Supply chain management attempts to place extreme emphasis on time and place through the tightening of the order cycle and improvement in distribution and delivery methods.

- World class supply chain management *flexes* by spending to the business; they flourish in good times and contract in bad times.

- The first step toward world-class supply chain management is an assessment of the current state. What level of efficiency or execution is evident at your company?

- Supply chain activities include order processing, customer service, forecasting, inventory control, inbound and outbound freight, physical distribution, and supply management.

- Supply chain management can improve speed to market and have a significant impact on profitability.

- World class supply chain management includes the axiom, "The customer is *usually* right," as opposed to always which works for Nordstrom's but can cripple other types of firms.

Exploratory Questions

- What evolution have you seen in terms of management structure?
- How has technology changed the way we do business?
- Have logistics costs dropped in your industry?
- What do you think the future is for supply chain management?
- What does the expression, "the world is shrinking" mean for supply chain management?
- Will supply chain costs continue to drop the next ten years?
- Will supply chain managers take on an expanded role in business?
- In your experience, what level of supply chain efficiency do most companies execute?
- Do you think all firms should go global with supply? Why or why not?
- What does the future hold for supply chain management?

Case Study – LBI Company

LBI is a publicly traded company in Michigan. They manufacture fine furniture and distribute through retail stores throughout the United States. LBI had numerous divisions and a fragmented headquarters staff that was looking after many of the company supply chain activities. LBI is an excellent run company that did not see the need for an overall supply chain strategy. Due to some acquisitions, the CFO requested a detailed look at the existing supply chain strategy with special emphasis placed on:

- Organizational design
- Division synergies
- Cost reduction
- Process improvement.

During the study, we uncovered the need for an overall Supply Chain Strategic Plan that would address these four major areas along with identifying the correct structure that would best fit with the strategy. As the saying goes, structure always follows strategy. Over the course of 18 months we worked with LBI to develop a cross-divisional strategic plan that included an expansion of the role of supply chain management, a change in managerial titles, and the establishment of key performance metrics that cut across divisional lines. In addition, we were asked to recommend specific tactical initiatives that might bring cost savings while we were revamping the network design. At the conclusion of the consulting engagement, the following results were realized:

1. A three-year Strategic Plan was developed and embraced throughout the various divisions
2. Key metrics were put in place to drive results
3. The organizational structure was revamped to best suit the new design
4. Three specific cost savings initiatives were uncovered that ultimately saved millions.

Case Study Questions:

1. Why do you think so much emphasis was placed upon the development of a Strategic Plan?

2. Why does structure always follow strategy?

3. Why do companies that are acquiring other firms go through such growing pains? What are the supply chain issues that may develop as a function of a new division being added to the mix?

2 PRESCRIPTION FOR SUCCESS

"A most important key to successful leadership is your ability to direct and challenge the very best that is in those whom you lead."

Anonymous

In the field of supply chain management, the key to success is to start with a plan. As the saying goes, *"Those who fail to plan, plan to fail."* The objective of this chapter is to provide a roadmap to follow that will ensure a step-change or transformational leap in supply chain performance. In this chapter, you will find a strategic plan template to use, an outline of the major issues that supply-chain managers are facing, and the ten steps to world class supply chain management. When these steps are implemented in earnest, good things will happen, specifically: A decrease in total order cycle time, an increase in in-stock percentage and on-time delivery, a reduction in inventory levels, and an overall decrease in total supply chain infrastructure and operational costs. The rest of the book will then provide the theoretical framework surrounding each of the ten steps.

What makes supply chain management so difficult? To begin with, it is the never-ending change of business development cycle which occurs in most businesses that impacts the overall supply chain network, making it very difficult to stabilize or keep aligned.

Secondarily, due to conflicting priorities and functional silos that exist in most organizations, attempting to minimize overall system wide costs while maintaining service levels is a daunting task. Finally, there is always a level of uncertainty and risk in any supply chain directly associated with the forecasting of customer demand and other external economic influences beyond the control of the supply chain group that make it extremely difficult to manage.

To that end, here are the major issues that a supply chain manager faces in these turbulent economic times:

Major Strategic Issues in Supply Chain Management

1. Aligning supply with demand and attempting to properly forecast to minimize inventory investment while maintaining appropriate in-stock levels. Managing production levels and inbound goods from suppliers is no easy task and requires a sophisticated forecasting method to ensure continuity of supply at a minimal investment.

2. Offshoring, outsourcing, and the need for just-in-time inventory have complicated supply chain management, making it both an art and a science. Lead time management from overseas, lack of third-party control, and uncertainty in transportation creates unprecedented risk. In addition, due the global nature of supply, many supply chains are now subjected to worldwide catastrophic events or natural disasters which fundamentally increase the odds of failure exponentially.

3. Distribution uncertainty. Transportation is impacted by a variety of factors including, rising ocean and freight rates, an increase in tariffs and customs/duties, an increase in the average time product is being held in customs, and a contracting of available freight carriers. This has caused a dramatic increase in the risk associated with overseas supply and a narrowing of the landed cost gap between foreign manufactures and the United States.

These three major issues make the competitive nature of supply chain management a difficult task to say the least. In fact, supply chain managers today must manage a number of functional areas to create a sustainable competitive advantage, including:
- Product Design and Specification Assistance
- Revenue Management Strategy and Assistance
- Network Design and Optimization
- Supply Management and Sourcing
- Strategic Supplier Relationships
- Offshoring and Outsourcing Strategies
- Inventory Investment and Control
- Distribution and Freight Management
- Key Performance Metrics and Management
- Information Technology and Integration
- Customer Service
- Reverse Logistics.

To attack these issues, here are the ten steps to supply chain effectiveness:

Exhibit 2.1 - World Class Supply Chain Tenets

Tenet	Sample Tactical Initiatives
• Develop a Strategic Global Vision.	• Develop a supply-chain plan • Globally source products • Set up global advisory board • Secure global distributors
• Use Strategic Supplier Relationships.	• Setup supplier task force • Use supplier performance scorecard • Integrate supplier systems • Recognize that workers and suppliers will become more mobile and global in nature

• Implement Critical KPI's to drive results.	• Develop EIS (see Ch. 10) • Track KPI's across entire supply chain • Solicit input from all levels
• Adopt an Inventory is Bad Mentality.	• Set goal of 98% accuracy • Use cycle counting • Strategically reduce safety stock • Recognize that product velocity, or "clock speeds" will determine the nature of supply chains
• Aggressively attack Distribution Costs.	• Eliminate unnecessary miles • Use on-board technology • Track driver productivity
• Be Information and Technology Driven. Recognize that AI (artificial intelligence) will become mainstream within most supply chains.	• Integrate systems across disciplines • Use load-building, routing, and warehouse technology to improve efficiency
• Design & Optimize the lowest infrastructure cost network.	• Minimize supply chain "touch-points" by reducing infrastructure through network rationalization modeling.
• Place Forecasting at the Top of your Priority List.	• Set target of >80% forecast accuracy across all SKU's. • Implement forecast champion to foster accountability. • Implement forecast accuracy incentives.

• Know the cost and tradeoff associated with your Customer Service Level. *Understand that service chains will become more important than product chains.*	• Develop in-stock % that makes business sense. • Understand the true cost of customer service (scrutinize order processing costs). • Know the cost of a backorder and reverse logistics.
• Don't forget about Warehousing & Material Handling.	• Set cost/hour and units/hour targets for the warehouse. • Set cost/hour goal for material handling units. • Use Technology to drive efficiency.

These ten steps provide the foundation for supply chain effectiveness. When implemented, these ten steps and corresponding tactical initiatives will result in the following:

1. A reduction in total order cycle time (TOCT) of 1-2 days
2. A reduction in obsolete and safety stock inventory of 10%-20%
3. A 20% reduction in distribution costs
4. A 10-30% decrease in COGS (product costs or cost of goods sold)
5. An increase in warehouse case/unit velocity of 15%
6. A 10% improvement in forecast accuracy
7. A dramatic improvement in order processing costs
8. A significant improvement (reduction) in the cash-to-cash cycle.

The first step to implementing the ten steps is the development of a Supply Chain Strategic Plan. The plan should be on a short time horizon; let's say three years due to the volatile nature of the economy which translates into consistent change. The Strategic Plan should at least include all the elements shown in following chart.

Exhibit 2.2 Strategic Plan Components

The steps to the strategic planning process include:

- Collect historical data and conduct data analysis.
- Perform an environmental scan and SWOTT analysis including:
  - Internal assessment of staffing and resources
  - External assessment of the general economy and regulatory environment
  - Major strengths of the organization
  - Major weaknesses of the organization
  - Major opportunities and threats, including competitive threats
  - Major industry trends that may impact the plan.

- Identify critical issues facing the organization.
- Document the top five goals/objectives of the organization.
- Develop the future vision of the supply chain.
- Construct the tactical mission statement and key objectives to accomplish.
- Formulate key tactical initiatives that attack each objective.
- Prepare the operational plan, including line-by-line costs and key assumptions and risks.
- Develop annual (three-year) targets for each major cost driver and performance indicator.
- Incorporate change and culture management into the plan.

One final thought about strategic planning and that is the supply chain plan must be clearly aligned with the overall goals and objectives of the company. This will ensure not only the acceptance of the supply chain plan, but will also create a continuity of purpose by making sure that all employees in the company boat are rowing in the same direction.

Conclusion

The development and monitoring of a supply chain strategic plan will prime the engine and create the roadmap for success. When developing a strategic plan, a supply chain manager should incorporate the ten keys to supply chain effectiveness. At the same time, it is critical to consider and include the major issues facing supply chain management in the plan. The two major learnings here are; globalize your supply chain strategy while using local execution of tactical initiatives to drive results, and remember that structure follows strategy. In other words, supply chain managers must develop a strategic plan before putting their resource plan together that will ultimately execute the plan. Following this prescription for success ensures continuity of supply, enhanced customer service, and the lowest overall infrastructure costs.

Chapter Summary

- Supply chain teams are facing a significant number of issues today, making the management of global supply and the execution of delivery more difficult than ever before.

- Supply chain management cuts across all functional disciplines, causing inherent conflicts that make streamlining of the overall network a difficult task.

- The first step to supply chain effectiveness is the development of a strategic plan.

- There are ten major steps to creating supply chain effectiveness. These steps, when implemented, will create a competitive advantage stemming from lower infrastructure costs and higher levels of customer service.

- Globalization has created a whole new set of variables to manage such as increased lead times, supply uncertainty, and risk management.

- Supply chain management can be summarized as the aggressive control of supply and demand.

- Properly managing the major tenets of supply chain management yields significant results including a reduction in overall infrastructure costs, a lowering of inventory investment, and an improvement in service levels.

Exploratory Questions

1. Why is a supply chain strategic plan so important?

2. What is meant by the expression, structure follows strategy?

3. What are the key elements of a strategic plan?

4. What are the major issues in supply chain management?

5. What are some of the factors that must be managed as it relates to uncertainty and risk?

6. Why is offshoring more difficult than it seems?

7. Why must a supply chain strategic plan be aligned with overall company objectives?

8. What might be the result of implementing the ten steps to supply chain effectiveness?

Case Study – AW Wine Company

AW Wine is a privately held company in Northern California. They distribute wine throughout the United States through retail/grocery stores and an Internet-based wine club. Due to the competitive nature of the wine business, AW was struggling with excess inventory, an increase in fulfillment costs, and old-school thinking in areas such as technology, and freight/transportation management. The venture capital group that owns AW requested a supply chain diagnostic, with special emphasis on the effectiveness of the supply chain, the application of technology, and the management and control of inventory.

During the assessment, the CFO expressed his desire to become world-class. In addition, he wanted to figure out a way to dramatically reduce on-hand inventory without compromising service. AW also wanted to cut the overall cost to warehouse and ship cases of wine. During the assessment, we discovered the following supply chain issues:

i. Excess inventory of $20 Million.
ii. Inventory accuracy rested at 89% (book-to-physical).
iii. Rising fulfillment costs, estimated to have risen by 13% over a 2-year period.
iv. Poor freight management practices and over-budget shipping costs.

v. Lack of supply chain technology; basically spreadsheets"R"us.
vi. Excessive order processing and customer service costs.

Instead of trying to suggest fixes for these issues individually, we decided to take a more holistic approach by recommending the implementation of an overall supply chain strategic plan that would attack the total supply chain. Using the ten steps to supply chain effectiveness as outlined in this chapter, we recommended the following changes:

1. The re-labeling of the excessive inventory which would allow AW to sell it at a major discount as the carrying cost of inventory was estimated to be approximately $3.5 million/year.

2. The implementation of a formal inventory control policy including weekly cycle counts with problem resolution, the identification of the top five reasons for inventory inaccuracy, and the stratification (ABCD) of the inventory.

3. Outsourcing of the fulfillment process, making the warehousing costs more variable.

4. Overhaul of the inbound supply process including the implementation of economic order quantity for materials, a strategic supplier relationship initiative, and the execution of an RFQ for all inbound freight.

5. A complete process mapping and enhancement initiative to the order processing and customer service functions.

6. The use of a more robust ERP (enterprise resource planning) system.

Two years after the conclusion of the project, AW reported the following results:
- A reduction of excess inventory of $10 million
- Inventory accuracy @ 96.7%

- The elimination of the annual physical inventory due to cycle counting
- A 6% reduction in order processing costs
- A reduction in freight cost/case of 16%
- A reduction of 13% in warehousing/fulfillment rates
- A 3% improvement in on-time delivery to customers.

Case Study Questions:

1. Why reasons could AW have for keeping such a large amount of excess inventory?

2. Why do you think fulfillment and freight are so often overlooked?

3. What other supply chain initiatives might be suggested to improve AW's situation?

3 SUPPLY MANAGEMENT: THE NEED FOR A GLOBAL OUTLOOK

"Supply chains cannot tolerate even 24 hours of disruption. So if you lose your place in the supply chain because of wild behavior you could lose a lot. It would be like pouring cement down one of your oil wells."

Thomas Friedman

At a recent supply chain conference I attended, one of the speakers boldly stated, *"It's not whether or not you think you should go global, it's inevitable. "*I echo this sentiment. Although global sourcing is often fraught with numerous problems, unless the United States becomes either incredibly more productive or figures out how to narrow the cost gap with foreign manufacturers, the need to source products and materials overseas is just going to continue. The goals of this chapter are to provide an appropriate method for fairly evaluating offshoring, to provide insight into the management and economics of the supply function, and to provide suggestions in areas such as quality and supply administration. In this chapter we will also discuss the need for the role of the supply function to be further integrated within the overall supply chain. By the end of this chapter you should have a better understanding of why offshoring is still in vogue and why the supply department needs to use key financial ratios to better manage this critical business activity.

The Role of Supply Management

Supply management spans functional boundaries and organizational borders. At the strategic level, supply management protects a firm from unexpected threats or shortages to inbound materials and supplies along with keeping cost-of-goods (COGS) pricing at a competitive level. The main goal of any supply department is to ensure a constant flow of goods and materials without disruption. At the tactical level, supply management is responsible for the purchasing of goods and materials, the relationship and management of suppliers, and ensuring a high degree of quality.

The supply department should be considered the central hub of activity in that it not only interfaces with all internal functional areas, but also has a relationship with most outside suppliers. In essence, supply management cuts across all departmental lines. The trick here is for supply management to focus on total lowest landed cost of ownership (TCO), being sure to consider the impact that buying will have on production, inventory, distribution/freight, and cash flow. The supply department cannot buy goods in a vacuum. There needs to be a decent level of integration between the supply group and the rest of the functional areas within the firm such that the rest of the organization fully supports the how, what, where, when and why decisions being made by the supply department. The ultimate role of the supply group should be crystal clear; lower total landed COGS, reduce inventory throughout the chain by buying smartly and economically, and ensuring a continuous flow of goods and materials with minimal risk. The secondary role of the supply group is to search the globe for the lowest cost, highest quality goods to ensure an uninterrupted flow of materials.

Exhibit 3.1 - The Important Role of Supply Management

Organizational Decision-Making

Although supply management should report directly to the senior supply chain executive, autonomy must be granted to supply managers to ensure an unbiased approach to decision-making. There has always been a debate about where supply should report; some saying Finance, others Production, while a few still maintain supply should stand alone. In my view, *where* supply reports is not the critical issue. Instead, how the supply department behaves is most important. As long as the supply group acts in a way that benefits the entire organization and not in just a self-serving way, it doesn't matter where it reports.

Centralized – Decentralized Approach

The other organizational design issue that are continually debated is whether centralized authority or decentralized decision-making is the better approach. Centralized decision-making exists when one person or supply group, typically located in headquarters, makes all the purchasing decisions, including those that impact the field locations. Supply activities are all directed and controlled by the main purchasing function. A decentralized approach exists when the field or other departments are granted the authority to make supplier and other purchasing related decisions. There are pros and cons to both approaches, with the main argument for decentralization being local service, shorter lead times, and faster decision-making. That being said, when functioning properly, a centralized approach may lead to increased profits. A properly structured and centralized supply group will create the following organizational benefits:

- **Leveraged volume.** Simply stated, volume discounts are possible when all company buying is tallied-up into one order. The economic power of an organization increases as the volume rises. For example, Wal-Mart, the world's largest retailer, buys at the most competitively priced level, due to the sheer volume of their purchases.

- **Reduction in duplication of effort and administrative burden.** Less chaos exists when orders are consolidated and the cost/purchase order dramatically decreases as you consolidate order processing. Other departments also benefit such as accounts payable and information technology as fewer suppliers translate into less invoices and reduced record keeping/reporting.

- **Standardization of specifications and consistent quality.** Consolidation allows for intense focus on standard product specifications and adherence to an overall supplier quality profile. Quality tends to increase as volume rises.

- **Decreased freight expense.** Rather than a supplier shipping numerous orders using many freight carriers or methods of shipment (LTL, FedEx, etc.), transportation savings will be realized through the consolidation of orders and shipping schedules.

- **Specialization.** Centralization breeds supply specialists whose main area of expertise is the art of purchasing. Specialists tend to buy better than untrained generalists.

- **Lower inventory levels.** Centralized control leads to a reduction in safety stock, increased inventory visibility, controlled lead times, and lower inventory carrying costs.

- **Reduction in supplier-related costs.** Suppliers are more apt to offer lower prices and better service when you help them lower their internal cost of doing business. Centralized supply means fewer sales calls, less order taking, fewer shipments, and less invoicing.

- **Better overall control.** A centralized approach is akin to the old saying, "the buck stops here. "**P**erformance usually improves when you assign accountability to one person or group.

Impact on the Bottom Line

Supply management has always been considered important because of its impact on the bottom line. Since cost of goods (COGS) represents a large expense, procurement is typically treated as an important function within the value-chain due to its effect on revenue and profit. This dynamic makes the supply group a necessary and highly-valued function within any company. In fact, in most manufacturing firms, the supply function is often viewed as a core competency. Why? The reason is simple. In most organizations, the supply group is accountable for spending more than half of every sales dollar on goods and services. As the supply group goes, so does the firm, meaning a well-run supply group might the difference between success and failure. A firm that simply tries to sell its way to profitability may eventually get there, but a firm that excels in supply management would be more likely to save its way to profitability at a faster pace.

In addition, supply management has a significant impact on sales, including:

- An increase in quality, therefore lower reverse logistics (returns) costs
- Creating pricing flexibility by reducing the total cost of ownership
- Speed-to-Market improvements
- Increase in customer satisfaction, therefore more repeat business
- Increased supply chain flexibility
- Overall reduction in total order cycle time (TOCT); from order to store-shelf.

Total Cost of Ownership

A strategic approach to supply management will yield a 20% or more reduction in the total cost of ownership. The total cost of ownership is described as the fully-burdened cost associated with acquiring, owning (including post ownership costs such as returns), and disposing of any material, equipment, finished goods, or services. There are eleven (11) main elements that make-up the total cost of ownership, including:

1. Product development, including engineering, specifications, and design costs.

2. Acquisition Cost, better known as the price paid for an item. This must include the total landed costs, including all taxes, fees, customs, duties, and most importantly, clearly delineated and understood freight expenses.

3. *Note:* As discussed in Chapter 10, one of the mistakes often made by supply groups is the buying of supplier goods on a delivered-price basis. The basic idea here is that delivered pricing is easier and less of a hassle. In addition, Finance tends to like delivered pricing since title to the inventory doesn't change hands until the product is received. However, as we will explore later, studies have shown that inbound cost of freight can be reduced by approximately 15% when the supply group negotiates the shipping rate.

4. The cost of quality evidenced by returns, defects, repeat business, etc. Statistical process control or SPC should be used to ensure that all materials and products meet stated quality targets.

5. Total cycle time in the chain. The shorter the cycle, the lower the cost.

6. The cost associated with risk, which typically manifests in larger inventories to protect against backorders.

7. Downtime costs. In a manufacturing environment, downtime represents a significant percentage of the overall cost of ownership. A few hours of downtime on a production line may cripple an organization's profitability in a given month.

8. Conversion costs. These costs include machine costs, product yield, scrap/waste, and rework.

9. Administrative and Non-Value Added costs. This includes all overhead to manage supply and all the non-value activities that occur in the chain, including the carrying cost of inventory. It might take six months for a case of Pepsi to hit the supermarket shelves and seven months to make it to your refrigerator, but it only takes a few hours to actually make the product. All of the wait and holding time within the value-chain is considered non-value-added.

10. Cost of Technology. This is the cost of systems, reporting, EDI, etc.

11. Post Ownership costs. This cost includes the cost of disposal, scrap, pure waste, the cost of customer service, and the cost of customer satisfaction (lost sales due to customers being unhappy with the product quality).

New Product Development

One activity that requires a great deal of time commitment on the part of supply management is the launching of new products. New product development, including the design, engineering, and quality profile required to successfully launch a product globally is a painstaking process that has more than 100 discrete steps. These steps fall into one of five (5) categories, including:

1. Product Development (proto-type development, CAD drawings, packaging, etc.)
2. Intellectual Property and Legal Protection
3. Marketing and Advertising Plan Development
4. Distribution and Market Penetration Strategy
5. Back-End Services Setup (fulfillment, returns, merchant account, customer service).

Supply management must be involved in each step of the process to ensure a high degree of quality and the lowest possible cost of ownership. Supply management must also get suppliers involved early on in the design process. At the design level, supply management should pay particular attention to lowering costs without sacrificing quality or performance. The new product development process is shown in Exhibit 3.2.

Exhibit 3.2 - Product Development Process

The primary role supply plays in new product development is to consider the tradeoffs associated with the six (6) main attributes that define a product, namely:
- Price
- Cost
- Availability and Degree of Substitution
- Reliability
- Quality
- Performance

The secondary role supply plays is to make sure that all products meet the objectives and specifications originally designed for the product. The major specification categories that need to be considered are shown in Exhibit 3.3.

Exhibit 3.3 - Categories of Specifications

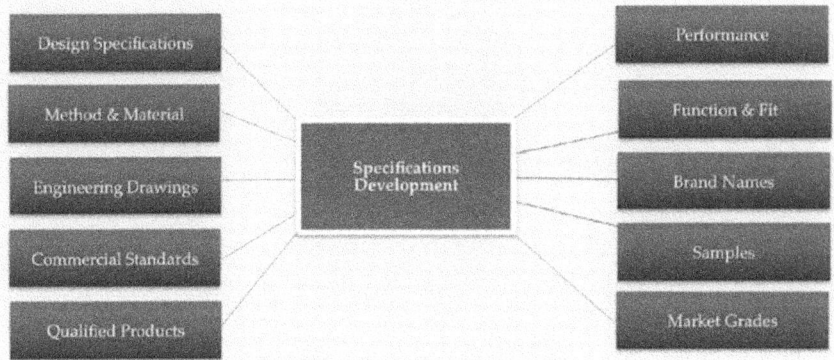

Source: *Supply Management, Burt, Petcavage, Pinkerton.*

Managing Quality

The evolution of manufacturing quality dates back to 1950, immediately following World War II. There have been many quality gurus who created a variety of quality management approaches that have been adopted throughout the world. The main founding fathers of quality include:
- W. Edward Deming
- Genechi Taguchi
- Masaaki Imai
- Phillip Crosby
- Joseph Juran

These men are credited with developing the major management approaches to quality including:
- Six Sigma.
- Total Quality Management.
- Continuous Improvement.
- DMAIC Cycle (define, measure, analyze, improve, control).
- Zero Defects.

The key to managing quality is to use the variety of tools and methodologies stemming from the quality management movement. These statistical process control (SPC) methods have become commonly known as the Seven Tools of Quality. These tools include:

1. **Pareto Charts**. A Pareto chart is a great tool to use when the process you are evaluating reveals data that are broken down into categories and you can count the frequency in which each category occurs. A Pareto chart helps to isolate the biggest contributors to a problem and shows exactly where to focus management efforts.

Exhibit 3.4 - Pareto Chart of Defects

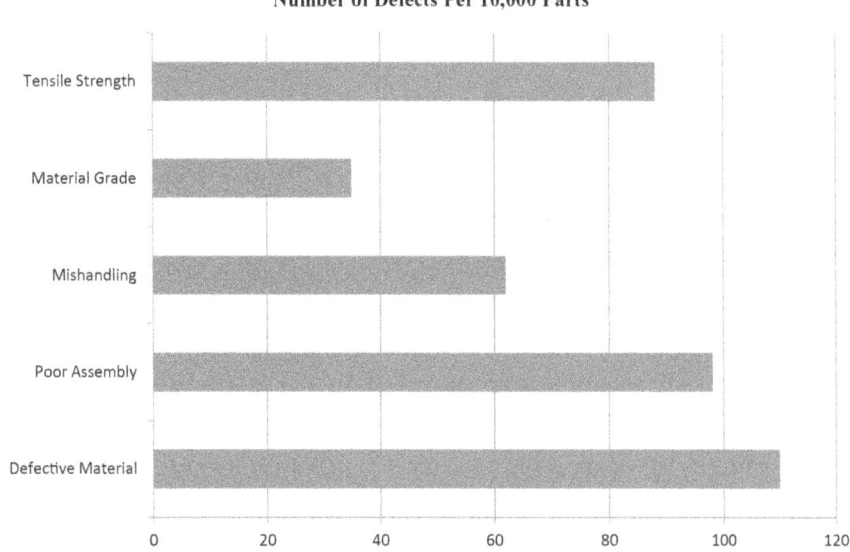

2. **Process Flow Charts**. According to the American Society for Quality (ASQ), a flow chart is a picture of the separate steps to a process placed in sequential order. The process described can be anything: a manufacturing process, an administrative or service process, even a project plan. It is best to use a flowchart:
    - To develop an understanding of how a process is completed.
    - To study a process for improvement.

- To communicate to others how a process is handled.
- When better communication is needed between people involved in the same process.
- To document a process.
- When planning a project.

A sample detailed flowchart of customer orders can be seen in Exhibit 3.5.

Exhibit 3.5 - Detailed Flowchart

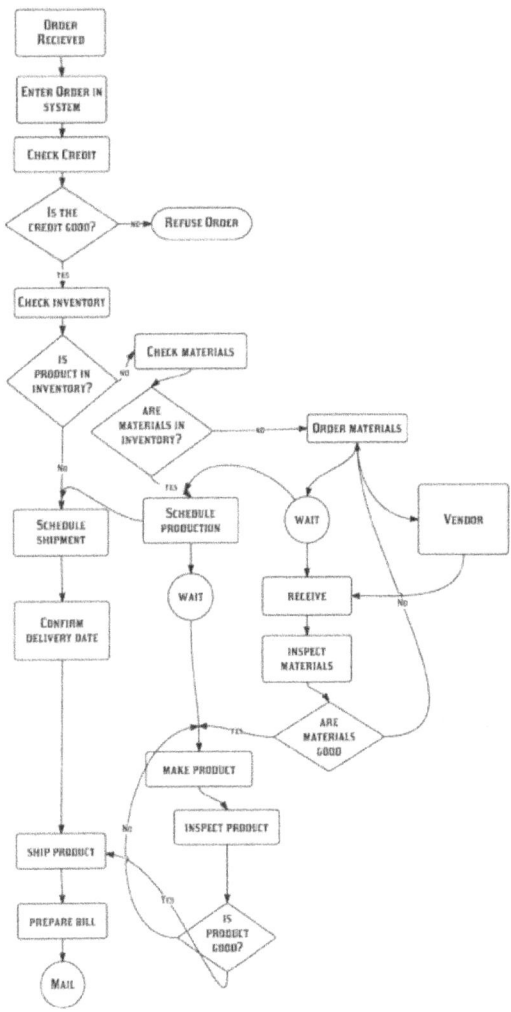

Source: American Society for Quality Website.

3. **Cause and Effect Diagrams.** A cause and effect diagram, also known as a fishbone diagram, is an excellent tool used to identify, sort and display all the possible causes of a problem or quality issue. It graphically illustrates all the root causes that influence a particular outcome. A cause and effect diagram should be used when you need to:
   - Identify the reasons for a problem
   - Evaluate existing problems so corrective action can be taken
   - Sort out or uncover a relationship between factors that impact a process.

Exhibit 3.6 - Cause and Effect Diagram

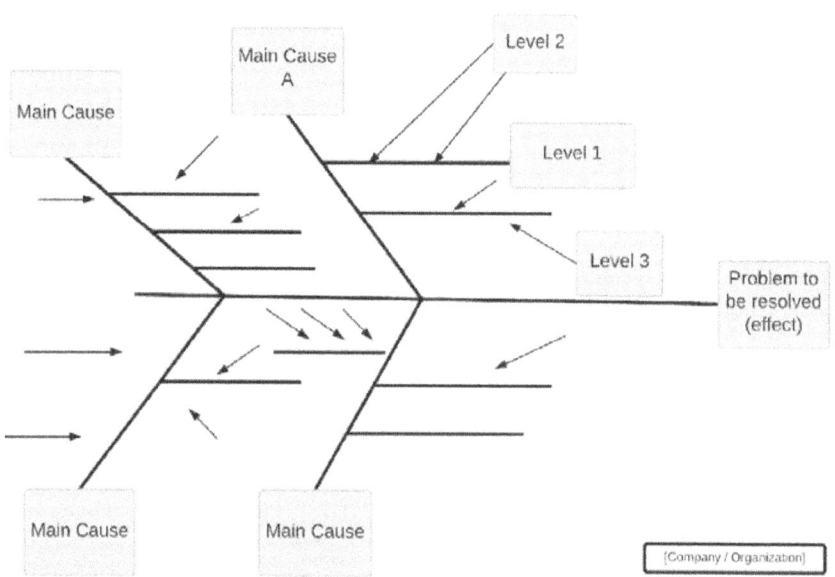

Source: Management Systems, Inc.

4. **Scatter Diagrams.** A scatter diagram is a tool used to analyze the relationship between two variables. It is used to either prove or disprove a cause and effect relationship. A scatter diagram will typically reveal a strong correlation between two variables. A scatter diagram can also be used to search for root causes of problems. Scatter diagrams are a direct result of regression analysis.

Exhibit 3.7 - Scatter Diagram

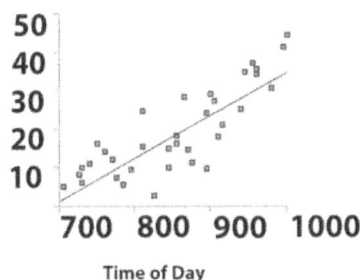

5. **Run Plots.** Run sequence plots are typically the first plots you create in exploratory data analysis (EDA). These plots quickly show data in a visual format and allow you to detect errors and relationship patterns. Run plots are graphs that display observed data in a time sequence.

Exhibit 3.8 - Run Plot Chart

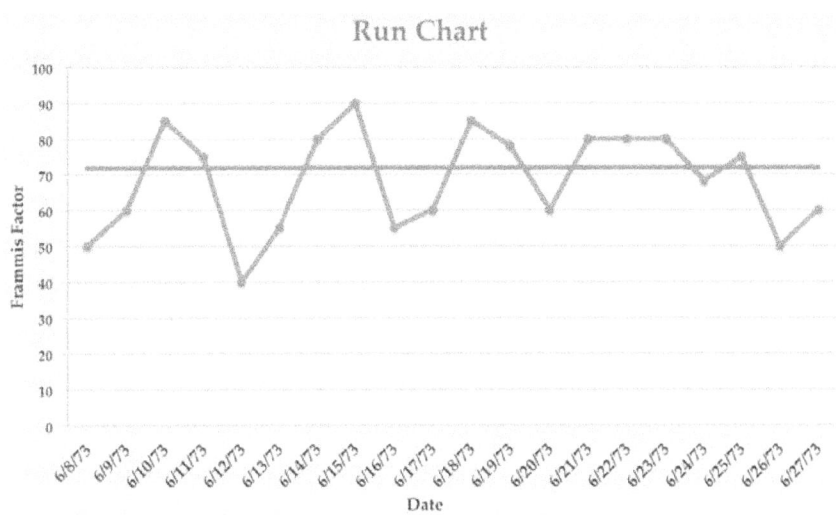

Source: Wikipedia.

6. **Frequency Histograms.** Webster's Dictionary states that a histogram is "a representation of a frequency distribution by means of rectangles whose widths represent class intervals

and whose areas are proportional to the corresponding frequencies. "A histogram represents the number of times something occurs. It can be used to ferret-out the main causes of a problem by revealing which cause occurs most frequently.

Exhibit 3.9 - Histogram.

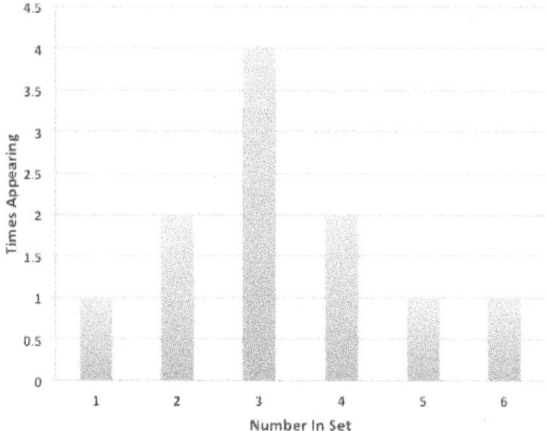

7. **Control Charts.** A control chart is a statistical process tool used primarily to determine whether or not a manufacturing process is within stated standards or limits. A control chart is a disciplined approach that enables better decision making regarding the control of a process.

Exhibit 3.10 - Upper & Lower Control Limit Chart

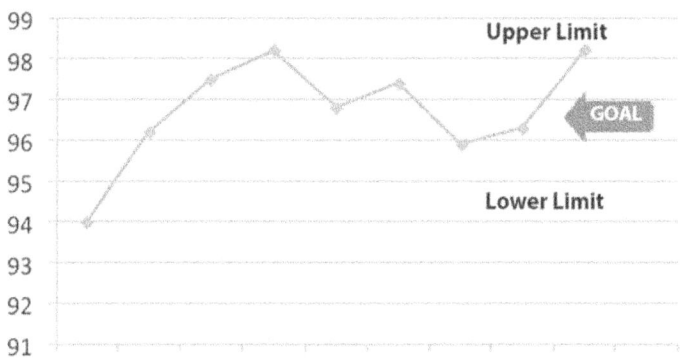

Global Sourcing and the need to go offshore

BusinessDictionary. com defines global sourcing as a procurement strategy in which a business seeks to find the most cost-efficient location for manufacturing a product, even if it's in a foreign country. Let's first discuss why global sourcing is in vogue. It's simple, lower total costs. Global sourcing is now the standard way of doing business in most industries. Why?Because you can expand your supplier base, gain access to advanced technology, and get superior quality. However, global sourcing should not be taken for granted. It is a lot of work and requires a significant level of expertise and experience to do it correctly. In fact, there are global sourcing agents or intermediaries that can assist in transitioning to foreign production. Another dynamic to consider is the "narrowing-of-the-gap" between China and other countries. This may dramatically change the way we do business over the next twenty years. But for now, global sourcing is still a critical function of a well-run supply department.

The first step when deciding where to source should be the development of a strategic sourcing plan. Within the sourcing plan should be specific tactical steps that allow for the transition from treating suppliers as vendors, to the more collaborative term, strategic partners. The key elements to a strategic sourcing plan are shown in Exhibit 3.11.

Exhibit 3.11 - Strategic Sourcing Plan Components

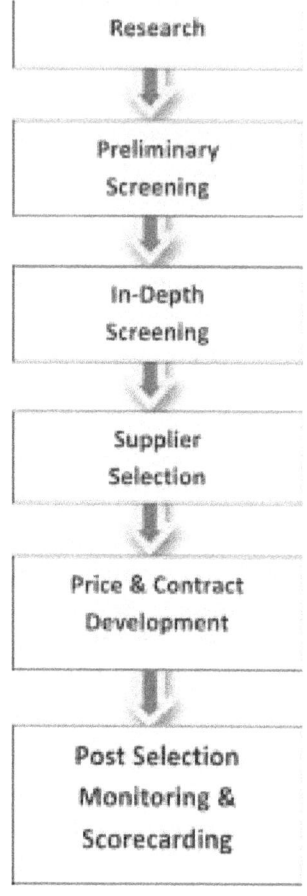

Strategic Sourcing Plan

Step 1: Researching Suppliers. The Internet has made this step quite easy as a few keywords into a search engine will produce a dozen potential suppliers for a given product or material. In addition to the web, you can gather supplier-related information from the following other sources:
- Industry Association Publications
- Trade Shows

- Industry Directories
- Industry Journals, Magazines, and Publications
- Catalogs
- Professional Supply & Procurement Organizations.

The purpose of this step is to establish a comprehensive list of potential suppliers.

Step 2: Preliminary Screening. After developing the supplier candidate list, the next step is the preliminary screening of the list. The objective here is to eliminate any and all suppliers that do not meet the minimum requirements for such things as financial stability, capacity, or quality. This is accomplished through supplier surveys, product sample review, and supplier on-site visits. The goal is to take the initial list developed in step one and pare-it-down to something more manageable.

Step 3: In-Depth Screening. After your candidate list has been streamlined, the next step is a more in-depth screen of potential suppliers. This step requires a more tactical review of candidates, including:
- Review of actual financial statements or bank references
- Review of Internet Data (blogs, bulletin boards, social media, etc.)
- Facility Visits
- Client References
- Quality Evaluation
- Capacity & Growth Analysis
- Review of Management Depth
- Flexibility and "Surge" Capabilities
- Application & Integration of Technology
- Reporting Capabilities
- Service Profile.

The intention behind step three is to narrow your potential supplier list to two to four candidates.

Step 4: Supplier Selection. After the list has been narrowed down, the next step is the formal evaluation and selection process. This includes requesting formal bids or proposals from the remaining candidates. In addition, here is where you use a formal decision matrix as a support tool to ensure a more objective decision. The decision matrix must include criteria associated with offshoring to a foreign country such as customs fees, taxes, freight, increased lead time and inventory requirements, criticality of the component, and most importantly, quality. A sample decision matrix is shown in Exhibit 3.12.

Exhibit 3.12: Supplier Decision Matrix

Supplier Evaluation Matrix

Decision Matrix

Rating	Description
0	No fit
1	Low fit
2	Fit
3	Good fit
4	Very Good Fit
5	Excellent Fit

Rating Scale

Decision Model		ALTERNATIVES					
		Supplier A		Supplier B		Supplier C	
Criterion	Weight	Rating	Score	Rating	Score	Rating	Score
Price	35%	4	1.4	2	0.7	3	1.05
RFQ Response	25%	2.95	0.7375	3.6	0.9	3.4	0.85
Quality	20%	3	0.6	3	0.6	3	0.6
Capacity	10%	3.5	0.35	4	0.4	3	0.3
Lead Time	10%	4	0.4	4	0.4	3	0.3
Total	100%	17.45	3.4875	16.6	3	15.4	3.1

Score = Rating * Weight

Exhibit 3.12: Supplier Decision Matrix, continued

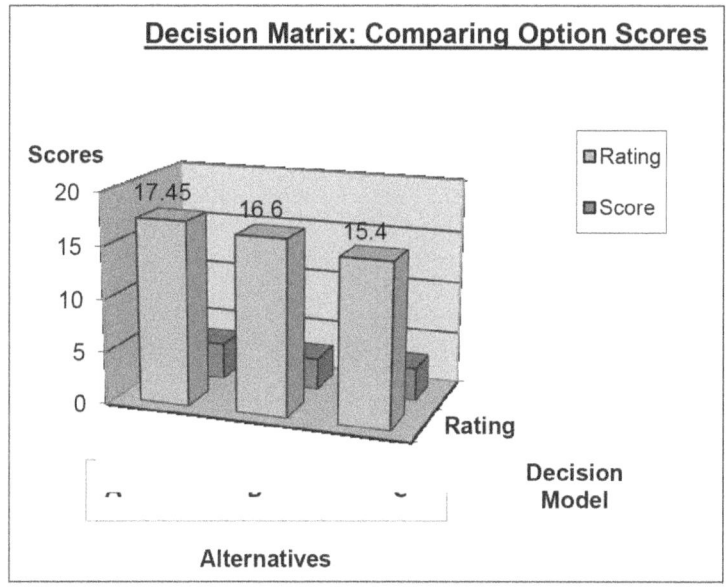

Remember, it is essential that you consider the factors that may change significantly when going offshore. When sourcing from a foreign country, quality may be suspect, lead times may triple, and inventory levels may rise due to higher minimum order quantities. You also need to consider some intangible issues that may develop such as:

- Communication Problems and Language Nuisances
- Cultural Issues
- Political Turmoil
- Currency, Exchange Rate, and Payment Transfer Issues
- Time and Geography Issues (time difference and distance)
- Contract Misunderstandings and Adherence Problems
- Catastrophic Events
- Governmental & Economic Instability
- Social Consciousness Concerns.

Step 5: Price & Contract Development. This step requires that a decision be made in terms of only accepting the most competitive bids or conducting a round of negotiations. Fundamentally, when you are dealing with high dollar value or complicated products (detailed and complex specifications), competitive bidding is the preferred method assuming there is an adequate number of suppliers in the category. When the price of a product is difficult to determine, or when service and quality are critical elements, negotiations are usually in order.

The purpose of this step is to establish the final pricing and contract terms.

Note: When developing contract terms, be sure to include the option of controlling the freight, language surrounding insurance requirements, including cargo liability, and key performance indicators (see Chapter 10).

Step 6: Post Selection Monitoring & Scorecarding. After awarding the contract to a supplier, the actual work begins. The objective should be to foster a strategic supplier relationship that considers the following factors:
- Fewer suppliers
- Information integration
- Supplier Managed Inventory (where appropriate)
- Continuous Improvement
- Total Supplier Involvement (design, specs, engineering)
- Single Source Buying
- Capacity Planning
- Environmental or Green Considerations.

In step six you should also develop a supplier scorecard to evaluate them on a quarterly basis. Evaluation criteria should include meeting capacity plans, on-time delivery, and quality. Ranking your suppliers via a formal scorecard will pay dividends.

The Economics of Supply Management

The last topic to discuss about supply management is managing cash. I believe that every manager who works in the supply department needs to take a mandatory finance course. At the same time, supply personnel should be well versed in distribution, freight, and inventory theories. The days of buying materials and goods simply by getting the lowest per unit cost are over. The Supply department needs to seriously consider the impact that every decision they make has on the other functional areas within the organization. Some of the questions that the supply group needs to consider include:

- Does the current order profile being used by Supply consider freight consolidation?
- Should all materials and goods be purchased on an FOB (freight on board) origin basis?
- Is Supply using blanket purchase orders and order consolidation to minimize costs?
- Does Supply consider the inventory/price tradeoff when buying?
- Is economic order quantity (EOQ) being used to determine ordering patterns?
- Does Supply fully take into account the carrying cost of inventory when buying?
- Does Supply track cost/purchase order (PO)?
- Has Supply been trained in the true cost of a backorder?
- Does Supply understand the impact they have on customer service?
- Has the supply group been trained in the importance of reducing total order cycle time?

Economic Order Quantity

When issuing a purchase order with a supplier, the procurement manager should consider the economics associated with small lot-size orders versus larger orders. The question here is whether the increase in per-unit cost due to smaller order quantities is offset by the reduction in inventory carrying cost. This is where the economic order quantity (EOQ) formula comes into play. EOQ considers the tradeoff associated with the cost of ordering against the carrying cost of the inventory on-hand. Exhibit 3.13 reveals the basic EOQ formula. There are more elaborate EOQ formulas that consider the cost of backorders or other factors, but this simple formula works in most cases.

Exhibit 3.13 - EOQ Formula

$$EOQ = \sqrt{\frac{2(\text{Annual usage in units})(\text{Order cost})}{(\text{Annual carrying cost per unit})}}$$

Source: InventoryOps.com

Annual usage or volume expressed in units

Order Cost is the sum of the fixed costs incurred each time an item is ordered. These costs are associated with the physical tasks required to process the order.

Carrying Cost per unit, also called inventory holding cost. Carrying cost is the cost associated with having inventory on-hand. In the EOQ formula, carrying cost is represented as the annual cost per average on-hand inventory unit. The primary components of carrying cost are interest (bank borrowing rate), insurance, taxes, and storage costs.

Calculating Inventory Carrying Rate (%):

The annual carrying cost of inventory is the sum of:
- Storage Costs
- Handling Costs
- Obsolescence Costs
- Damage Costs
- Administrative/Overhead Costs
- Loss/Pilferage Costs
- Interest or the cost of money

Next, divide these total costs by the Average Inventory Value. Then add the Opportunity Cost of Capital (the return you could reasonably expect if you used the money elsewhere). Finally, add insurance and taxes. The total should be greater than 15%. The inventory carrying costs is then calculated by multiplying the inventory carrying rate by the average inventory value.

Cost of a Backorder

The definition of a backorder is the cost incurred when a business is unable to fill an order and must complete it at a later date. A backorder cost can be discrete, as in the cost to replace a specific piece of inventory, or intangible, such as the effects of poor customer service. Backorder costs are usually computed and displayed on a per-unit basis. The cost of a backorder is calculated as follows:

- **Call center/customer service expenses** – at least one additional call to the call center to inquire of order status or provide instructions as to the disposition of the backordered item. This expense should include the per call expense associated with the phone operator, supervision, and of telecommunication.
- **Freight cost** – the incremental freight cost incurred to ship a backorder separate from the original order.
- **Packaging materials** – The cost of additional packaging and shipping materials such as corrugated, envelopes and any cushioning materials required. This cost is incurred as an additional cost due to the assumed second shipment of the backordered item.
- **Warehouse processing costs** – The cost to process the backorder as another warehouse order. As such, costs including direct labor, indirect labor, and occupancy costs are included in the warehouse processing costs.
- **Backorder notification costs** – FTC requirements for a backorder notification consists of the cost elements for postage, prep and processing time, and the cost of any documents/forms.
- **Other costs** - In addition, there are some intangible costs to consider including:
- **Cancellations** – 80% of cancelled orders are due to backorders. This impacts gross margin.
- **Lost goodwill and future sales** – The impact on a customer who has experienced a backorder is one that is constantly debated. The consensus is that backorders rank as one of the top reasons, next to price, returns convenience, and service that cause customers to stop buying from a company. The

value of those lost sales is calculated in different ways by each company.
- **Lost cost of initial customer acquisition** – The added cost of losing a customer is the initial cost of acquiring that customer in the first place. Included would be costs to print and mail catalogs, rental of lists, maintenance of web sites, customer service, etc.
- **Incremental inbound freight cost for expedited receipts** – Some companies, in the interest of maintaining good customer relations, will expedite the receipt of backordered items to facilitate their shipment.
- **Expedited outbound freight** – Some companies spend additional freight dollars to deliver backorders with expedited delivery options.
- **Lost Demand** – One cost of a backorder comes when a customer decides not to order if an item is not in stock. Some companies with sophisticated systems track this lost or phantom demand.

Source: A Study of Backorder Costs For Non-Store Retailers by Kline Management Consulting, F. Curtis Barry & Company.

Managing Inbound Freight

The final economic consideration associated with supply is inbound freight. It shocks me that so many companies are still buying goods and materials on a delivered price basis. Suppliers are simply not in the freight business. There is usually a 15% reduction in inbound freight costs when you move away from delivered pricing. At a minimum, the supply group should conduct an analysis that evaluates the difference between the delivered price and the F.O.B. origin price (whereby you control the freight).

In addition to freight control, the supply department should dictate the freight delivery instructions via a formal routing guide as shown in Exhibit 3.14.

Exhibit 3.14 - Inbound Routing Guide

SUPPLIER INBOUND FREIGHT ROUTING INSTRUCTIONS

ABC COMPANY

Date:_____

DM asks your cooperation and compliance with the following routing instructions. Our traffic Management Program is designed to provide ABC company with the best overall rates and services. Non-compliance with these instructions or unauthorized use of non-listed carriers will result in a chargeback for any additional costs an charges to ABC Company.

<u>Instructions:</u>
- Clearly mark each carton with shipper and consignee name, shipping address, and ABC Company purchase order number(s).

- Indicate the total number of cartons, number or pallets and the purchase order number(s) on our carrier's Bill of Lading.

- Palletize and shrink-wrap all cartons whenever possible. Combine multiple orders on one Bill of Lading when shipping to the same address.

****ABC Company client code (FM14) must be included in the Customer # section of Bill of Lading***

CARRIER SELECTION

- **Shipments under 200lbs -** (individual cartons must not exceed 70 lbs)
  - United Parcel Service

- <u>**LTL-200 lbs to 6,000 lbs:**</u>
  If more than 6 pallets or over 650cubic ft. call DM Transportation for routing 888-399-0162

- <u>**Shipping From:**</u>
  CT, DC, DE, MA, MD, ME, NH, NJ, NY, OH, PA, RI, VA, VT

  XYZ Motor Freight
  (Contact your local terminal)
  www.nemf.com

Shipping From: All Other States – Direct Points Only •Large LTL or Truckload – 6,001 lbs & Above & Expedited Services		ABC Express (Contact your local terminal) www.roadway.com DM Transport. MGT Services Dispatch@dmtrans.com (610-367-0162)
SHIPPING TO & BILL TO:	Follow ABC Company PO Instructions	**If the selected carriers cannot pick up directly from your point of origin, contact DM.** Special purchase order instructions or delivered pricing agreements will override the above. Please direct any traffic questions, routing problems, or services issues to DM Transportation Management Services
BILL FREIGHT CHARGES TO:	ECFA 13016 Eastfield Road Huntersville, NC 28078	DM Transportation management Services is a full service logistics company serving the Direct Marketing and Retail industries. www.dmtrans.com EMAIL: dmtrams@dmtrans.com

Source: Courtesy DM Transportation.

Conclusion

Globalization is here to stay and supply managers need to embrace this aspect of the economy. Global sourcing will continue to become increasingly more competitive as foreign countries jockey for position and attempt to overthrow China as the main global supply source. The Supply function must take-on this sourcing challenge as supply management is an essential business function and the area within the overall supply chain that has the most impact on profitability. The critical issues in supply continue to be global sourcing, outsourcing, strategic supplier relationships, and managing the total cost of ownership. Supply managers must be well-versed in all areas within the supply chain and must make decisions that benefit the entire organization. In addition, supply information needs to be assimilated across the enterprise and backwards integrated with suppliers. The key data elements to be managed in supply are price, quality, inventory, and freight.

Chapter Summary

1. Supply management plays a significant role in overall business and supply chain strategy.

2. Supply management must make decisions that benefit the entire organization.

3. The total cost of ownership (without sacrificing quality) must be the driving force behind global sourcing.

4. Centralized procurement can yield significant dividends but must include local preferences and service requirements.

5. There are more than 100 discrete steps to the new product development process.

6. A major focal point of the supply group needs to be delivering a quality product. The quality team should use the seven tools of quality and get everyone involved in the quality process.

7. Global procurement starts with a six-step strategic sourcing plan. An evaluation of global sourcing must include the

increase in lead time and inventory requirements, along with the impact on product quality.

8. Supply managers must be trained in the economics of supply management including the carrying cost of inventory, the cost of a backorder, and economic order quantity.

Exploratory Questions

1. What role should supply management play as it relates to overall business strategy?

2. How does supply impact overall company profitability?

3. What is meant by the total cost of ownership?

4. What are the pros and cons of centralized procurement?

5. What role should supply play in new product development?

6. How can supply management help to measure quality?

7. Why is the delineation of inbound freight so important?

8. What are the critical considerations surrounding global sourcing?

9. What role should supply management play in inventory control?

10. Why should all supply managers be well-versed in Finance and Economics?

Case Study – Snorefreenow.com

Snorefreenow.com is a direct response product that alleviates snoring. The company is located in Las Vegas, Nevada but has fulfillment set-up in Yucca Valley, California. Snorefreenow is sold through catalogs, the Internet, and some retail stores. The Snorefreenow product consists of ten total components, including packaging, and is currently sourced in the United States. Due to pricing pressure from the catalog houses, the CEO requested an evaluation of global sourcing for all ten components. The objective was to determine the impact that global sourcing would have on COGS (cost of goods sold) and quality. The CEO wanted to ultimately reduce the cost of goods without sacrificing quality so he could pass along the cost savings to the catalog houses through reduced pricing.

During the evaluation, we collected the following COGS data:

Product Component	Sourcing Location	Minimum Order Quantity	Current Lead Time	Total Price/Unit
Oral mouthpiece	Los Angeles, CA	1,000	2 weeks	$2.65
Insertion tool	Los Angeles, CA	1,000	2 weeks	$0.86
Dental case	La Habra, CA	500	1 week	$0.43
Clean & Fresh 2 ounce bottle	Los Angeles, CA	500	5 days	$0.17
Bottle Cap & Label	Los Angeles, CA	500	5 days	$0.05
Bottle Shrink Wrap	Los Angeles, CA	10,000	5 days	$0.01
Clean & Fresh Ingredients	Del Rey Beach, FL	10 Cases	2 weeks	$0.57
Package Insert	La Habra, CA	2,500	3 weeks	$0.04
Retail Box	La Habra, CA	2,500	3 weeks	$0.97
Brochure	La Habra, CA	5,000	3 weeks	$0.78
				$6.53/Unit

We also reviewed the existing quality profile of the product as defined by:
- Number of customer complaints – less than 1%
- Return % - less than 3%
- % Manufacturing Defects – less than 2%.

The perceived quality was quite high as the number of complaints was negligible, as was the return and defect rates. The company was not experiencing any significant quality-related problems.

The next step to the engagement was to research alternative suppliers for the ten components, considering all the factors required to make a well-informed decision. The CEO was adamant that price alone was not to be the determining factor for the decision. After considerable research and the development of a simplified strategic sourcing plan, we eventually compared the existing COGS price structure to several alternatives. The primary sourcing alternative was identified to be the Country of China. The comparison between the current sourcing and China follows:

Product Component	Sourcing Location	Minimum Order Quantity	New Lead Time	Total Price/Unit
Oral mouthpiece	Shanghai, China	5,000	6 weeks	$1.05
Insertion tool	Shanghai, China	10,000	6 weeks	$0.15
Dental case	Shanghai, China	5,000	4 weeks	$0.26
Clean & Fresh 2 ounce bottle	Shanghai, China	5,000	3 weeks	$0.09
Bottle Cap & Label	Shanghai, China	5,000	3 weeks	$0.02
Bottle Shrink Wrap	Shanghai, China	10,000	3 weeks	$0.005
Clean & Fresh Ingredients	Shanghai, China	10 Cases	6 weeks	$0.40
Package Insert	Shanghai, China	5,000	6 weeks	$0.02
Retail Box	Shanghai, China	5,000	6 weeks	$0.78
Brochure	Shanghai, China	10,000	6 weeks	$0.65
				$3.425/Unit

On the surface, the move to China would save more than $3/unit, making it difficult to ignore. However, the decision was made to pilot the idea by conducting a test of quality. Minimum order quantities were purchased on all products with the exception of the oral appliance. The CEO simply did not want to send the mouthpiece to

China out of fear of being copied or knocked-off. In addition, the oral appliance is the core component with exacting specifications that are required to create product efficacy. The balance of the components was tested over a six-month period. Afterwards, the quality profile was extrapolated to be as follows:
1. Expected customer complaints – 5%
2. Return % - 6%
3. Defect Rate – 8%.

This forecasted decrease in quality was alarming and caused the CEO to rethink the idea. The quality issue was exacerbated by two other factors. First, the increase in lead time, which would dictate a more precise ordering process to ensure zero backorders. Second, the additional inventory investment that would be required due to an increase in minimal order quantities. There would be a definite increase in inventory carrying costs.

Based upon all the data, the CEO decided to only go offshore with two components, namely the bottle and insertion tool. He believed that these two items would have a negligible effect on quality.

Case Study Questions:

- Do you agree with the CEO's decision?

- Why was lead time and inventory such a cause for concern?

- Why do you think quality was chosen over cost savings?

4 OUTSOURCING

"Outsourcing and globalization of manufacturing allows companies to reduce costs, benefits consumers with lower cost goods and services, causes economic expansion that reduces unemployment, and increases productivity and job creation."
― Larry Elder

Companies outsource many of their supply chain functions such as warehousing and distribution for a variety of reasons. Although it is hard to explain, outsourcing seems to go hand-in-hand with downsizing and business reengineering. Many executives believe that unless your primary business is physical distribution, you should leave the shipping to the experts. Does it have to be this way? Can outsourcing and in-house logistics survive together in some delicate balance?

By the end of this chapter, you should be able to articulate the reasons why many organizations outsource. You should have a good grasp of the pitfalls associated with outsourcing, and you should be able to perform a detailed evaluation of in-house versus outsourced supply-chain activities.

The Definition of Outsourcing

Businessdictionary. com defines outsourcing as:

Contracting, sub-contracting, or "externalizing" non-core activities to free up cash, personnel, time, and facilities for activities where the firm holds a competitive advantage.

Why Consider Outsourcing?

As Exhibit 4.1 shows, the topic of outsourcing has attracted considerable attention in the past thirty years. Outsourcing is an attractive alternative for many organizations as they attempt to deal with such situations as eroding profit margins, declining market share, increased competition for corporate funds, and globalization of the world economy. There are some sound reasons why many companies have chosen to outsource one or more supply chain functions. To that end, outsourcing has many benefits, including the following:

1. It can provide off-balance-sheet financing
2. It encourages a firm to stick to its core competency
3. It may provide a competitive advantage
4. It can eliminate or shield organizations from restrictive government regulations
5. It may enhance access to improved information technology
6. It might transfer certain liabilities (Environmental Protection Agency [EPA] and others).

Exhibit 4.1 – History of Outsourcing in the United States of America

1850's	Industrial Revolution marked a fundamental change in manufacturing processes including company specialization in functions and activities, and outsourcing to increase quality and reduce costs

Late 1970's	The Japanese invasion of auto and heavy equipment manufacturing causes rust-belt manufacturers including GM, Ford, Chrysler, Caterpillar, Deere, Case, etc., to lose billions of dollars. In order to compete on quality and price, U. S. manufacturers aggressively began outsourcing parts, components, complete models etc., to others. Outsourcing has been very effective and successful in these industries.
Early 1980's	U. S. auto and heavy equipment dealers begin outsourcing trucking, engine, and undercarriage rebuilding, electrical and hydraulic component rebuilding, specialized machining, payroll, software development, etc. Outsourcing has been very effective and successful at the reseller level.
Early 1980's	Trucking industry deregulates with bloody results. For example, of the 100 largest trucking companies in 1979, less than twenty survived to compete in 1994. The 80% kill rate indicates that most trucking companies could not adapt to free market competition. Today, trucking rates are so low that many companies outsource interstate trucking and most outsources intrastate trucking.
Mid-1980's	In response to globalized markets, industrials begin outsourcing plant and mobile asset maintenance and repair activities. Industries include steel, chemical, power petroleum, pulp and paper, food and beverage. Outsourcing has been very effective and successful in these industries.
Later 1980's	In response to a declining tax base, budget cutting, and Republican control, the U. S. government begins outsourcing fleet and facility maintenance and management activities. Hundreds of fleet departments are outsourced. Results are bloody and mixed. Most turnkey outsourcing of fleet departments

had not lasted five years before being brought back in-house. Are government fathers using turnkey fleet outsourcing to cause change and cost reductions?

Early 1990's The federal government, including military bases and defense contractors, begins rapid downsizing. Defense contractors find it extremely difficult, if not impossible, to convert products, services, technology, and culture, and achieve cost competitiveness in order to compete in the private sector. Several fleet and facility maintenance contractors previously focused on military base contracts begin entering the private sector and competing for fleet and facility outsource contracts.

Mid-1990's Communications companies and gas and electric public utilities continue deregulation activities. Fleet and facility departments are beginning to be outsourced. Results are bloody. Will public utility senior managers use turnkey outsourcing to cause change and reduce costs . . . or will public utility fleet managers make the required changes?

2000 -2013 4PL's come into vogue, using improved technology and systems integration to lure more and more companies toward outsourcing. The majority of Fortune 500 companies have outsourced one or more activities by the end of the 90s.

Source: Kelly Walker & Associates, "Outsourcing was a Hot Topic in Las Vegas and Colonial Williamsburg." *Utility & Telephone Fleets*, September/October 1995.

Ask any chief financial officer why outsourcing is well received, and you'll be given these three reasons:

1. Outsourcing avoids long-term financial commitment in times of economic uncertainty.

2. It eliminates the hidden cost of ownership.
3. It reduced the need for precious corporate capital and could improve the company's return on assets. It is no wonder that more than half of 200 medium-size companies recently surveyed stated they already outsourced at least one function (see Exhibit 4.2).

Exhibit 4.2 - Percentage of Medium Sized Firms that Outsource one or more activities.

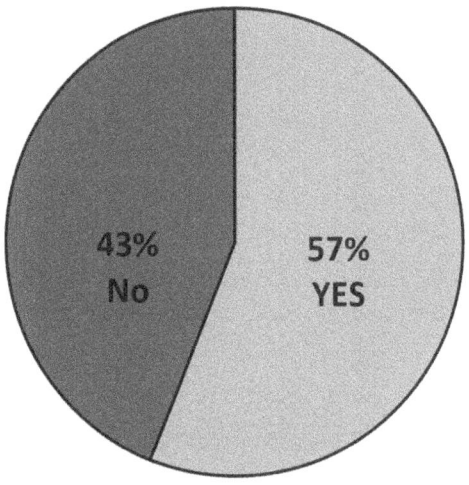

Two additional dynamics are contributing to the outsourcing fad – industry trends and the challenges facing supply chain managers.

Distribution industry trends include the following:
- Seamless stream of fully integrated management information
- Staffing the delivery function (drivers and vehicles) at only 80% of the demand
- Faster turnover of assets to reduce failures, obsolescence, and increased costs
- Enhanced flexibility to accommodate growth
- Slashing of inventories.

Challenges facing supply chain managers include:
- Constant pressure to reduce costs
- Rapidly changing technology

- Retention of quality drivers
- Government regulations
- Customer expectations of faster, better, and lower-cost delivery.

When Does Outsourcing Make Sense?

Outsourcing makes sense in organizations that have functional silos, conflicting goals among departments that give each department a separate agenda and cause them to pull in different directions. Functional silos usually exist in firms that do not use general managers, but instead have department heads for each major function within the company (i. e., sales and marketing, manufacturing, finance, and distribution). Outsourcing may help minimize the conflict inherent in this situation.

Outsourcing makes sense when your existing labor environment is poor and your organization's work rules are unreasonable. If capital is hard to come by, outsourcing can provide a mechanism for getting new equipment and turning over assets every few years. It can also help you access improved technology from third-party suppliers.

With all these reasons in mind, should a supply chain manager just throw in the towel and outsource? Absolutely not. Outsourcing has its pitfalls, but if the economics of outsourcing make sense for your firm, you should embrace the concept. Third-party suppliers can be strategic partners rather than adversaries. If supporting an in-house function is no longer feasible, outsourcing may be the next best thing.

When Does Outsourcing Fail?

Outsourcing should not be taken lightly. Handing over your business to a third-party who may not fully understand yo ur corporate structure or culture can be very dangerous if not handled properly. Outsourcing usually fails under the following conditions:
- Your evaluation of suppliers is poorly handled
- There is a lack of senior management support
- You choose the wrong partner

- There is a lack of mutual trust
- Short-term thinking takes over
- Lead-time for start-up is insufficient
- Quality is considered less important than price.

Companies outsource a variety of activities, including; private fleet management, order processing, inventory control, warehousing, information technology, and electronic data interchange (See Exhibit 4.3). Alternatives to fleet outsourcing include full-service leasing, dedicated contract carnage, finance lease with contract maintenance, for-hire and contract carriers, owner-operators, and freight management services (mode selection, freight auditing, and outside carriers). The need for continued outsourcing is evidenced by the recent growth within the 3PL and 4PL industry (third and fourth party logistics).

The recent growth projections of the major outsource categories are as follows:

Full-service leasing – 3-5%
Dedicated contract carriage – 4-7%
Warehousing – 6-8%
Third-party logistics – 10-15%

If these growth rates are maintained, more than 80% of the Fortune 500 companies (with supply chain networks and vehicles) may outsource one or more activity by the year 2020.

Exhibit 4.3 Outsourcing by Business Segment.

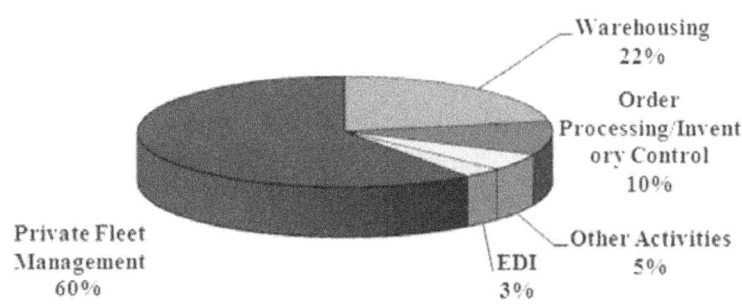

A Delicate Balance

The objective of any supply chain network design is to provide the lowest overall infrastructure cost. For example, using distribution as the function in question, one must consider the overall distribution landed cost associated with product delivery to a customer. From a distribution perspective, optimizing the transportation network and thereby lowering delivery costs can best be realized when a balanced approach is used. Balancing a distribution network involves a detailed analysis of each lane (or individual route) of traffic. The main question posed by the balanced network theory is: What mode of transportation (i. e., private fleet, dedicated contract carriage, or for-hire) should be used to produce the lowest overall system cost?

Many factors go into this equation. Current driver wage scale, age of equipment, specific traffic lanes traveled, mileage patterns by route, and so on, should all be taken into account. In a typical delivery environment, it is usually advantageous to use a private fleet when the vehicles "come home" every night and stay close to the origination point (i. e., routes traveled less than 100 miles per day, round trip). This dynamic helps explain why leasing has not totally infiltrated the light-to-medium duty truck (LMV) market. Outsourcing to a dedicated carriage provider works well when backhauls can be secured to offset costs and when the existing network environment is cost prohibitive (i. e. poor work rules, terrible union relationship; old expensive equipment; no technology). For-hire carriage, depending on the lane of traffic, can work well in a variety of situations.

The key is to find the correct mix of for-hire, dedicated, rail, or private fleet that lowers overall distribution costs. The lane-by-lane cost analysis will identify the mix. The analysis should consider the following:
- The cost of each lane after net-backhaul revenue is factored in
- The average length of haul that affects vehicle life cycles and diver costs (teams)
- The true, total cost of distribution, including fixed and variable expenses, supervision, and so on.

After properly identifying the total costs associated with the private fleet, you can solicit cost proposals from both for-hire and dedicated carriage providers.

In an LMV environment, the leverage point is different. The analysis shifts to individual route optimization. The question becomes: What mix of financing or ownership and vehicle specifications, by route, will provide the lowest network costs?

Number of miles, and cases or cube must be taken into account to determine the individual profitability of each route. If cases are not distributed, but instead the vehicle is used exclusively for service (such as in the telecommunications and utility industries), the analysis calls for an in-depth study of fleet size, utilization and costs.

The same kind of logic can be applied to any of the other supply chain functions that are being considered for outsourcing. The metrics will obviously be different, but the thought process and design analysis can still be applied.

Strategic Alliances with Third-Party Suppliers

Third-party suppliers are not the enemy. If used appropriately, they can be invaluable resources for technology, equipment, and information. Before you enter into a partnership agreement with a supplier, look for clues that characterize suppliers who are first-rate, including:
- They insist on learning about your business before discussing price
- They suggest route rides, plant tours, and a visit to your headquarters
- They have a quality program in place
- The supplier team is always prompt for meetings and appropriately prepared
- Their presentations are first class
- They suggest you contact both existing and past customers for references
- They belong to and support more than one trade association

- When you phone the vendor, someone answers by the second ring and quickly transfers you to the appropriate person
- They have direct access to the latest technology and can demonstrate it at your first meeting
- They have a formal problem resolution report that gets senior management's attention.

Strategic alliances between third-party suppliers and supply chain managers must be nurtured. During the first ninety days of the relationship, be sure to demand formal status meetings take place every other week. The learning process is two-way. Offer to go to the supplier's headquarters and visit its most technologically advanced facility. Get a list of the key people you should know within the firm.

How to Properly Evaluate Outsourcing

An outsourcing evaluation consists of these six (6) major steps:
1. Assess the current operation and identify activities that are candidates for outsourcing.
2. Define key objectives, performance measures, and overall expectations of the project.
3. Develop a request for proposal or quote (RFP/RFQ) that includes the key criteria for
4. evaluating the supplier.
5. Identify first-rate third-party providers. The step should always include site visits, tours of the supplier's headquarters, and a formal interview of the actual personnel to be involved in the program.
6. Negotiate the deal.
7. Develop a formal implementation plan.

Exhibit 4.4 shows a step-by-step approach to evaluating outsourcing. Identifying key objectives and expectations is the most important step in your outsourcing analysis. You must have a clear and concise description of the current and desired state of operations before the analysis can proceed. Use the following criteria when considering any third-party provider:

- The firm's qualifications and reputation
- Management depth
- Industry experience and relevant client references (past and present)
- "Bricks and mortar" (network infrastructure...number of depots, etc.)
- Strategic direction
- Financial stability
- A documented quality process in place
- Surge capabilities to accommodate growth or short-term needs
- Ability to handle labor relations issues
- Range of services offered
- Cultural fit with your company
- Willingness to agree to a continuous improvement in costs and service
- Cost and potential savings.

Develop an evaluation matrix that compares the suppliers against such criteria and a rating scale that rates them accordingly. Weigh each major criterion so that the most important aspects of the analysis point to the best vendor. For example, 20% of the weight might be placed on cost and potential savings. An additional 10% might be placed on range of services offered (see Chapter 3, Exhibit 3.12 for an example of a decision matrix).

In order to compare supplier quotes meaningfully, you must ensure that they are based on the same elements. Some third-party suppliers of supply chain services quote "naked rates. " These rates exclude some aspects of the costing structure (e. g., in a full-service lease, some vendors may leave out washing or vehicle substitutions). After comparing the costs of each supplier, qualitative factors must be introduced. Sample qualitative factors include the following:
- Cultural fit
- Employee morale
- Resistance to change
- Management's tolerance for risk.

After choosing a supplier, develop a formal implementation plan that includes a contingency or backup plan should the effort fail.

Exhibit 4.4 Outsourcing Methodology

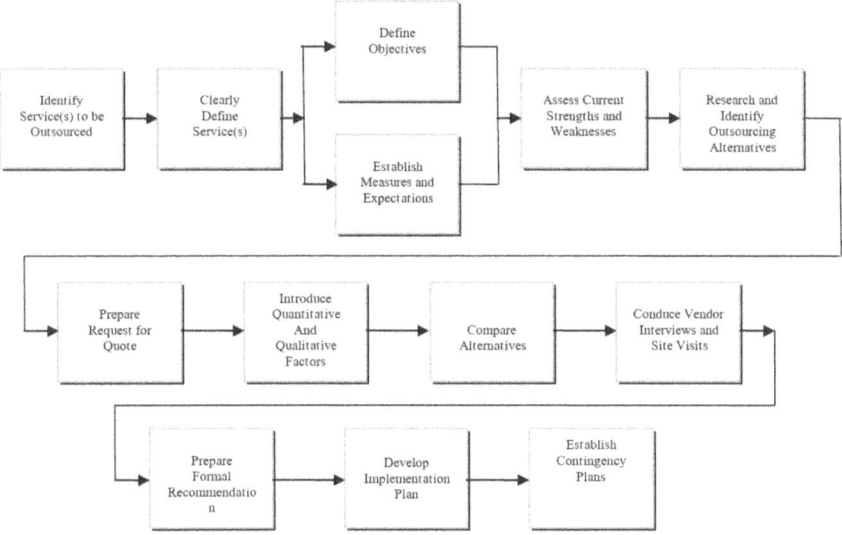

Developing an RFP/RFQ

The outsourcing request for proposal and/or request for quote process consists of seven (7) main steps:
- Define the requirements and scope of the RFP/RFQ.
- Develop the key objectives and outcomes of the RFP/RFQ.
- Develop and send out the RFP/RFQ including a realistic time-frame for completion.
- Carefully evaluate the bids using objective and weighted criteria(each criterion should be weighted based upon the importance to your organization) such as:
  - Quality of the Solution
  - Cost
  - Cultural Fit
  - Financial Stability
  - Customer References
  - Services Offered
  - Industry Reputation and Experience

- Application of Technology
- Reporting and KPI (key performance indicator) Application
- Terms and Conditions.

* Select an outsourced partner.
* Develop a statement of expectations for both sides.
* Finalize the outsourced relationship through a formal agreement including performance metrics.

The RFP/RFQ should employ a table of contents that includes:

Sample RFP/RFQ Table of Contents

1. Structure of the RFP 2
    1.1. Key sections of the RFP 2
    1.2. Statement of Purpose 2
    1.3. Background Information 3
    1.4. Scope of Work 3
    1.5. Outcome and Performance Standards 4
    1.6. Deliverables 4
    1.7. Term of Contract 4
    1.8. Payments, Incentives, and Penalties 5
    1.9. Contractual Terms and Conditions 5
    1.10. Requirements for Proposal Preparation 5
    1.11. Evaluation and Award Process 5
    1.12. Process Schedule 6
    1.13. Questions Conference 6

How to Keep It In-House

If keeping supply chain activities in-house is your goal, the following activities will help you achieve it:
- Perform a benchmark study that clearly indicates your organization is the best in its class
- Use activity-based costing to squeeze out every ounce of cost from each process within your span of control
- Get the finance department to confirm your assessment of the true cost of the supply chain

- Conduct a strategy session to determine the best use of company capital resources
- Perform a comprehensive cost study to determine how your organization stacks up against the 3PL (see Exhibit 4.5)
- Implement incentive programs to create excitement and recognize star performance.

Exhibit 4.5: The Cost of In-House Transportation compared to Dedicated Carriage.

IFMC. INC.

TABLE 1: PRIVATE FLEET VS. DEDICATED CONTRACT CARRIAGE

PROJECTED COST

		Annual Cost ($)	Budgeted for Next year
1 EQUIPMENT COSTS:			
A.	Lease Payments on Equipment (fixed & mileage)		
B.	License & Registration Costs		
C.	Sales Tax		
D.	Property Tax		
E.	Equipment repair for damages & accidents		
F.	Rental charges for equipment and accidents		
G.	Painting, Lettering, & Decal Expense		
H.	Vehicle depreciation, if owned		
I.	Vehicle washing		
J.	Technology Costs (fixed)		
K.	Substitute vehicle rental expense		
L.	HVUT		
	Total Equipment Costs		
2 Material Handling Equipment:			
A.	Pallet Jacks		
B.	Load Bars		
C.	Straps and Tarps if Required		
D.	Hand Trucks		
	Total Material Handling Equipment		
3 Driver Costs:			
A.	Wages		
B.	Payroll Taxes		
C.	Workman's Compensation		
D.	Medical Bills		
E.	Vacation & Holiday Pay		
F.	Holiday Bonuses or Other Incentives		
G.	Drug Tests & D.O.T. Required Medical Exams		
H.	Uniforms		
I.	Disability Pay		
J.	Pension 401k Plan		
K.	Life Insurance		
L.	Drive Travel Expenses and Tolls, Hotel, Etc.		
M.	Safety Programs (awards incentives)		
N.	Training Cost		
O.	Recruiting Costs		
P.	Temporary Labor		
	Total Driver Costs:		

Exhibit 4.5: The Cost of In-House Transportation compared to Dedicated Carriage, continued.

PROJECTED COST

	Annual Cost ($)	Budgeted for Next year
4 Mechanic Costs:		
A. Wages		
B. Payroll Taxes		
C. Workman's Compensation		
D. Medical Bills		
E. Vacation & Holiday Pay		
F. Holiday Bonuses or Other Incentives		
G. Drug Tests & D.O.T. Required Medical Exams		
H. Uniforms		
I. Disability Pay C54 Pay		
J. Pension 401k Plan		
K. Life Insurance		
L. Tools, Uniforms, Supplies		
M. Safety Programs (awards incentives)		
N. Training Cost		
O. Recruiting Costs		
P. Temporary Labor		
Total Mechanic Costs		
5 Insurance (if self insured, this must be allocated):		
A. Liability Insurance		
B. Physical Damage/ Theft Insurance		
C. Cargo Insurance		
D. Cost of Deductibles on Actual Occurrences		
E. Attorney's Fees in Defending Legal Suits		
Total Insurance:		
6 Fuel and Road Expenses:		
A. Actual Cost of All Fuel Used		
B. Fuel Taxes		
C. Ton Mile and Third Structure Taxes		
D. Tolls		
E. Drives Telephone Call or Pagers		
Total Fuel and Road Expenses:		

	Annual Cost ($)	Budgeted for Next year
7 Management Costs:		
A. Wages of Managers and Clerical Staff		
B. Payroll Taxes of Managers Staff		
C. Vacation & Holiday Pay		
D. Workman's Compensation		
E. Medical Benefits		
F. Costs of Processing Payroll		
G. Renting Costs		
H. Management Time & Safety Policy Meetings		
I. Management Information Systems (MIS) Expenses		
J. Clerical and Temporary Labor Costs		
K. Arbitration/ Union Grievance/ Attorney Fees -Labor issues		
L. Compliance and Parking Violations, Other Fines		
M. Fleet Administration (.05-5% of ACQ Cost)		

Exhibit 4.5: The Cost of In-House Transportation compared to Dedicated Carriage, continued.

	Annual Cost ($)	Budgeted for Next year
8 Maintenance & Shop Expenses		
A. Shop Fixed or Rental Expenses (Building, Equip., Parking Lot)		
B. Variable Expenses (Utilities, etc)		
C. Maintenance - (shop, van, parts, lease etc.)		
D. Fuel parts and Tire Inventory Carrying Costs		
E. Supplies		
F. Garage Insurance		
Total Maintenance & Shop Expenses:		
Grand Total All Costs:		
Total miscellaneous Expenses		
Total Costs Of Private Fleet Operation		
Cost= Private Fleet operation + Lost Earnings*		
Less = Current Net Backhaul Revenue		
NET FLEET OPERATIONS COST		

*lost earnings on capital investment, using company weighted cost of capital

Performance Indicators
A. Annual Miles
B. Annual Net Sales
C. Annual Cases or Pounds
D. Cost as Percentage of Net Sales
E. Cost Per Case or Pound
F. Cost Per Mile

Conclusion

Can a supply chain manager share the same house with a third-party logistics provider? The answer is yes. Supply chain managers who have their act together from a cost and service perspective have nothing to fear. Even if a company does decide to outsource for capital or other reasons, a strong supply chain manager will be placed in another function, supervise the third-party, or be granted a promotion for being a good corporate steward. In addition, it does appear that outsourcing is here to stay as organizations continue to struggle with the lack of capital, pressure from unions, a poor economy, and the need to stick to their core business.

Chapter Summary

- A strategic tactic that many organizations use is sticking to what they know best.

- The majority of Fortune 500 companies outsource one or more activities.

- The definition of outsourcing can be stated as contracting, sub-contracting, or "externalizing" non-core activities to free up cash, personnel, time, and facilities for activities where the firm holds a competitive advantage.

- Outsourcing should be considered in an organization where functional silos abound.

- Many outsourcing projects fail due to a poorly conducted evaluation or an apples-to-oranges comparison of costs.

- There are six major steps to the outsourcing process that should be carefully followed when evaluating a third-party supply chain provider.

- A carefully constructed decision matrix should be used to compare potential third-party suppliers.

- Outsourcing should be viewed as an opportunity not a failure.

Exploratory Questions

1. Why do may organizations use outsourcing as a strategic tool?

2. What are the major drivers behind the outsourcing movement?

3. What causes outsourcing to fail?

4. What are the six major steps to the outsourcing process?

5. What criterion should be considered when evaluating 3PL's?

6. Why do you think so many Fortune 500 firms outsource non-core activities?

7. What qualitative factors must be considered when outsourcing?

Case Study – DMN Media Group

DMN Media group delivers periodicals and magazines throughout the Southwestern United States. Due to pressure from the transition to Internet-based news, DMN was suffering from reduced circulation and profitability. The DMN supply chain network consisted of a large plant with an attached warehouse and more than 100 delivery vehicles. Senior management had identified rising distribution costs as a major contributor to the decline in profitability. The CFO decided to bring-in outside consultants to study the alternatives associated with the delivery system. The objective was to determine the feasibility of outsourcing the transportation to a lower cost third-party. The CFO wanted to ultimately reduce the cost of delivery while maintaining service. In addition, the CFO wanted to conserve capital dollars so they could be used for higher return projects.

During the evaluation, we collected the following data:
- Insufficient dock space at the warehouse was causing severe congestion
- Employee morale was low due to wage freezes
- Restrictive work rules dictated paying a four-hour minimum to drivers
- Vehicles were well past their economic life and out of warranty
- Driver productivity was in question due to low daily stop count
- Lack of technology was causing supply chain blindness
- Supply chain costs increased an average of 6% per year for three years.

The project consisted of evaluating the feasibility of outsourcing the delivery system to a third party. An RFQ was used as the method to compare the third parties to the in-house cost and service for delivery.

Six potential third parties were evaluated and a decision matrix was used by the project team to conduct the detailed comparison of data. The evaluation ultimately pointed to outsourcing as a viable alternative. The comparison of the in-house cost of delivery to the third party that was chosen revealed the following:

- Due to the elimination of the restrictive work rules and the use of part-timers, the third party would reduce costs by $2.0 million per year.

- The 3PL would implement automated dispatch, on-board truck technology, and computerized routing to further reduce costs.

- The 3PL agreed to a three-year continuous improvement program that demanded an additional $1.0 million in annual savings.

- After the initial operational assessment by the 3PL, a regional distribution center was recommended along with the conversion to tractor trailers (from straight trucks). This significant change eventually saved DMN Media $6.0million per year.

Case Study Questions:

1. Why do you think so many companies allow restrictive work rules to creep-in and cause higher costs?

2. Why does it often take an outside point of view to change the way a company does business?

3. Why do many organizations neglect technology as a source of productivity?

4. Why are consultants often used to study an organizational problem?

5 ORDER PROCESSING AND CUSTOMER SERVICE

"Sales without Customer Service is like stuffing money into a pocket full of holes."

David Tooman

The Institute for Supply Chain Management (SCM) offers this definition of SCM:

> *Supply Chain Management is the integration of key business processes from end-user through original suppliers that provides products, services, and information that add value for customers and other stakeholders (see Exhibit 5.1). The key words here are business processes, and within every business, the process starts with an order. Once an order is placed by a customer, the supply chain management process begins.*

USING YOUR SUPPLY CHAIN AS A COMPETITIVE WEAPON

Exhibit 5.1 - Supply Chain Management Business Processes

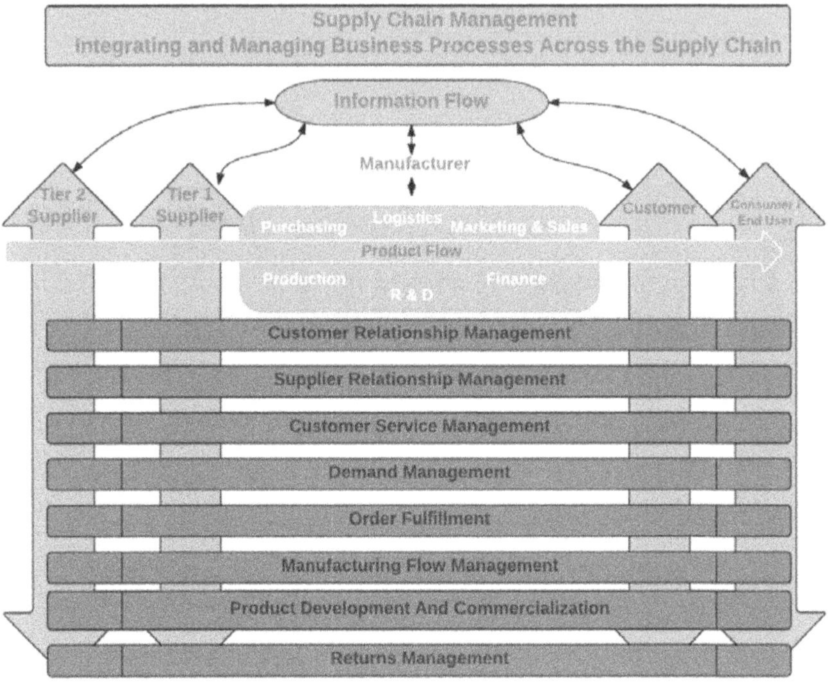

Supply Chain Management
Integrating and Managing Business Processes Across the Supply Chain

- Information Flow
- Manufacturer
- Tier 2 Supplier
- Tier 1 Supplier
- Purchasing
- Logistics
- Marketing & Sales
- Customer
- Consumer / End User
- Product Flow
- Production
- R & D
- Finance
- Customer Relationship Management
- Supplier Relationship Management
- Customer Service Management
- Demand Management
- Order Fulfillment
- Manufacturing Flow Management
- Product Development And Commercialization
- Returns Management

Source: Institute for Supply Chain Management.

An order should be considered a celebration as it connotes customer confidence, yet in all my years of SCM consulting, the art of order processing is the one activity that is most often overlooked by management. This chapter will delve into topics such as the true cost of an order, defining your customer service policy, the perfect order, and the *real* cost of customer service.

The Definition of Order Processing

Order processing, or order fulfillment as it is also know, is the tracking and monitoring of customer orders from receipt to delivery. Order processing produces the data for order fulfillment. The ordering process generally consists of the following steps which should be documented through a flowchart or process flow diagram:

1. **Receipt of the Order.**
2. **Customer Credit Check.**
3. **Inventory Determination.**
4. **Production or Order Pulling.**
5. **Shipment and Delivery.**
6. **Customer Billing.**
7. **Post Sale Follow-Up.**
8. **Reverse Logistics (if required).**

To successfully implement a flexible supply chain management system, a centralized approach to order processing should be used such that customers receive their orders as efficiently from the global marketplace as they do from the local supply chain. I know, easier said than done, but this simple concept is crucial as the global nature of your supply chain should be invisible to your customers.

The True Cost of an Order

You would be surprised how many companies do not know their true cost to process an order. One of the problems is that we have been taught the old adage, "the customer is always right." Well, I submit that it is better to operate under the assumption that the customer is usually right. It is simple too expensive to give customers the Nordstrom's treatment in each and every case. As shown in Exhibit 5.2, the cost of customer service gets ridiculously expensive above 95%. In fact, it has been estimated that for every percent above 95% customer service as defined by the in-stock percentage coupled with on-time delivery, that the corresponding impact on the total supply chain can be as high as 15% due to the extreme levels of inventory required to execute this level of performance.

This doesn't mean you should deny your customers excellent service. What it does mean is that you should carefully evaluate the cost of customer requests. Some customer requests that require scrutiny include:
- Customer order change requests*
- Partial pallet orders if full pallets were baked into the pricing
- Below minimum order quantity requests

- Mixed pallet orders
- Expedited service if standard shipping was quoted.

Note: Some of my clients for example allow customers to place orders on Monday, then change or cancel the order as often as the customer wishes during the balance of the week. While this is great for customer service, it wreaks havoc on the rest of the supply chain and is extremely costly to execute. At a minimum, a hard cutoff for orders should be used along with an added customer charge for any abuses associated with the excessive changing of orders. The question I am asking here is this: "If a customer orders on a Wednesday, then changes the order three times by Friday, and demands delivery by Sunday. Is this okay?" Simply put, it's only okay if the customer pays for this level of service.

Exhibit 5.2 - Customer Service Tradeoff

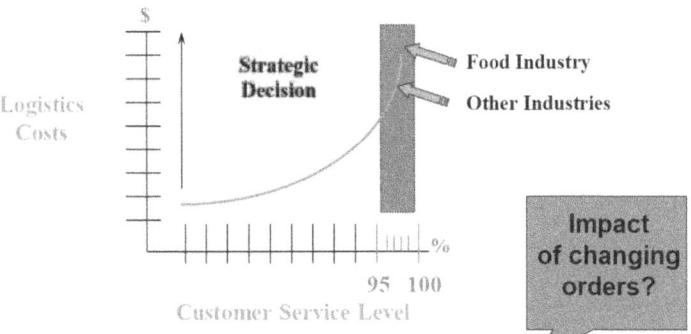

Struggle may exist due to logistics mandates.
Seemingly ridiculous logistics decisions would be questioned by any third-party provider.
Intense customer focus and high switching cost probability creates higher delivery costs.
Other industries often question the extreme cost of marginally incremental customer service.
Companies are desperately attempting to cope with this paradigm shift.
Lack of local control is causing frustration.

When calculating your processing cost per order, you simple take the total cost to process all orders (CSR's and any other staffing related to order processing including an allocation for supervision, telecommunications costs, any customer response related technology expenses, inbound call center expense, cost for faxes and EDI costs, etc.) and divide those costs by the total number of annual customer orders. What you are attempting to calculate here is the total hours it takes to completely process a customer order. For example, let's say a company processes 10,000 orders for the entire year. This company has two CSR's and 20% of a supervisor's time allocated to order processing.

> Total Orders = 10,000
> CSR's wages, benefits, and all other forms of compensation = $40,000/CSR = $80,000
> Supervisor's allocation @ $20,000
> Technology costs estimated to be allocated at $10,000/Year
>
> Total Costs estimated to be $110,000, therefore, the total cost/order is:

$110,000/10,000 = $11/order, including the cost of customer service.

Of course with the use of EDI and in larger companies whereby the order total may be 150,000 orders, the total cost per order will be significantly less. It is the understanding of your company cost to process an order that is important here as due to the number of variables, the cost per order will vary significantly depending upon the size of the firm.

Order Entry Methods - Receiving Orders

When receiving orders from customer or placing orders with suppliers, a few methods can be used, including:
- Verbal orders
- Email
- Fax
- Phone
- Mail
- Internet
- EDI (electronic data interchange).

The problem with accepting all forms of orders is the inherent cost associated with each individual method. This is not to say you should reject orders of a certain kind but instead, consider creating an incentive for your customers to use EDI or internet based ordering. Faxed, verbal, and emailed orders should be minimized. Exhibit 5.3 reveals the various order entry methods along with their keys to success and application.

Exhibit 5.3 - Order Entry Methods

Order Entry Method	Description	Keys to Success	Application
Mail	Order forms received through the mail and manually entered into order processing system.	Scanning & Imaging of forms to automate order entry.	When customers do not have access to automated order entry systems.
Telephone	Orders received by phone and entered into the order processing system by a customer service representative (CSR).	Telephone keypad method (no human interaction). Keep prompts limited and instructions simple.	When range of order entry is limited or when specialized information is needed from a CSR.
Fax	Order forms received by fax.	Using OCR (optical character recognition) to enable direct order entry from faxed forms.	Where order information is captured on 1 page and customers have readily available access to a fax machine.
EDI	Orders received through EDI Protocol directly from the customer's system.	Fast download protocols directly linked to order entry system without human intervention.	When customers already use EDI technology and have excellent familiarity with these types of transactions.

Internet (e-commerce)	Orders received through the company website and shopping cart.	2 click ordering capabilities and guest log-in possibility.	When customers prefer to use Internet-based ordering of individual units.
Email	Orders received by customers to a CSR email address.	Fast turn-around with backup email to ensure quick processing.	When customer does not have access to other forms of technology.
Verbal	Manual (verbal) orders received by sales reps.	Hand-held technology used by sales reps to speed processing.	When field sales reps are used and customers do not have access to technology.

Source: Adapted from Supply Chain Strategy, Edward H. Frazelle, Ph. D.

Order Pattern Recognition

Last year while travelling to Argentina, I attempted to purchase something immediately following my exit from the airplane. My debit card got declined so I called my bank to figure out what went wrong. The bank representative explained that there was nothing wrong with my debit credit card and that I had sufficient funds in the account to cover the purchase. Naturally, I then asked why the card got declined. The bank representative responded by stating that they found it highly unusual that I was buying something using this debit card while in a Foreign Country (I normally used a credit card and not this debit card). They suspected fraud so they declined the purchase hoping I would call to clear-up the matter. In this case, the bank's debit card pattern recognition software had detected an aberrant transaction and wanted to verify that I was the person using the card. This kind of software yields big dividends in the areas of order processing and fulfillment, inventory control, and customer service.

Customer Credit Verification

In his excellent book, *Supply Chain Strategy*, Dr. Edward Frazelle states that:

> "Prior to any order release or inventory commitment, a near real-time (online and/or instant check) customer credit verification must take place to ensure payment." He goes on to say that customers should be classified as:
>
> - Green-Light Customers (those with excellent payment histories)
> - Yellow-Light Customers (those with good-to-average payment histories)
> - Red-Light Customers (those with poor payment histories).
>
> Yellow and red light customers should be carefully checked and limited such that payment can be secured.

Source: Supply Chain Strategy by Dr. Edward Frazelle, page 87.

Order Batching and Changes

Orders should be batched, picked, sequenced, and shipped to minimize total supply chain costs. What you are attempting to do here is satisfy customer response and delivery times while simultaneously reducing the cost of warehousing and distribution. The following factors must be considered when processing orders:
- The optimal pick wave assignment in the warehouse (orders to be picked together to reduce costs). The goal here is to reduce the number of material handling or warehouse touches as each and every time you touch a pallet or a case costs your company money.
- The optimal customer delivery sequencing to be loaded into trucks to minimize off-load times.
- The optimal shipment mode(less-than truckload or LTL, truckload, rail, etc.).

- The optimal individual customer delivery frequency to minimize the number of outbound loads.
- The optimal number of stops or deliveries per load.
- The optimal route to use to make deliveries (this will be explored further in another chapter).
- On-time departure and customer delivery time requirements.

Order batching should be performed online and in real-time wherever possible to eliminate human touches/intervention. Once orders are assigned, order releases to the WMS (warehouse management system) and TMS (transportation management systems) should be performed in a real-time, automated, and integrated fashion to reduce overall costs.

Order changes should be part of your customer service policy. Order changes should be considered prior to releasing the order to the warehouse. Once orders have been picked and staged, additional order changes should carry some sort of additional charge (I realize that this upsets customers at times, so at a minimum, maybe a charge should be considered after the order is loaded on a truck). If the order change causes a delay in shipment, the order should be entered as a new order so as to not delay existing customer orders. Although this does fly in the face of providing excellent customer service, the point here is that we are attempting to reduce supply chain costs. Of course, I do not advocate upsetting your customers, just training them on the added costs.

The status of each and every order should be communicated to customers in a timely fashion. If there are any exceptions to the originally agreed upon contents, timing, or terms of an order, prompt communication to the customer will ensure a high-degree of satisfaction. In addition, any major impact on costs should be discussed with the customer to ultimately arrive at an agreeable additional charge if any.

Customer Response Systems

Customer response systems (CRS), also known as customer relationship management (CRM) systems are one of the hottest areas within global supply chain management due to their vast impact on the total enterprise. CRM's encompass a wide array of company activities, including:
- Order entry and processing
- Customer information or database harvesting
- Customer contact management
- Order and customer activity profiling
- Order pattern recognition
- Open order status
- Active versus inactive customer management
- Customer service policy and management
- Customer satisfaction measurement
- E-Commerce integration.

Most CRM systems have the ultimate goal of establishing a personal relationship with each customer. For example, have you ever received a direct mail piece stating, "Happy Birthday, please come in for a 25% discount to celebrate your special day. " This is a form of customer relationship management.

The Perfect Order Concept

The perfect order is defined as a customer request that is *perfectly*:
- Entered
- Processed
- Filled
- Picked
- Packed
- Shipped
- Delivered
- Communicated
- Invoiced
- Documented.

I know...this is really difficult to execute. But as the old saying goes, "It is better to be approximately right than precisely wrong. " Let's suppose that each of these ten activities has a 97% accuracy rate or conversely a 3% error rate. What this would calculate to mean is that approximately 30% of the time (to keep the math easy as statistically it is somewhat different due to weighting and the true method of statistically calculating error rates) orders are inaccurate in some way, shape or form.

Calculating your perfect order performance requires the following mathematical formula:

Perfect orders = $\prod_{(n=1 \text{ to } N)} P_n$, whereby Pn = the individual performance associated with the ten activities involved in perfect order performance. $\prod$ is expressed as 3.1415.

Exhibit 5.4 reveals a Perfect Order Reporting document that can be used to compare locations in a multi-DC environment.

Exhibit 5.4 - Perfect Order Reporting

Perfect Order %	Atlanta	New York	Baltimore	Denver	Overall
% of Order Entered w/o Error	97	95	99	96	97
% of Orders filled 100%	91	99	93	95	92
% of Orders Shipped On-Time	97	95	98	94	96
% of Orders w/o Damage or Shortages	99	98	96	97	98

% of Orders Collected within Financial Guidelines	90	89	93	94	92
% of Order w/o Returns or Complaints	91	92	89	94	92
Perfect Order TOTAL	94	93	95	96	95

Defining your Customer Service Policy

A customer service policy defines how a company intends to treat its customers. It is the contract between the supply chain and the marketplace. The customer service policy dictates the targets and goals you have set to obtain a high-degree of customer satisfaction. The customer service policy identifies the customer requirements for every area within the supply chain including supply, inventory, order processing, warehousing, and distribution. A sound customer service policy reflects three things:

1. A focus on inventory velocity and total order cycle time compression.
2. Measures of customer service success.
3. Minimum order quantities, expected fill rates, and aggressive response times.
4. What you are trying to answer here is what level of service will provide the highest degree of customer satisfaction while still meeting all the financial objectives within your business model. The real question is whether or not your company can provide Nordstrom-level service without breaking the bank. If you cannot provide extreme levels of customer service, a more definitive approach to a customer service policy is in order. The policy should address what you are, and are not willing to do for customers.

Key Measures of Customer Success

In order to truly understand the level of service being provided, it is important that key measures be tracked and monitored for continued progress. Customer response measures should include:
- Order entry accuracy = orders entered precisely as defined by customers/total orders
- Invoice accuracy = invoices perfectly matched to customer requirements/total invoices
- Order fill rate = total units (cases) shipped/total units (cases)
- On-time delivery % = orders delivered within minutes of customer desired window/total orders
- Damage % = orders delivered without in-transit damage/total orders shipped
- Claims-free shipment % = orders delivered without any shipment-related claims/total orders
- Total order cycle time (in days) = the time elapsed from customer order to delivery date

A Word about Reverse Logistics

One of the most important aspects of providing service is the understanding of *why* customers do certain things, including:
1. Returning items.
2. Complaining about product quality.
3. Demanding improved service.

Simply stated, product returns are too expensive and need to be minimized. In fact, in many cases it is often better to tell customers to keep the item and not deal with all the reverse logistics associated with processing a return. The first step to understanding this is documenting why customers are returning items and/or complaining about product quality. Exhibit 5.5 reveals the reasons why customers call.

Exhibit 5.5 - Reasons Customers Call

 # Complaints

Reason	# Complaints
Where is my order?	25
Late delivery	16
Product quality	6
Need Instructions	10

After documenting the reasons why customers are complaining, the next step is to uncover the root causes of the complaints. Was it something the warehouse did incorrectly or did the freight carrier make a mistake? Then list the underlying issues associated with the complaint and determine the resolution for each complaint. In addition, you should assign a cost to remedy each complaint.

As mentioned, returns can be very expensive so minimizing reverse logistics should be a major focal point of any supply chain. To keep returns to a minimum, keep your return policy simple. For example, "no returns for made-to-order products." For all other products, a 15% restocking fee plus the actual return shipping cost will be deducted from your refund.

CONCLUSION

Creating customer value should be the main goal behind every supply chain. Supply chain management greatly affects customer satisfaction, which in turn, impacts repeat business. Order processing and customer service are two critical functions within supply chain management that can make a difference. The key to improving service is to increase inventory velocity while compressing total order cycle time. Minimizing the supply chain "touch-points" associated with order processing while monitoring critical customer service measures will create a competitive point of difference. In addition, paying strict attention to perfect order execution will make it difficult for customers to switch to a competitor.

Chapter Summary

- Supply Chain Management starts with a customer order which should be celebrated.

- Order processing is a critical front-end business process that has major downstream supply chain impact.

- The true cost of an order is underestimated 80% of the time.

- Supply chain managers need to adopt the philosophy that the customer is *usually* right.

- The key to supply chain management is increasing inventory velocity while compressing total order cycle time.

- Perfect order execution will improve customer satisfaction.

- Defining your customer service policy and measuring its effectiveness will create a competitive advantage.

Exploratory Questions

1. Why do many organizations accept every kind of customer order?

2. What is meant by the expression, the customer is *usually* right?

3. How do you define the Perfect Order?

4. What are the two (2) keys to supply chain success?

5. Why is minimizing reverse logistics so important?

6. What is meant by supply chain "touch-points?"

7. Why is it so important to carefully define your customer service policy?

Case Study – NMC, Inc.

NMC was a California based direct marketing firm that specialized in "As seen on TV" products. Most of the products marketed by NMC were advertised on television. These impulse-type products have historically been riddled with a high rate of return due to consumer remorse post purchase. In NMC's case, the return rate was rising at an alarming rate as was consumer complaints. The return rate was estimated to be 17% of total orders. This alarming rate of returns was also causing Better Business Bureau complaints, and even a few Attorney General issues. At the same time, company profitability was at a historic low.

The CEO decided to hire a consulting firm to study the reverse logistics problem. The project mandate was to uncover the major causes of returns and make subsequent suggestions to increase consumer satisfaction. The CEO wanted to ultimately increase profitability while improving customer service.

During the evaluation, we collected the following data:
- Returns were driven primarily by perceived value (quality) issues
- NMC had changed suppliers and moved offshore to China to secure most goods
- Reasons for consumer complaints were not being tracked or managed.
- Customers were allowed to return without a restocking fee or return shipping expense
- Interruptions in supply and increased lead time from China were causing shipping delays
- Supply chain costs had increased an average of 3.6% per year for five straight years.

The project consisted primarily of evaluating the reasons for consumer returns. During the study, quality and sourcing issues with China became apparent. The evaluation ultimately pointed to poor quality as the source of consumer complaints. The majority of the returns were caused by the following:

- An average total order cycle time of six weeks from order to delivery. In fact, we uncovered a direct correlation between order delays and returns.

- Perceived quality was determined to be the number-one cause of consumer complaints.

- The product defect rate per 1.000 units had increased 24% since the Chinese supplier was introduced.

- The process used to choose the Chinese supplier was sub-par and did not include a first-run quality inspection.

The fix was rather easy. We reviewed product specifications and engineering, including visiting the Chinese supplier and working together with them to improve product quality. We reviewed the causes of product defects and conducted a focus group to solicit consumer input. We also developed a formal customer service policy that included a return restocking fee and shipping charge (only after the quality problem was addressed). NMC started to track and monitor causes for defects and returns and put forth a concerted effort to reduce supply lead time and total order cycle time.

Case Study Questions:

1. Why do you think so many companies do not pay attention to reverse logistics?

2. What does this case study suggest as it relates to moving supply off-shore?

3. What steps should NMC take to make sure this problem doesn't happen again?

4. How specific customer service measures should NMC monitor?

6. FORECASTING AND DEMAND PLANNING

"Forecasting is the art of saying what will happen, and then explaining why it didn't!"

Anonymous

When describing the criteria for successful real estate investing, the saying goes, "location, location, location. " In the field of successful supply chain management, it can be stated, "forecasting, forecasting, forecasting. " In Chapter 5, we discussed that all supply chain activities start with an order. I stand corrected. In fact, supply chain activities really start with a forecast. Forecasting, which is akin to looking into a crystal ball, has been the nemesis of many companies, typically having an accuracy rate of only 75% due to new product introduction, poor or insufficient historical data, or inadequate statistical modeling tools. This chapter delves into the art and science of forecasting and demand planning. I will provide the variety of methods that can be used to forecast demand, along with a set of statistical tools to employ to bring an increased level of sophistication to your forecasting.

Definition of Forecasting

Forecasting is the statistical method used to predict future events or results based upon historical data. Business. com defines forecasting as: A planning tool that helps management cope with the uncertainty of the future, relying mainly on data from the past and present and the analysis of trends. While both of these definitions work, the key words within these definitions are method, tool, historical, uncertainty, and future. To keep it simple, forecasting should be viewed as a glimpse into the future based upon history. Forecasting is fundamentally based upon *known* historical demand plus the judgmental prediction of *unknown* emerging or new products.

The Immutable Laws of Forecasting

There are some forecasting absolutes, including:
1. Most forecasts are wrong.
2. The shorter the time horizon, the more accurate the forecast.
3. Forecasts are less accurate at the SKU level and more accurate at the *family* level.
4. The more history, the better the forecast.
5. Forecasts will help or hinder with production scheduling and inventory levels.

Why Bother Forecasting?

Forecasting is the backbone of supply chain management in that it can lead to an increase in inventory availability and a higher return on assets. Forecasting can be used to assess capacity requirements, develop budgets and capital plans, assist with hiring and staffing decisions, predict materials and production requirements, and for assessing long-term resources. Unless you can build to order, proper forecasting will dramatically improve the execution of your supply chain activities.

The Benefits of Forecasting

Proper forecasting will lead to:
- A reduction in inventory investment
- A decrease in safety stock (safety stock is normally based upon three times the standard deviation of the forecast error; therefore, for every $1 you cut in forecast error standard deviation, you cut $3 in safety stock)
- An increase in perfect order performance
- A shorter cash-to-cash cycle
- A reduction in backorders
- An improvement in customer satisfaction
- A higher fill rate
- An increase in revenue and margin.

In fact, based upon a study of 118 companies conducted by my consulting firm, a dramatic improvement in forecasting was the single most important improvement a company could make to reduce overall supply chain infrastructure costs. This study also uncovered the following:

1. Even high-performing firms have some excess and obsolete inventory.
2. Best in class companies still experience a 4-7% out-of-stock level.

Causes of Forecasting Inaccuracy

So, why do even some of the best companies experience problems with forecasting? Simply stated, forecasting issues are primarily caused by the uncertainty of market demand and the fickle nature of customer buying behavior. In addition, the major causes of forecast inaccuracy include:

- Functional silos. Due to a difference in the way the various departments within an organization are rewarded, conflicting priorities and goals often get in the way of proper forecasting.

- The process used to forecast. There are many ERP systems (enterprise resource planning) that have sufficient built-in forecasting algorithms to accommodate most organizations. Yet, forecasts remain inaccurate in many cases due to the who, what, when, and how a forecast gets put together.

- The lack of sufficient technological application and integration across the enterprise which causes spreadsheets"R"us.

- Lack of a forecast champion and/or accountability. Should only sales develop the forecast? Should the senior-level team dictate the forecast? Should Finance be intimately involved in forecasting? Where should the overall accountability of forecasting be placed? It is usually best to have a functional team develop a forecast, and then assign a forecast key-holder who has the ultimate responsibility for the accuracy of the forecast.

- The belief that forecasting is a ridiculous exercise. This sort of denial creates a half-hearted effort whereby the team only goes through the motion but doesn't dig into the details to ensure a sound forecast.

- Overstating sales to appease the board, senior executives or stockholders. I once resigned from a company where I was a vice president due to this exact issue. In this case, my boss at the time, who was the CEO, demanded that my division budget an 8% increase in sales during a flat market and lousy economy. My entire management team meticulously developed our forecast which called for a 5.2% increase in sales, which we considered a stretch goal. We knew that budgeting an 8% increase would ensure that we spent the entire next twelve months "explaining away poor performance. " We also knew that none of us would get a bonus given this unrealistic expectation.

- Ignorance of Industry and Economic Trends. Trend analysis plays an important role in forecasting. Is the GDP (gross domestic product) expanding or contracting? Is inflation on the rise? Is unemployment higher than normal and is consumer confidence below prior year? Are you in a mature industry experiencing stagnant sales? Many in academia believe that a simple formula for forecasting is:

F = historical demand + growth in GDP + seasonality factor.

I submit that there is a lot more to forecasting than the understanding of GDP and seasonality. In fact, a much better indicator than GDP would be specific industry growth or decline.

- Catastrophic events that cause major problems with supply and demand. Consider the earthquake that devastated Japan. Toyota had all kinds of problems securing parts after that event, which I am sure wreaked havoc on their ability to forecast.

The Challenges of Forecasting

You will face numerous challenges when attempting to forecast, including:
- The lack of availability of sophisticated statistical models
- Data integrity problems, particularly at the SKU (stock keeping unit) level
- Insufficient management and customer input
- Lack of functional integration (technology) across the company
- New product introduction, product turnover, or product mix changes
- Uncoordinated marketing and sales promotions
- The need to consolidate numerous forecasts across many divisions or functional areas.

Types of Forecasts

Forecasting is used primarily to get a futuristic look into demand, price, and supply. The demand is usually in terms of company and market level sales. Price forecasting includes the prediction of product pricing, the cost of debt (money), and the cost of materials and services. Supply forecasting includes the cost of commodities, raw materials, and labor. Forecasting can also be used for capacity planning, distribution network design, and production planning.

Forecasting can even be used to have a little fun. Imagine trying to forecast or predict the number of points Los Angeles Lakers superstar Kobe Bryant will score in his next basketball game. There are some who would take the easy way out and just use his historical points scored average to predict his next game. More often than not, this approach would result in a wrong answer. Just like in the game of business, basketball has its art and its science. In order to properly predict Kobe's next game, we would need to include the following quantitative and qualitative factors in order to get a more precise forecast:

- Kobe's overall points scored average
- His points scored average against the team he will be playing next
- Kobe's general state of health (any injuries that may hamper his play)
- Kobe's scoring average against the defender in the next game
- A decision surrounding whether Kobe will play the role of facilitator or scorer
- Kobe's scoring average on the precise day of the week and time of day for the next game
- A look at the starting five to see if other player issues may change Kobe's role
- The average number of minutes Kobe plays against this opponent.

As you can see, even something as fun as predicting Kobe's points scored number can be quite complicated. Now, just imagine trying to predict the sales of a company that has introduced three new products, has four divisions, seven vice presidents, and just acquired another company. Easier said than done!

Approaches to Forecasting

There are two (2) main approaches to forecasting; the quantitative approach and the qualitative approach. The quantitative approach is best used in a mature industry (company), when historical data are readily available, and when the situation you are attempting to forecast is stable (e. g., all things being equal, base Pepsi-Cola will generally increase as a function of the growth in population). The quantitative method does not work well in a wildly fluctuating situation. Instead, the qualitative approach should be considered. The qualitative approach is best used when there is situational ambiguity, poor or insufficient data, and where the situation requires some intuition and experience. These two methods should be used in combination due to forecasting being both an art and a science. The best approach is to start with the quantitative approach then filter the answer by adding qualitative factors that may change the results.

The quantitative approach to forecasting uses data at its foundation; specifically, historical demand, seasonality adjustments, general economic data such as the Gross Domestic Product (GDP), inflation, and industry growth or decline statistics. After these data are gathered, statistical modeling such as linear regression is used to "predict' the future or next likely data point(s). The qualitative approach to forecasting uses a less scientific method and involves gathering data from a variety of sources including:
- Judgment of an expert group
- Feelings or intuition
- Perception
- Subjective input
- Experience
- A review of previous similar product launches.

As mentioned, it is usually better to use a combination of both approaches (quantitative and qualitative) when attempting to see into the future. Due to basic unpredictability, be sure to have a contingency plan as, remember, most forecasts are wrong. Along with these high-level approaches, there a few types of forecasts that most organizations must execute.

Demand Forecasting

There are two (2) types of demand forecasts; overall market demand and company-level demand. Overall market demand helps an organization decide the share of market they will attempt to command. Firm level demand takes into account the variables that impact product specific forecasting. Within most supply chains, customer demand for the majority of products doesn't vary much yet inventory levels, in-stock percentages, and backorders often fluctuate quite considerably. For example, with most mature products, retail sales will remain steady with the exception of any seasonality. However, at the distributor level for the same product, demand may fluctuate.

Supply Forecasting

In some cases, forecasting supply is more important than predicting customer demand. An interruption in supply can cripple a company's sales by slowing down the flow of inbound goods. This has become increasingly important due to the global nature of supply. Demand may vary at the supplier level, even though customer orders are seemingly constant. This phenomenon is called the *bullwhip effect*. The bullwhip effect is defined as the variability that takes place when moving backwards up the supply chain, from customers to suppliers. The impact that this variability has on a typical supply chain includes increased safety stock levels, an increase in capacity requirements, and inconsistency in order frequency at the supplier and distributor levels.

Supply chain variability is caused by many factors, including:
1. Poor inventory control practices.
2. Long lead time, which forces an increase in safety stock requirements.

3. Inconsistent ordering patterns.
4. Inconsistency in supply.
5. Price fluctuations, which causes the downstream effect of "stocking-up" to avoid a price increase.

In order to reduce variability, supply chain management must focus on the following:
- Ensuring consistency in supply through strategic partnering with suppliers.
- Working to reduce lead time wherever possible by managing freight, customs, and order processing.
- Reducing uncertainty by centralizing demand information.
- Managing capacity and production to ensure appropriate inventory levels.

Price Forecasting

Most organizations need to forecast prices for key raw materials, components, sub-assemblies, and/or commodities. This often dictates a practice called *forward buying,* wherein you buy larger quantities that require inventory storage in an attempt to protect against an increase in price. At the same time, organizations need to forecast selling prices for individual products, along with discounts and allowances that may raise the forecast requirement. Regardless, part of the forecasting process is to consider the impact that inbound goods and selling price may have on the need for overall supply and inventory.

Methods to Improve Forecasting

In his excellent work, *Supply Chain Strategy*, Dr. Edward Frazelle, states that the following principles are used to attack the sources of forecast inaccuracy:
- Forecast elimination, by using a build to order strategy wherever possible
- Forecast Measurement, whereby accuracy is monitored and rewarded

- Forecast Accountability, by assigning a forecast champion who is responsible for accuracy
- Capturing True Demand, at the customer level
- Forecast Information Sharing with suppliers and customers
- Event Calendaring, whereby the forecast is tied to certain events that drive sales
- Pattern Recognition, by using linear regression to uncover noticeable patterns in the data
- Rewarding Forecasting Accuracy, by modifying bonus and pay structure to create forecast accuracy incentives.

These eight methods, when employed diligently (at least the majority of them) will improve forecast accuracy by at least 25% and will eliminate the allusion of forecast excellence. Forecast accuracy is calculated as:

Forecast Error = Actual Demand – Forecasted Demand (usually shown as a percentage)

When there are data over a number of periods, you can also measure the mean forecast error and the mean absolute deviation by using the following formulas:

Mean Forecast Error Formula:

$$MFE = \frac{\sum_{i=1}^{n}(E_i)}{n}$$

Mean Absolute Deviation Formula:

$$MAD = \frac{\sum_{i=1}^{n}|E_i|}{n}$$

Remember, safety stock is usually calculated as three times the standard deviation of the forecast error. Therefore, it is essential to tighten the forecast error wherever possible.

Tools for Forecasting

There are a variety of qualitative and quantitative tools available to help with forecasting, including:

Qualitative Technique	Overview	When Used	Procedure
Jury of Executive Opinion	Combines input from key industry decision makers and influencers	No historical data available No causal data	Brainstorming sessions and quarterly forecast meetings
Delphi Method	Judgmental Group Think	Group members first work individually, then collectively to reduce personal bias	Panel of experts surveyed in round-robin fashion normally using a facilitator
Leading Indicator	Based upon industry and general economic trends	When externally influenced by the economy or specific industry trends	When results tend to be seasonal in nature; uses industry trends to predict future results.
Life Cycle Analogy Method	Data from similar and/or previous product used to determine growth	When a new product is being introduced and no data are available	Determine the pattern of the similar product data and use intuitive judgment to predict results
Time Series Modeling (see Exhibit 6.1)	Distinguished between random fluctuations and true changes in demand	Based upon simple pattern of data; uses moving or weighted averages	Develop chart of data points and time (periods or months) and predict next logical data point

Qualitative Technique	Overview	When Used	Procedure
Curve Fitting	Approximates basic trends in historical data	Long-range planning	Identifies a curve or trend that matches a series of data points
Input-Output Models	Used to identify linkages between data sets	When products are comprised of several sub-assemblies	A quantitative economic technique that identifies and quantifies the interdependencies between different sets of data
Linear Regression Analysis (see Exhibit 6.2)	Used to predict next most logical future data point	When historical data are available and abundant	Gather historical data and use software program
Exponential Smoothing (see Exhibit 6.3)	Special form of moving average modeling similar to time series	When there are spikes or outliers in the data	Develop a chart of weeks of data then apply smoothing constant

In general, the selection of the appropriate modeling technique can be guided by the stage of the product's life cycle. New products require the use of more judgmental and qualitative techniques due to the lack of data. Semi-Mature products should use simple time series modeling. Mature products that are rich with historical data should use more quantitative causal models such as linear regression analysis. The two (2) modeling tools I use most often are Linear Regression and Time Series (Moving Average and Weighted Average) Modeling. The formulas and an example of the outputs realized from these modeling techniques are shown in Exhibits 6.1 and 6.2.

Exhibit 6.1 - Time Series Modeling

Simple Time Series Output graph showing trend.

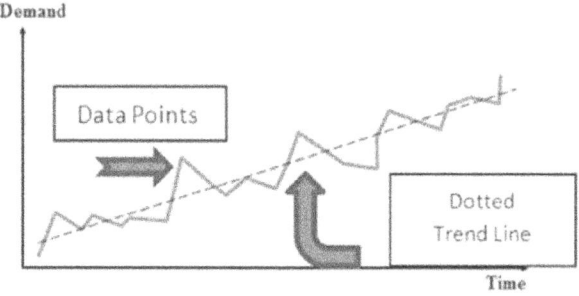

Time Series Moving Average Formula: whereby F = forecast, D = demand, N = number of months or periods.

Month	Demand
1	10
2	13
3	9
4	8
5	11
6	13
7	14
8	11
9	12
10	10
11	8
12	?

$$F_{t+1} = \frac{\sum_{i=1}^{n} D_{t+1-i}}{n}$$

3-Month Moving Average Prediction for Month 12, assuming no seasonality is: (12+10+8)/3 = 10

Time Series Weighted Moving Average Formula: whereby F = forecast, D = demand, W = weighting factor.

Month	Demand
1	10
2	13
3	9
4	8
5	11
6	13
7	14
8	11
9	12
10	10
11	8
12	?

$$F_{t+1} = \frac{\sum_{i=1}^{n} W_{t+1-i} D_{t+1-i}}{\sum_{i=1}^{n} W_{t+1-i}}$$

3-Month Weighted Moving Average using factors of: 0. 6, 0. 3, and 0. 1.
(12*. 6)+(10*. 3)+(8*. 1)/(6. +. 3+. 1) = 11

Exhibit 6.2 - Linear Regression Analysis

Formula: y = a + b(x), whereby Y = predicted variable (i. e., demand), X = predictor variable.

Simple Linear Regression

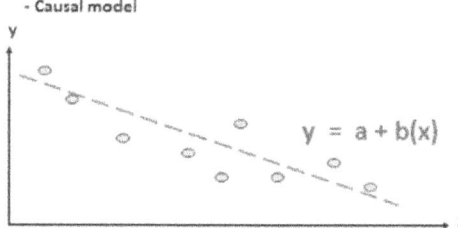

- Assumes linear relationship
- Causal model

y = a + b(x)

Exhibit 6.3 - Exponential Smoothing

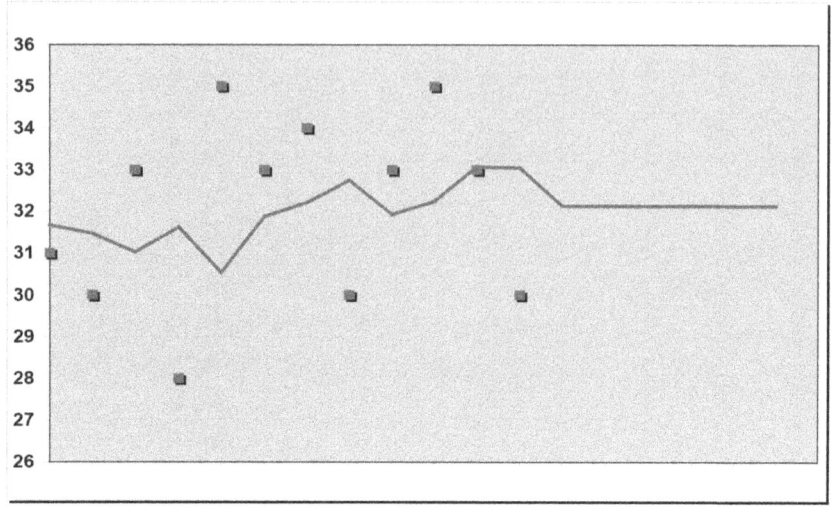

The formula for exponential smoothing is:

$$F_{t+1} = \alpha D_t + (1 - \alpha) F_t$$

Where:

F_{t+1} = the forecast for the time period t + 1 (the new forecast)

F_t = the current forecast

D_t = the actual value for the time period t

α = smoothing constant used to weight the current forecast and time value

Most of these modeling methods can be performed using Microsoft Excel™ or SPSS™. There are also numerous off-the-shelf software programs that can be used to forecast results.

Conclusion

In supply chain management, everything starts with a forecast. When the forecast is inaccurate, the negative downstream effect is quite considerable. When the forecast is sound, the rest of the supply chain works in concert and performs at a higher level. Forecasting is both an art and a science and can be the difference between mediocre performance and "step-change" results. Forecasting is akin to being a fortune-teller who attempts to get rich by predicting the future. Ninety percent of the time the fortune-teller is wrong with the exception of some random chance that simulates success.

Forecasting mature products is much easier to accomplish, since typically these products are rich with historical data. New product forecasting is where the system breaks-down. Across most industries, total forecast accuracy is in the area of 70%; meaning that 30% of the time, the forecast is wrong. This is somewhat misleading as new product forecast accuracy is wrong the overwhelming majority of the time. Finally, the bullwhip effect causes increased variability as you move backwards up the supply chain, causing increased operational inefficiency.

Chapter Summary

- Most forecasts, particularly new product sales predictions, are wrong.

- Inaccurate forecasting has a large negative impact on the downstream functions within the supply chain.

- The bullwhip effect causes increased variability on the front-end of a typical supply chain (small changes in customer demand often creates large front-end order variations).

- Forecasting is an art and a science and should incorporate both quantitative and qualitative methods to improve accuracy.

- Large amount of historical data increases forecast accuracy.

- Many companies give off the allusion of forecast excellence; in reality, the majority of firms perform inadequately in the area of forecasting from a supply chain standpoint.

- Simple time series modeling and linear regression can be useful tools to improve forecasting.

Exploratory Questions

1. Why is forecasting so difficult?

2. What are some of the major challenges associated with sound forecasting?

3. What are the key benefits to improving forecast accuracy?

4. Why should a supply chain manager consider using both quantitative and qualitative methods when conducting a forecast?

5. Explain why functional silos causes a decrease in forecast accuracy.

6. Discuss the bullwhip effect and its impact on supply chain variability.

Case Study & Questions

PSC, Inc. is a California based company that specializes in unique, high-end cameras that are truly one-of-a-kind. The company is run by a group of brilliant scientists and inventors who decided to diversify their product offerings by introducing a novel product under the new company banner SK Robotics. The new product, called the Robot, is an under-vehicle inspection device that reveals drugs or bombs. It is used primarily in the surveillance and counter-terrorism industries. Since the Robot was a unique product with few competitors, forecasting sales was difficult. The partners at SK Robotics had the following questions:

1. Would the industry accept this kind of device since the current technique was still the old "stick-and-mirror?"

2. What kind of sales can be expected from the Robot, considering that it is a new product?

3. How can SK Robotics do a better job of forecasting results, considering there was no sales history?

4. Does using the results from similar product categories make sense when attempting to forecast sales for the Robot?

5. How can a firm predict best-case, expected-case, and worst-case scenarios?

The project consisted of conducting a market analysis and providing a sale's forecast prediction for the Robot. Since there was no historical data, we chose to use only qualitative methods to arrive at our conclusions. After considerable thought and debate, the team decided to use several forecasting tools to accomplish the project goals, which was to answer the questions put forth by the executive team. The forecasting tools included:

- *Jury of Executive Opinion.* We started out by developing a set of standard questions that were consistent with the questions the executive team wanted answered. We then interviewed the key executives at SK Robotics. We then developed a list of influencers in the surveillance and counter terrorism industries. We used the same set of questions and interviewed ten of the main influencers within each of the industries. After this, we formulated a set of conclusions that came from these interviews. These questions and conclusions were to be used for the Delphi method of forecasting as it provided a good foundation.

- *Delphi Method.* We formed a task force of that consisted of a cross-section of people within and outside the industries in question. We were even able to convince a competitor to sit on the task force. We facilitated a round-robin type brainstorming session that fielded the standard set of questions we developed, paying particular attention to whether or not the conclusions that resulted from the opinion interviews had any validity.

- *Leading Indicators.* We used a modified version of a traditional leading indicator analysis. The team decided to consider the following data as part of the leading indicator analysis:
    - General Growth in GDP in the United States
    - General Economic Data such as CPI (inflation), PPI (producer price index),
    - Capital Spending
    - Growth in the Surveillance and Counter Terrorism Industries
    - Estimate of the Number of Organizations currently using the stick and mirror approach
    - First Year Sales for similar products and products within similar categories
    - Price points for similar products
    - Number of airports in the USA currently performing random entry inspections.

Based upon the interviews, the brainstorming session, and the data collected, we were able to successfully forecast the launch of the Robot. Of course, the forecast wasn't perfect as there were unexpected international sales and some governmental regulatory hurdles that needed to be overcome.

Case Study Questions:

1. What is the danger of using solely quantitative forecasting techniques when predicting sales?

2. What assumptions must be understood when using similar product results to forecast sales on a new product?

3. What events might have derailed the forecast?

4. After the first year of history, what quantitative method could be used to forecast the following year sales?

7: INVENTORY MANAGEMENT AND CONTROL

"We want to turn our inventory faster than our people."
James Sinegal

All inventory is bad. Get rid of all of it, I say. Of course, I mean this figuratively, not literally. Although I make these comments rather tongue-and-cheek, the point here is that most businesses simply have too much inventory. As of this writing, there is about $1 trillion dollars of inventory in the United States alone. The old adage, only the strong survive clearly applies here. He or she who has the least inventory wins, case closed. The era of carrying a ton of safety stock, introducing numerous products without strategic thought, or carrying a few more items, *just in case*. Those days are over. It is way too expensive to carry excess inventory with the estimated carrying cost ranging from 15-35% annually. That's right, if you carry an average of $5 million of inventory on-hand, it is costing you an additional $1 million/year (at 20%) just to store it, handle it, count it, etc.

By the end of this chapter, you will learn:
- Why we hold inventory
- The true cost of inventory

- Why 95% accuracy is not good enough
- The causes of inventory inaccuracy
- The major drivers of inventory
- How to set up a sound inventory policy
- The need to improve forecasting
- The cost of customer service and its impact on inventory
- The critical tenets of inventory
- The importance of using inventory KPI's (key performance indicators)
- Inventory management challenges
- Why you should completely eliminate taking physical inventories
- The top technologies for Inventory Control.

What is Inventory Management?

Inventory management is the process of planning, establishing, controlling, and monitoring of inventory in a way which results in minimized costs, shorter delivery times to customers, and increased perfect order performance (perfect throughout the entire supply chain). In addition, inventory management must include the balancing of cost and service; that is, to employ the lowest cost of inventory that meets or exceeds your customer service requirements.

Misconceptions about Inventory

There are a number of misconceptions that exist about inventory control, including:

1. The higher the inventory level, the higher the customer service level.

    Reality: Most companies that hold large amounts of inventory are storing it in the wrong locations and in the wrong individual inventory item amounts. So, despite carrying a lot of overall inventory, the corresponding customer service level in many cases is poor.

2. Carrying increased inventory levels reduces customer stock-outs.

   Reality: The problem with this statement is that it requires SKU-level forecasting and in-stock perfection. When a customer reaches for the regular bag of potato chips, it is usually on the shelf; however, when that same customer reaches for nacho cheese and jalapeno chips, the cost of always carrying that secondary flavor (that doesn't sell nearly as much as the regular chips) is too high.

3. Inventory is like insurance; "you need it when you need it."

   Reality: Just like carrying a $10 million life insurance policy on yourself when you have no heirs, no debts, and no philanthropic beliefs, carrying a ton of inventory just-because is like being over-insured. It is simply too costly.

4. Inventory only relates to finished goods.

   Reality: Inventory consists of any item you buy, sell, store, produce, or even count, including raw materials, sub-assemblies, or components.

Let me be clear here by stating that the goal is not merely inventory minimization. The objective should be to carry the lowest amount of inventory that results in the highest level of customer service at the lowest cost.

Why do we hold Inventory?

Most companies are holding excessive inventories for all the wrong reasons. In a recent survey (see Exhibit 7.1), a supply chain consulting group uncovered why most firms are carrying too much inventory.

Exhibit 7.1: Reasons for Inventory.

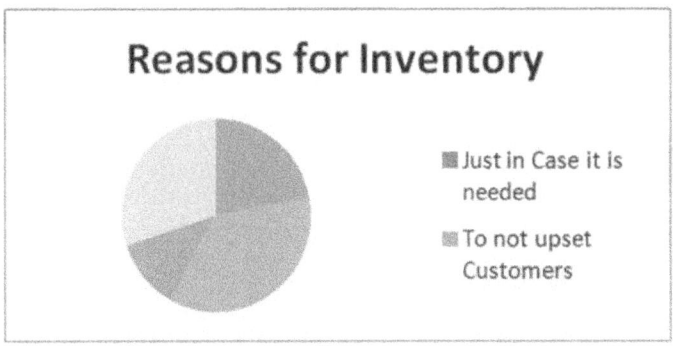

Source: IFMC, Inc. survey of 132 companies.

Exhibit 7.1 reveals that 70% of the reasons behind holding inventory are highly subjective in nature. No science or strategic thought is being used when formulating most inventory policies. In order to better control inventory, you need to eliminate all the emotion surrounding customer service and deal with the new realities of business, namely:

- Only the strong will survive (strong in service and lowest in cost to serve)
- Most industries will see further collapse through consolidation
- It's no longer if you will go global, it's when
- Progressive firms use critical performance metrics (analytics) to manage their business
- If your company is large, act like it. You can't simply behave like you are still pushing a cart down the street selling vegetables.

These realities dictate taking a strong position on inventory levels based upon information and a keen sense of what customers truly want and need. *Just because* is no longer an acceptable means of managing inventory.

Types of Inventory

There are a few types of inventory that most businesses carry in order to satisfy customer requirements, namely:

- Demand inventory, which is expected to sell and to fulfill existing or future orders.

- Lot-sized inventory, which results from producing or purchasing to receive productivity or cost savings.

- Anticipated inventory, which is inventory you anticipate selling at some time in the near future, hopefully based upon historical demand and strategic thought.

- Hedge inventory, which is purchased due to anticipated raw material price increases, industry driven price increases, or predictions surrounding the general economy.

- Safety stock inventory, which is nothing more than protection against stock-outs and backorders. This is the inventory that is usually questionable and based upon a "just-in-case" mentality.

The Psychology of Inventory

There is a simple reason why most companies pile up or even horde their inventory. I call it the "hope-it-will-sell-fallacy." Sales pressure causes the organization to stockpile inventory, hoping customers will buy. This is especially prevalent when a new product is introduced. As a result, many business owners and senior management teams sit in fear of running out of inventory. The pervasive motto seems to be let's keep a few extra on hand to make sure we don't upset our customers. This is primarily due to the "I want it now mentality" that exists in society today. What is interesting about that flaw in logic is that studies have shown that when consumers want a product bad enough, they will wait for it. Take the luxury brand Prada. One of their premium pairs of sunglasses proved so popular that consumers often had to wait 2-3 weeks to get a pair; which they did without argument! Of course, this is not to say you should make your customers wait, especially if you have a non-branded or run of the mill type product. What I am saying is that inventory should be managed without all the emotional hogwash typically attached to this function. In addition, it is critical to understand that inventory is all about three things:

1. Increasing velocity throughout the supply chain.
2. Obtaining better than 95% inventory accuracy levels (book to cycle-count/physical).
3. Using key metrics/analytics to drive inventory policy.

What is interesting about inventory psychology is that approximately every seven years when the economy swings from good to bad, the majority of businesses shred inventory as a first step move to reduce the cost structure. What should that tell us? It's simple. Act like the economy is lousy all the time. This mentality will create a foundation for caution which will make a manager think twice before ordering more inventory.

Inventory Policy Challenges

There is a great deal of pressure being placed upon the supply chain function of most organizations which is causing a re-examination of inventory policy. These challenges include:
- The need for a shorter cash-to-cash cycle
- Pressure to increase the return on invested capital
- Intense competition which leads to market pressure to reduce prices
- Eliminating stock-outs and backorders
- Increased global competition which is driving down pricing
- A more discerning and sophisticated customer
- The increased pressure to source products globally to lower material costs.

These challenges are forcing most companies to re-examine not only their overall inventory strategy, but also the need for inventory itself. Many smaller firms are considering alternatives to carrying inventory such as a made-to-order strategy or a drop-ship type arrangement similar to those used by some large e-commerce based companies. In addition to these external challenges, there are some internal struggles facing most organizations today, including:
1. Functional silos due to the lack of cross-functional support and/or lack of common goals and objectives (and conflicting reward systems).

2. The complicated nature of setting individual customer and inventory item-level service levels.
3. The lack of sound historical data which makes cost to serve modeling difficult.
4. Antiquated application of technology which makes data mining impossible.
5. Lead time variability at the supplier and customer level.

The increased pressure being placed upon most supply chains is dictating a close look at two major inventory strategies. These two strategies, which are outlined later in this chapter, include reducing inventory carrying costs through supply chain design and optimization (lowering infrastructure costs), and cost-to-serve modeling which includes aggressively reducing lead times from suppliers and to customers and adjusting customer delivery frequency and minimum order quantities.

Inventory Drivers

As shown in Exhibit 7.2, inventory levels are driven by a variety of organizational edicts or problems.

Exhibit 7.2 – Inventory Drivers.

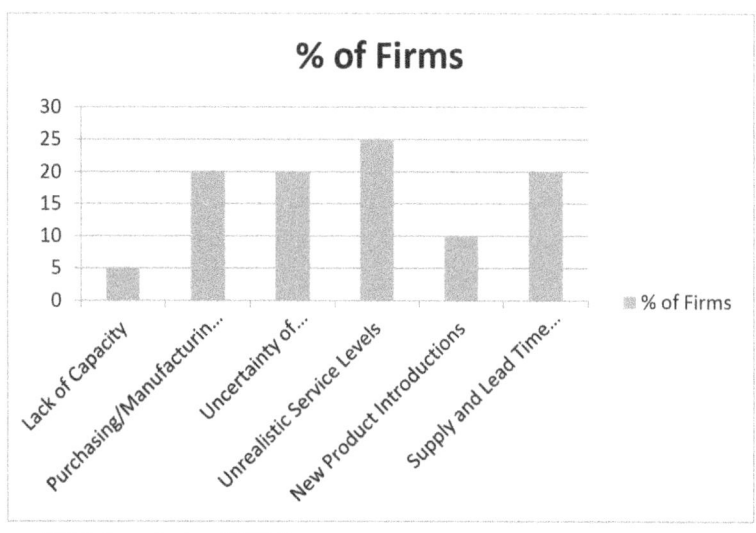

Source: IFMC, Inc. study of 132 firms.

What is most interesting about this chart is that 90% of the drivers cited are controllable. Functional silos need to be eliminated by using a common reward system across the enterprise. Capacity must be strategically planned out for at least a five-year horizon. Customer service levels, including delivery frequency should be optimized such that you service your customers at the lowest cost/highest service level, and new products should be introduced methodically and with cross functional involvement. In addition, purchasing must work in concert with Finance to obtain supply at the lowest cost yet minimal inventory levels.

Causes of Inventory Inaccuracy

As you can see, inventory control is a highly complex subject that is impacted by many internal and external forces. These forces also impact inventory accuracy. As I have stated, 95% accuracy is just not good enough. Imagine if we accepted 95% accuracy elsewhere. We'd have a mess on our hands. For example, if we accepted 95% accuracy in hospital cardiology wards, 5% of patients might undergo major heart surgery unnecessarily! So, what are the major causes of inventory inaccuracy?

Major Causes of Inventory Inaccuracy

1. Parts moved w/o proper documentation (transaction).
2. Parts not received correctly from Supplier.
3. Supplier sent different count than on packing slip w/o verification count.
4. Lack of proper picking usually associated with insufficient training.
5. Incorrectly accounting for scrap/waste.
6. Inter-company transfers w/o proper documentation.
7. Lack of cycle counting and poor use of annual physical counting of inventory (using temporary and untrained personnel to count at the end of each fiscal year).
8. Basic human error due to the lack of technology being employed (it is estimated that for every 300 keystrokes of a computer keyboard, a human error occurs).

Identifying these causes and sharing them with everybody within the firm who has a stake in inventory control will go a long way to improve the process. A simple chart like Exhibit 7.3 should do the trick. The chart shows the number of times a reason occurred during a physical count of inventory.

Exhibit 7.3: Reasons for inventory inaccuracy

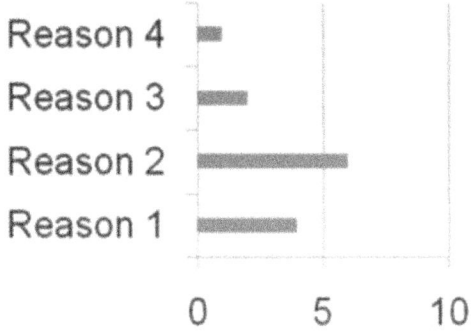

Benefits of Improved Inventory Accuracy

There are two primary benefits associated with improved inventory accuracy. First, having greater inventory accuracy makes an organization more responsive and reliable to their customers by ensuring the right products in stock at the right levels. Secondly, increased inventory accuracy improves financial performance by reducing end of year inventory write-offs associated with missing or misplaced inventory.

The Impact of Customer Service

One of the most often cited reasons for excessive inventory is the need to keep customers happy. There is a belief that the more inventory I keep, the happier my customers will be (the theory being if I keep a lot of inventory, I will run out of items less frequently). In fact, this mentality of keeping customers happy and the old saying, "the customer is always right" has thrown many a company into bankruptcy. Of course you want to keep your customers happy, but a better saying to adopt is the "customer is *usually* right. " This allows for the occasional pushing back on customers when they are being completely unreasonable. Having a Nordstrom's-level customer service policy may make customers smile, but you simply cannot adopt this philosophy in a low margin business.

Here are the main customer service related supply chain tasks that cause inventory variability and higher costs:

1. Not using a hard order date/time cutoff, thereby allowing customers to order whenever they want and with as many order changes as they want.

2. Allowing customers to order below the minimum order quantity that allows for targeted profitability.

3. Allowing customers to order mixed pallets or a variety of inventory items that require increased warehouse time without charging for it.

4. Still using old-school methods of accepting customer orders which are riddled with human error (fax, email, verbal, phone).

5. Setting up delivery frequencies that are simply over-servicing the customer.

6. Allowing customers to squeeze delivery windows into smaller and smaller time windows.

7. Setting up customer in-stock/availability targets that are too aggressive for the current supply chain and technology.

Of course, I am not saying we should dismiss with all the wants and desires of our customers. That would be heresy. Instead, what I am saying is that there is a true need to work with customers to create a delicate and enhanced balance of service and cost. For example, during a supply chain consulting engagement at a $400 million firm in Texas, my group stumbled upon the fact that customers were asking why our client was coming to their stores so frequently.

This led to analyzing delivery frequency. What we found was our client was going to stores 27% of the time when the customer did not even need product. This may cause some level of customer goodwill, but clearly our client was over-servicing the network. My recommendation here is to survey the top 10% of your customer base and ask them how you can work in concert to improve service yet lower costs. You will be surprised by what they tell you. If you do not ask your customers for help, you will never know if they are willing to support a slightly different method of ordering or delivery.

True Cost of Carrying Inventory

The cost of inventory is much more than just the cost of the goods itself. For every dollar of inventory you carry, you will experience carrying costs of at least 15%. In fact, most experts in the supply chain field estimate the carrying cost of inventory to be between 15-35%. One of the reasons for this wide range is interest rates and the cost of borrowing. As the cost of money rises, carrying costs increase. Generally speaking, as of the writing of this book, carrying costs are estimated to be around 17%, depending upon your firm's cost of money. As elaborated in Chapter 3, the carrying cost of inventory includes:

- Storage Costs (warehousing, public storage, storage rental space)
- Handling Costs (material handling)
- Obsolescence Costs (holding useless inventory)
- Damage/Waste Costs (defects, unusable returns)
- Insurance and Taxes
- Administrative/Overhead Costs (supervision, clerical, inventory control)
- Loss/Pilferage Costs (theft, shrinkage)
- The Cost of Money (inventory investment, interest, borrowing costs)
- Inventory redeployment and transfer costs.

As shown in exhibit 7.4, there is evidence that most companies understand that inventory is not only illiquid, but often the first thing to go when downsizing. When the U. S. economy crashed in 2008, corporate America responded by shredding millions of dollars of inventory in an attempt to reduce costs.

Exhibit 7.4 – Inventories Climb to Recession High

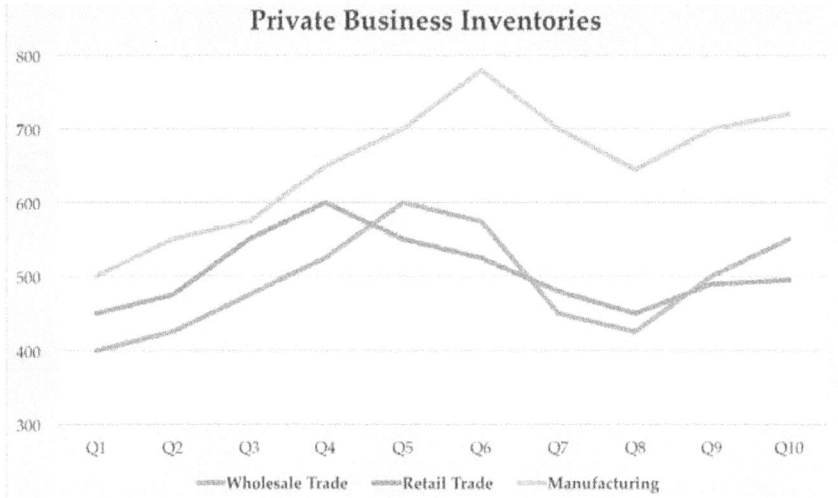

Now that we understand all the idiosyncrasies surrounding inventory control, let's start discussing the ways to control and manage it. Let's start with the two (2) major inventory strategies mentioned earlier:

Design and Optimization

The topic of supply chain design and optimization is covered later in Chapter 12. However, since network design is important to the overall success of your inventory control program, a brief explanation of its importance and relevance to inventory control is in order.

Supply chain design and optimization is fundamentally about employing the least amount of infrastructure (warehouses, trucks, etc.) while delivering superior customer service at the lowest cost. Most organizations neglect to continually and strategically review their network infrastructure. This leads to the following issues:
- To many facilities or distribution points
- Excessive inventory

- Inventory deployed in the wrong location
- Customers being serviced from the wrong distribution center
- Too many inactive SKU's (stock keeping units or inventory items).

As shown in exhibit 7.5, the more facilities you have in the network, the more inventory you will tend to carry. Having more locations, however, will reduce distribution cost/unit delivered as you are theoretically closer to the customer. The trick is to employ the least number of facilities which results in the lowest overall infrastructure costs at the highest service level. The service level must include an attempt to hold the least amount of inventory without sacrificing customer service. This will yield lower inventory carrying costs. In addition, ensuring that all inventory items are situated in close proximity to the right customer will also help to improve inventory control.

Exhibit 7.5 - The Impact of Locations on Inventory

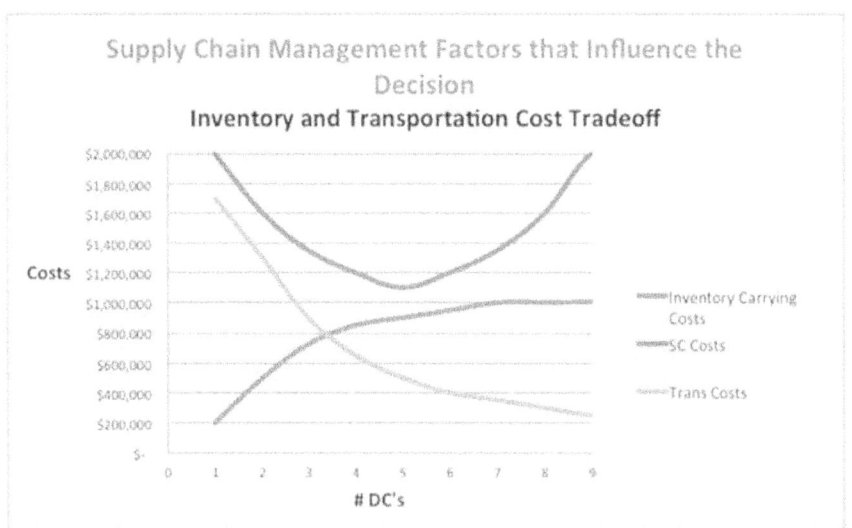

Cost-to-Serve Modeling

The second strategic initiative that helps to control inventory is cost to serve modeling (CTS). CTS modeling analyses each and every customer at the item level to ensure profitability. By carefully evaluating all of the costs associated with servicing individual customers, you will uncover which customers require the most attention. Often times a simple reduction in delivery frequency or the raising of minimum order quantities can improve the profitability picture. You will be surprised how often customers will be willing to modify their service profiles resulting in a win/win situation.

Exhibit 7.6 - IFMC, Inc. Cost-to-Serve Model
Product Pro-Forma (P&L of True Costs)

PRODUCT/
SKU #:_____

Suggested Retail Price	$0.00
Case Quantity	0
Case Projections	10,000
Minimum Order Quantity	0
Economic Order Quantity	0

	Units	Cases	$$$$	% of Gross Sales
Manufacturer's Selling Price	$2.72	$16.32		
Gross Sales	60,000	34,000	$554,880	
Cost of Goods				
Material Costs	$1.42	$8.52	$289,680	52.21%
Packaging	$0.00	$0.00	$0.00	
Distribution & Freight	$0.00	$0.00	$0.00	
TOTAL COGS	$1.42	$8.52	$289,680	52.21%
GROSS MARGIN	$1.30	$7.80	$265,200	47.79%
Sales Deductions				
Discounts	$0.05	$0.30	$10,200	1.84%
Term Discount	$0.03	$0.19	$6,460	1.16%
Mark-Downs	$0.00	$0.00	$0.00	
Other Deductions	$0.00	$0.00	$0.00	
TOTAL DEDUCTIONS	$0.08	$0.49	$16,660	3.00%
NET SALES	$2.64	$15.83	$538,220	97.00%
NET SALES MARGIN	$1.22	$7.31	$248,540	44.79%

Marketing & Advertising Expenses				
Advertising	$0.00	$0.00	$0	
Allowances	$0.14	$0.14	$8,100	
Promotions	$0.00	$0.00	$0	
Feature Ad	$0.42	$0.74	$25,020	
Display/POP Materials	$0.00	$0.00	$0	
TOTAL M&A EXPENSES	**$0.55**	**$3.31**	**$33,120**	**5.97%**
Selling Expenses				
Brokerage Costs	$0.14	$0.86	$29,240	
Slotting Fees	$0.00	$0.00	$0	
Samples	$0.03	$0.18	$6,120	
Ticket & Invoice Adjustments	$0.03	$0.18	$6,120	
TOTAL SELLING EXPENSES	**$0.20**	**$1.22**	**$41,480**	**7.48%**
Order Processing/Transaction Costs (include mixed pallet fees)	$0.00	$0.00	$0.00	
Warehouse Expenses (includes lumper fees)	$0.00	$0.00	$0.00	
Inventory Carrying Costs	$0.00	$0.00	$0.00	
Pallet Fees if any	$0.00	$0.00	$0.00	
Deployment Expenses	$0.00	$0.00	$0.00	
Transportation/Freight to Customer	$0.24	$1.41	**$47,940**	
Overhead (admin, customer service, etc.)	$0.00	$0.00	$0.00	
Interest Expense	$0.03	$0.16	$5,440	
TOTAL ADMIN	**$0.26**	**$1.57**	**$53,380**	**9.62%**
OPERATING INCOME	**$0.20**	**$1.21**	**$120,560**	**21.73%**
Delivery frequency in number times/week	2x/week			
Total Order Cycle Time to customer (lead time	10 days			

Next, let's discuss some tactical inventory initiatives by reviewing the major tenets of inventory control.

Inventory Control Tenets

1. Adopt the mentality that **all** inventory is **bad**. Remember, act like the economy is always lousy. When in doubt, get rid of it.

2. Conducting Annual Physical Inventories is like using a slide ruler today to do Math. Cycle counting is the only way to control loss. Cycle counting is the periodic (daily, weekly, bi-weekly, or monthly depending upon the number of inventory items you have) counting of inventory with special emphasis on immediate problem resolution. Essentially, you are going to count your inventory (using highly trained individuals) much more frequently to ultimately eliminate the need for an annual physical count. You should set rules for the number of times you count each SKU (stock keeping unit) depending upon its criticality to the overall business. The more critical, the more times you count it.

    - Cycle Counting

ITEM	Counts/Year	Quantity	Total Counts
A	4	150	600
B	2	100	200
C	1	700	700
		Total Counts/Year	1,500

    D items, which are basically obsolete, should only be counted in an attempt to get rid of it.

3. 95% Inventory Accuracy <u>not good enough</u>. The inventory accuracy target of book-to-physical should be 98%. This requires a great deal of employee training. It should not be ok to write off inventory at the end of every year.

4. Stratifying the Inventory into manageable categories (A,B,C,D) is the only way to truly understand what is

USING YOUR SUPPLY CHAIN AS A COMPETITIVE WEAPON | 129

happening. Inventory stratification segments the inventory into the following categories:

A items are fastest moving
C items are the slowest moving
D items are obsolete
B items are everything else.

- ABC Stratification

    1. Segment inventory items by:

        - Monetary value
        - Usage
        - Criticality in the Production Process
        - Difficulty to procure (lead time)

General Rule of Thumb:

20% of your Inventory Items will account for 80% of Volume
20% of Inventory will account for 60% of your Profit

- ABC Stratification

    A items: Top 10% - 15% of Volume
    C items: Bottom 60% - 80% of Volume
    B items: The balance of the items unassigned
    D items: Worthless inventory – not required

- Focus on A item control & critical components

- Assign A items closest to dock – and secure
- Measure accuracy: part #, location, count

The key here is to meet with your Finance team to determine the best way to stratify the inventory as some firms prefer volume to be the determinant while others choose dollars as the main factor (some choose to segment both ways). In light of increased globalization of supply, you may also want to include global supplier lead times and quality such as defects/1,000 units in this stratification. You may need to increase your inventory level based upon extremely long global lead times and a higher than normal defect rates. Hopefully, your company is also willing to invest in an MRP/DRP, or advanced planning system that will enhance inventory control. In addition, as explained in the setting inventory control section of this chapter, you should also be sure to set-up your inventory control policy across multiple echelons or supply chain stages while simultaneously including demand variability in the policy/equation.

5. Obsolete inventory typically represents 10% of total value. It should be thrown away, donated, heavily discounted, or even given to employees, whatever. Smart firms evaluate the cost of holding this useless inventory for sometimes years versus donating it and taking a tax write off.

When analyzing inventory, a good place to start is segmenting the inventory into simple categories as shown in Exhibit 7.7.

Exhibit 7.7 - Major Categories of Inventory

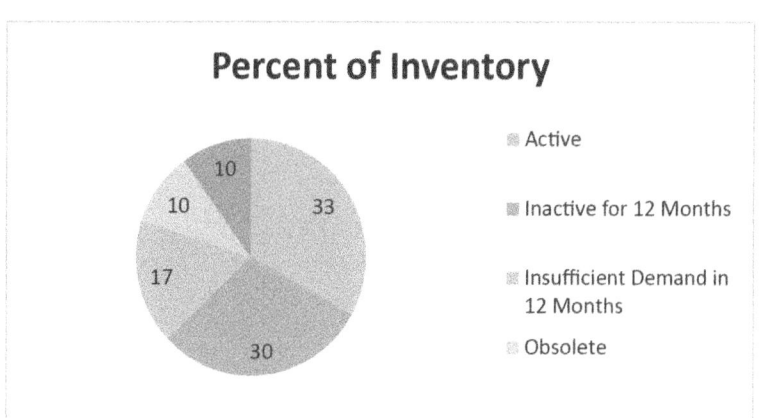

6. Implement Inventory Key Performance Indicators by tracking:

    1. 99.9% Bill of Material Accuracy (BOM).
    2. 99.5% Master Schedule Accuracy.
    3. 100% Inventory Location Accuracy (flow diagram, staging).
    4. 99% Cycle Count Accuracy.
    5. <3% Obsolete Inventory.
    6. 99.8% Purchase Order Accuracy.
    7. >90% PERFECT ORDERS.
    8. Inventory Turns Target – as close to 12 as possible but highly industry dependent.
    9. 95% Forecast Accuracy.
    10. 100% Substitution Reporting.

7. In addition, waste/damage/theft needs to be aggressively managed to less than 1% of the total. Remember, it's all about velocity when it comes to inventory control. Using weeks of supply rules without including variability of demand is a sure way to screw-up the inventory. Progressive firms use a combination of weeks of supply, demand variability, seasonality, advanced planning, and inventory stratification to set-up the inventory policy control limits.

8. Inventory must be managed at the SKU Level. If you do not manage inventory at the SKU (individual inventory item level), you will lull yourself to sleep thinking your inventory process is in control. For example, during a physical count of inventory at a client site, the following results were uncovered:

Item Number	Book Count	Physical Count	Difference
1	126	122	-4
2	212	194	-18
3	324	351	+27

4	76	81	+5
5	942	906	-36
6	111	104	-7
7	23	28	+5
8	1004	1023	+19
9	301	270	-31
10	11	4	-7
TOTAL	3,130	3,083	-47

Wow, 98.5% accuracy! Of course, not really as when you look at the individual items, there are obvious problems that must be corrected.

9. Inventory Control starts with a solid forecast. When it comes to Supply Chain Management, there are two absolutes. Most companies carry too much inventory, and most forecasts are wrong. In our database of more than 300 companies across the United States, there is an average forecast accuracy of only 70%. Better stated, 30% of the time, the forecasts are inaccurate! Most companies set their safety stock at three times the standard deviation of the forecast error. If you reduce the standard deviation by $1, you will reduce the safety stock by $3. As mentioned earlier, most progressively run companies use a combination of weeks of supply, variability of demand, seasonality, and inventory stratification to set-up the inventory control policy.

10. Supply (Purchasing) must have accountability and take responsibility for Supplier Inventories by using EOQ and ROP (Reorder or Trigger Points). Purchasing from suppliers must include the downstream impact that supplier inventory may have on manufacturing, inventory, warehousing, material handling, and distribution.

11. Inventory Management requires Process Control and Training as discussed in Chapter 3. Start by mapping out each and every process step within the major functional areas within

the supply chain. List each step to the process, the amount of time for each step, and then assign a cost to each task. Next, try to eliminate, simplify or optimize each step within the process (ESO).

Finally, let's review some industry best practices for enhanced inventory control.

Inventory Best Practices

1. Supplier-Managed Inventory (SMI). Supplier replenishing inventory to min/max levels.
2. Produce to order or using supplier drop-ship and consignment arrangements.
3. Cross-docking, where inventory moves in and out of the distribution center with essentially no human touch.
4. Implementing an inventory managed risk program that acknowledges shorter product life cycles and global competition. Use modular/component designs to reduce risk.
5. Using a centralized hub to store finished goods that have a high degree of variability.
6. Inventory Profitability Analysis by Customer and SKU.
7. Advanced planning MRP/DRP...including variability across multiple echelons/stages within the chain.
8. Inventory Reward System/Accountability – assign an Inventory Champion and implement a forecast and inventory accuracy reward system for the entire organization.
9. Using in-transit inventory as a virtual warehouse.
10. Inventory postponement wherever possible (last minute addition of sub-assemblies or components).

Technologies to Support Inventory Control

Improving inventory control effectiveness takes velocity, visibility, and collaboration. In order to accomplish a high degree of supply chain success, companies must employ the appropriate amount of technology to achieve best in class performance. Using ten to fifteen spreadsheets to manage a business is not only unsophisticated, but also prone to human error. Today's technology allows for the evaluation of tradeoffs and the analysis of what-if scenarios. Technology also provides complete order and inventory visibility throughout the supply chain.

Some of the technology being used to enhance inventory control includes:
- Visibility systems
- Lean synchronization technology
- Sophisticated WMS (warehouse management system) with postponement capabilities
- Sourcing simulation tools
- Item level and finished goods optimization tools
- Event management systems.

Unfortunately, even though we have access to a great deal of technology today, more than the majority of firms lack sophisticated supply chain and distribution technology that makes a difference. Even companies that employ a robust front-end purchasing and accounting system often lack real time inventory and order visibility. In addition, most sophisticated front-end systems still require some level of customization in order to accomplish total inventory tracking and control.

Establishing a Sound Inventory Policy

Setting up an Inventory Control Policy should be driven by five (5) variables:
1. Variability of demand.
2. Variability of supplier lead time.
3. Desired service level.
4. The global nature of supply (length of lead time, quality profile).
5. Frequency of review.

Simply stated, a network that consists of all domestic-based suppliers in close proximity versus a globally based supplier network dictates a completely different set of inventory rules. The more variable the demand, the higher the inventory level. The more intense the service level, the higher the inventory level. The longer the lead time, the higher the inventory level. This variability should cause a continuous review of your inventory control policy; a minimum of every six months. In addition, most progressive firms use a combination of weeks of supply, demand variability, seasonality, advanced planning, and inventory stratification to set-up inventory policy control limits.

The major steps to setting up an inventory control policy include:

Step 1
Gather data, including supplier volumes and lead times, demand by inventory item, seasonality and variability data by SKU, and individual customer service levels. This data are the starting point and will provide a snapshot of the demands being placed upon the supply chain. These data will also help to set up inventory "trigger" points whereby your system will dictate the need for inventory based upon a pre-determined set of rules.

Step 2
Set up a policy that limits the amount of people who have access to the inventory. In addition, keep a record of who has access to all secure areas. Most companies underestimate the impact that theft has on inventory loss. In fact, it is usually a good idea to install security cameras and keycard-access entry points in all inventory storage areas.

Step 3
Implement an iron-clad receiving procedure for all raw materials and finished goods. It has been estimated that 25% of all inventory problems start at the receiving dock. Be sure to section off designated areas for each SKU and clearly label each section. All employees should be trained on exactly where to place each inventory item and the rationale behind the warehouse layout. Either weigh or scan all incoming pallets/product and double verify that all goods received are in the correct count and type.

Step 4
Create a comprehensive purchasing plan that takes advantage of just in time and economic order quantity techniques. Use blanket purchase orders wherever feasible to combine supplier ordering into as few PO's as possible. Take advantage of quantity discounts but be sure to include the impact on inventory carrying and warehousing costs before you make larger purchases.

Step 5
Create an inventory demand schedule that covers each month of the coming year. Be sure to take into account seasonal fluctuation in demand and any other event driven variability that exists. Use this demand schedule after adding some judgment to calculate the optimal re-order points and maximum stock levels for each inventory item.

Step 6
Create an automated, system-generated notification system that alerts management when an inventory item has fallen below its re-order point or conversely, when it has reached its maximum stock level.

Step 7
Process map (flow chart) the entire supply chain to document all the steps within the buying, receiving, ordering, warehousing, inventory, and distribution processes. Establish formal and written procedures to ensure the timely processing of all paperwork, including purchase orders, inbound receipts and inventory counts.

Step 8
Set up a formal cycle count procedure that includes:
- Precise put-away and pick procedures
- Pinpoint accurate counting procedure that includes definitions for all inventory items
- Training of all employees conducting the cycle counting
- Formal problem resolution process
- Posting of results.

Step 9
Set targets for inventory accuracy, inventory turnover, and receiving accuracy. In addition, set acceptable levels for items out of stock (availability) and backorders. The point here is that on some inventory items it may be acceptable to allow a few backorders and/or out-of-stocks. Yes, this is counter-intuitive to good customer service. That is true. The reality is that for some unpopular and less important inventory items is simply better to go into backorder than keep excess items on-hand.

Step 10
Set up a continuous versus periodic monitoring system and bi-annual review of your inventory policy. Goals and key ratios should be monitored every month with the appropriate action steps taken to correct any deficiencies.

Conclusion

We need inventory to meet and exceed customer requirements. But that doesn't mean we should keep 20% excess inventory in safety stock to make 100% sure we always have enough. In fact, I maintain that safety stock is for wimps. If you are utilizing sound just in time inventory principles and communicating the cost of doing business with your customers, there is a happy medium between keeping too much inventory and having a dissatisfied customer. The trick is to find the right balance. Fundamentally, inventory should be managed in a way that results in:
1. Having less on-hand.
2. Causes it to move faster throughout the supply chain (increasing velocity).
3. At least 98% accuracy (book-to-physical).

Chapter Summary

- All inventory should be suspect and looked at through a pair of critical glasses

- Inventory accuracy needs to be better than 98%.

- Eliminate safety stock until it hurts.

- Inventory must be managed at the SKU (stock keeping unit) level.

- Most inventories have 10% obsolescence (get rid of the dead wood).

- Use economic order quantity and reorder trigger points to order stock.

- Eliminate physical inventory and replace it with cycle counting.

- Stratify the inventory into ABCD categories and include both volume and dollars.

- Inventory starts with a forecast. Make sure you challenge the forecast five times!

- When in doubt, reduce inventory and increase the turnover rate.

Exploratory Questions

1. How does the customer service policy impact inventory control?

2. What are the major causes of inventory inaccuracy?

3. What are the benefits of a sound inventory strategy?

4. Why does cycle counting improve inventory accuracy performance?

5. Why is it occasionally acceptable to have a backorder?

6. Why is the understanding of the carrying cost of inventory so critical to business?

Case Study and Questions

Discount Mavericks, Inc. (DM, Inc.) is a direct marketing company that as a fulfillment center located in Salt lake City, Utah. They carry four major product lines and a total of twenty-two inventory items (aka, SKU's). The total amount of inventory on-hand averages $2.3 million. The existing inventory policy was fraught with all the tell-tale signs of inefficiency, including: too many backorders, not having the *right* inventory, excessive customer complaints, the need to count inventory to account for lost product, and inventory accuracy at only 86%. In fact, at the end of each year, DM, Inc. would write-off a significant amount of money associated with inventory book-to-physical shortfalls.

DM, Inc. was struggling with poor cash flow, an increase in customer complaints, and a lousy balance sheet that reflected too much inventory considering the size of the company. The Director of Business Development and the CFO called us in to conduct a high-level assessment of their Inventory Management Program.

Our diagnostic consisted of a thorough review of the entire supply chain with special emphasis on inventory control and purchasing techniques. We reviewed the following data:
- Two year history of customer complaints
- 120 days of PO's
- Inventory level by SKU
- Backorders and out-of-stocks for the previous six months
- Current inventory policy and procedures
- Application of technology
- Inventory reports

The main finding was the lack of technology and too many touches. The entire business was being run using spreadsheets. There was also a lack of sound purchasing practices, with most buying being done in a highly reactive and rushed fashion. Inventory control consisted of only an annual physical count, using temporary employees as the main counters. After reviewing the major causes of customer complaints, we uncovered that most issues were related to 'where's my stuff?" Customers were not getting their products in a timely manner due to consistent backorders and temporary out of stocks.

After careful consideration and considering the extent of the supply chain issues, we recommended that fulfillment be outsourced to a third-party (3PL). The third party would take over all buying, warehousing, inventory control, and shipping responsibilities. The 3PL would also employ technology in lieu of spreadsheets. This was the fastest and least expensive way to fix all the problems.

Case Study Questions:

1. What are some of the alternative solutions that could have been implemented instead of outsourcing?

2. What specific inventory targets should DM, Inc. track?

3. How does DM, Inc. ensure that the outsourcing effort is a success? What safeguards can they put in place to protect their assets?

4. Why do so many companies use spreadsheets instead of technology to manage results?

5. How should DM, Inc. handle the existing customer complaints?

8 LOGISTICS AND DISTRIBUTION MANAGEMENT

"Most senior executives don't realize that they are in the distribution business; they just happen to be delivering a certain type of product..."

Dr. Tony Vercillo

Logistics and distribution management is the final frontier for most organizations. Logistics is the last bastion of customer service. In most cases, distribution (delivery and transportation) is not considered a primary business function, but instead merely a support function and a necessary evil. However, as globalization continues to shrink our world, logistics and global distribution are becoming more critical business functions that require a detailed understanding of the overall supply chain. The purpose of this chapter is to introduce you to the numerous concepts involved with managing logistics and physical distribution. This chapter delves into the strategic importance of distribution and underlines the key measures that drive distribution results. This chapter will cover the following topics:
- The definition of logistics and distribution
- The criticality of logistics
- Logistics decision areas
- The basic distribution system

- Approaches to physical distribution
- Mode selection
- Inbound and outbound freight management
- Private fleet management
- Reverse logistics

By the end of this chapter, you should be able to design an appropriate distribution strategy, choose the correct mode of transportation, aggressively manage inbound freight from suppliers, and decide between a private fleet or a third-party delivery method. In addition, you will be able to design an appropriate reverse logistics system that reduces the cost of returns and damage.

Definition of Logistics

Logistics is the efficient and integrated inbound, outbound and reverse flow of goods, services, and information from the point of origin to the final destination for the purpose of meeting or exceeding customer expectations. Companies rely on logistics to manage their supply chain partners and to provide information and critical performance metrics to ensure business success. Logistics has to do with managing complex interdependencies between suppliers, company infrastructure, and customers.

Logistics covers a wide range of business activities, including:
- Order processing
- Inventory management
- Warehousing
- Transportation
- Material Handling
- Packaging
- Information systems
- Customer service

The Criticality of Logistics

Organizations are finally starting to realize the important role that logistics plays in reducing the cost infrastructure, and with improving service performance, customer satisfaction, and overall company profitability. Logistics has evolved from a tactical function into a strategic imperative. The impact that logistics has on an organization's infrastructure cost can be on the order of a 10%-35%. This can translate into higher levels of profitability if managed aggressively. In fact, total logistics costs typically rank second only to raw material costs when analyzing total cost of goods sold (COGS).

Logistics management can improve many areas within the supply chain, including:
- Reducing supplier lead times
- Reducing total order cycle time
- Reducing overall investment in inventory
- Increasing on-time delivery performance
- Improving perfect order performance
- Enhancing customer satisfaction
- Reducing the cost of reverse logistics

Logistics Decision Areas

As mentioned earlier, logistics has to do with the physical flow of goods and information. To that end, these flows of goods and information require infrastructure. The supply chain and logistics infrastructure requires decisions that impact cost and profitability. These decisions include:

Network Design, or the number of and location of plants, warehouses, and suppliers:
- How many warehouses do we need?
- How many suppliers should we use?
- Where should plants and warehouses be located?
- Which warehouses should service which customers?

Transportation mode, such as trucking (LTL, truckload), rail, air freight, pipeline, or water (ocean freight):
- Which mode provides the best balance of cost and speed?
- How do I minimize the number of shipments?
- How do I reduce supplier lead times?
- How can I consolidate loads to minimize less-than-truckload shipments?
- How do I minimize outbound miles?

Capacity planning, including the size of warehouses, plant capacity and speed, truck or container size:
- How large should my warehouses be?
- How fast should my production line be?
- How large should my trucks or trailers be?
- How many and how large of containers should I bring over from global suppliers?
- How fast does product need to get to me and to customers?

The Basic Distribution System

A basic distribution system consists of four (4) major dependencies:
1. Suppliers (raw materials, components, sub-assemblies, etc.)
2. Manufacturing/Production
3. Warehousing
4. Customer or end-user.

Exhibit 8.1 - Major Logistics Dependencies.

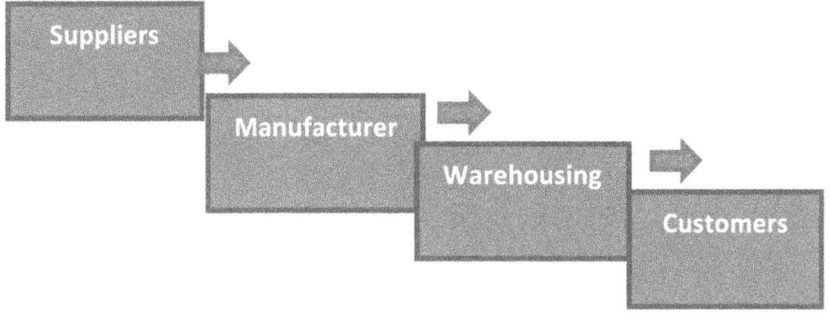

Due to e-commerce, not every distribution system has all four dependencies, but the majority of basic distribution systems within large organizations have these points of origin and destination. The trick to employing the right distribution system is to answer this simple question:

"How do I eliminate or minimize the number of overall supply chain touch points?"

Each of these points of distribution results in humans, machines, or robots "touching" the product. With every touch comes the probability for errors and added costs. Therefore, the ultimate distribution network has few or no suppliers, no production, no warehouses, and no trucks! When I was a Division Manager at PepsiCo, I used to always say that the ultimate goal of our distribution network should be to eliminate all the infrastructure such that when a consumer turns on his or her faucet in their home, Pepsi comes out! The point here, of course, is to minimize the number of suppliers and facilities yet still meet or exceed customer expectations.

Approaches to Physical Distribution

There are two (2) primary approaches to physical distribution; direct shipment, or the inventory storage method. The direct ship approach entails the product being shipped directly from the manufacturer or supplier to the end customer. Companies such as Amazon and EBay have made this approach quite popular. The inventory storage approach consists of shipping from the supplier or manufacturer directly to an intermediate point such as a warehouse or depot prior to shipping to the end customer. There are a few factors that will dictate the type of approach to use, including:
- Is the product made to order or made to stock?
- Do your suppliers have drop-ship capabilities?
- Do you ship locally, nationwide, or internationally?
- Do you employ a push or a pull strategy?

The direct shipment approach attempts to bypass warehouses and distribution centers (DC). When you employ the direct shipment

method, the manufacturer or supplier delivers products directly to the end user. This approach results in a few efficiencies, including:
- Shorter lead times
- Lower costs since you avoid the expense associated with a warehouse or DC
- Less prone to error due to the reduction in distribution "touch" points.

The primary disadvantage of the direct ship method is the lack of freight consolidation opportunities, or risk pooling (described later in the book) as there is no central warehouse. Another disadvantage may be higher transportation costs as some suppliers or manufacturers might choose to use smaller freight loads (or less-than-truckload) going to a larger number of locations. Direct shipments are preferable when short lead times are critical such the perishable food industry. In addition, when retailers demand full truckloads, direct shipments are often used as there is less need for an intermediate storage facility.

The inventory storage method is used when lead time is considered less critical and when being closer to the customer is deemed imperative. Inventory storage is heavily dependent upon the following factors:
- Lead time required by customers which dictates the inventory holding strategy
- Stock availability policy and the acceptance of backorders
- Centralized versus decentralized management structure
- Single or multi-location deployment
- Push or pull inventory strategy
- Cross-docking
- Transshipment
- Risk pooling or freight consolidation desirability.

Customer expectations often dictate holding inventory close to the majority of the demand. Corporate mandates such as 95% in stock availability and zero backorder tolerance also create the need for inventory storage. The advantages of the inventory storage method is that the product is closer to the customer (increased response time) and in-stock availability rates tend to be higher, thereby increasing customer satisfaction. The disadvantage of the inventory holding method is the cost to carry the inventory, including the cost of obsolescence.

In a centralized management structure, optimization decisions are made for the benefit of the entire supply chain. In a decentralized management structure, decisions are made for the benefit of local optimization. The more decentralized the management structure, the more likely a multi-location strategy is deployed.

A multi-location network consists of numerous points of origin and destination. The goal of the distribution network is to provide customers with the fastest response time at the lowest cost (that meets corporate profitability goals). The trick here is balancing the inventory while meeting the peak and low season demand requirements. Exhibits 8.2 and 8.3 reveal a typical multi-location network.

Exhibit 8.2 - Multi-Location Distribution Network (7 DC's scaled by outbound truckloads).

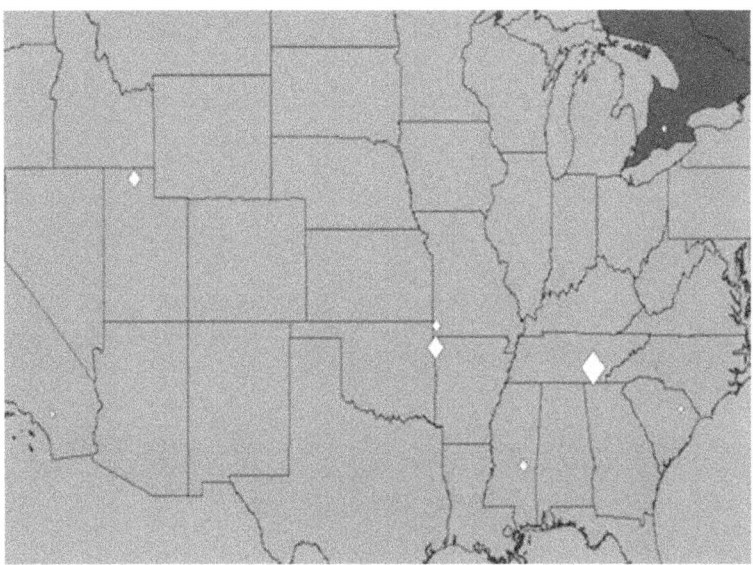

Exhibit - 8.3 Multi-Location Distribution Network (including outbound shipments).

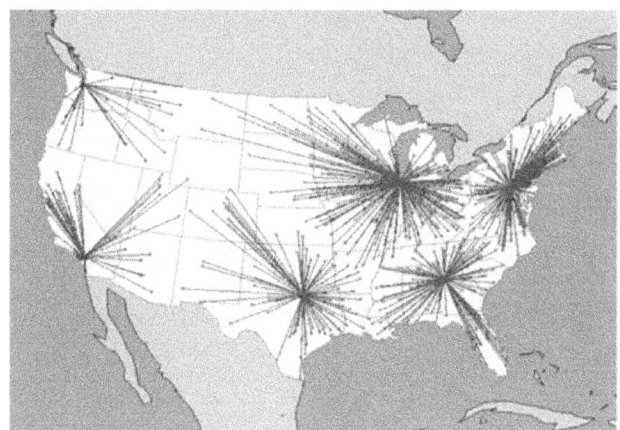

Source: Designing and Managing the Supply Chain, Simchi-Levi, Kaminsky, Chapter 3.

There are two (2) approaches to distribution that can be followed to achieve a balanced inventory and the appropriate level of safety stock. These approaches are the push and pull distribution systems. The push approach send products from the production point to the distribution centers based upon typically a regional a sales forecast. The pull approach consists of the distribution centers demanding product based upon actual demand.

Exhibit 8.4 - Push and Pull Distribution Methods.

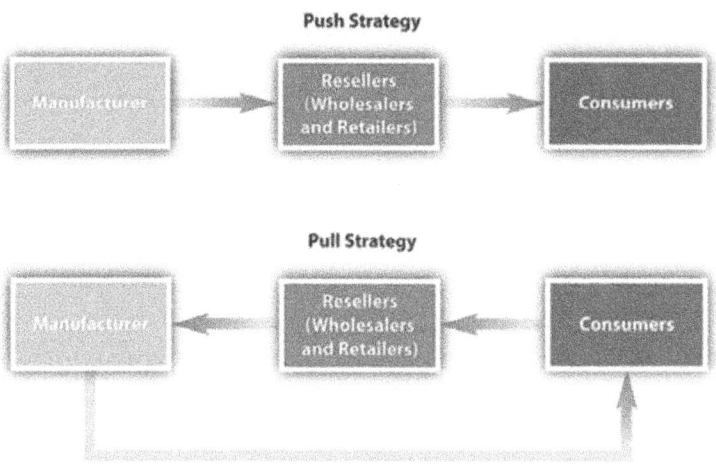

The disadvantage of a push system is the lousier the forecast, the larger the inventory. In addition, under the rules of a push system, the more DC's in the network, the larger the inventory due to an increase in local safety stock requirements. In a push system, the distribution centers need to be sensitive not only to total forecast inaccuracies, but also must deal with local sales fluctuations. The advantages of a push system are the deployment of smaller warehouses, an increase in customer satisfaction, and larger truckload shipping.

In a pull system, a customer order generates production at the plant. The inventory is "pulled" through the supply chain based upon demand at the consumption point. The disadvantages of a pull system are larger plant-based inventories, lower customer service levels, and the likelihood of less-than-truckloads movements. The advantages of the pull system include less inter-DC shipments, a reduction in safety stock, and the possibility of avoiding the warehouses by using direct to customer shipments.

Push-Pull System

The reality in supply chain management is that most distribution networks use some sort of hybrid Push/Pull approach. The benefits of the push/pull approach include:
- Higher degree of truckload shipments between plants and warehouses
- Reduced inter-DC inventory transfers
- A decrease in total system safety stock
- Often utilizes direct shipments from plants to customers
- Increase in service levels.

Cross-Docking

In a cross-docking arrangement, warehouses are used solely as a coordination point and not to store inventory. In a typical cross-dock type warehouse, goods are delivered from the manufacturer or supplier then shipped to customers or retailers as fast as possible and without much human intervention. In theory, in a cross-dock situation, product is not stored but instead, transferred to the shipping department immediately. Cross docking reduces the carrying cost of inventory and also decreases lead times. The downside to cross-docking is the heavy investment required to accomplish the in and out nature of the inventory transfer. In fact, cross-docking requires a nimble and highly responsive transportation system and the integration of information systems across the supply chain.

Transshipment

When advanced and integrated information systems are in place, a transshipment strategy may be in order. Transshipment allows for shipment of goods between facilities in an attempt to fulfill some immediate customer need. Retailers will often use transshipment to accommodate urgent customer requirements by utilizing inventory visibility to gain access to other retailer's stock. While this strategy is considered important by some retailers, it must be controlled tightly to avoid the double shipping of goods.

In addition, within a multi-location distribution network, internal transshipment must be avoided wherever possible. Excessive transshipment within a supply chain usually means inventory is being deployed incorrectly.

Risk Pooling

In any supply chain, regardless of which inventory deployment strategy is being used, there is a need to control demand variability wherever possible. One of the best ways of controlling variability is through the concept of risk pooling. Risk pooling attempts to aggregate demand across all locations, thereby reducing system wide variability. Demand fluctuation is reduced in aggregate as high demand from one customer is usually offset by low demand from another customer. This tends to reduce safety stock requirements across the network and decreases total average inventory. For example, in a centralized distribution network that pools the inventory, the main warehouse may serve all customers, which tends to lead to less system variability. Normally, this demand variability is measured by the standard deviation or the coefficient of variation.

The standard deviation measures how much demand tends to vary around the average, while the coefficient of variation is the ratio of standard deviation to average demand as expressed by the formula:

Coefficient of Variation = Standard Deviation\Average Demand

Choosing the Right Distribution Strategy

Selecting the right distribution strategy can be quick tricky and requires a detailed look at the entire supply chain. In fact, in most cases, a varying approach based upon the product type or product family is normally employed. The factors that influence the choice of strategy include customer demand and variability, the location of the customers, the required service level, and the infrastructure costs.

Exhibit - 8.5 Distribution Strategies

Strategy Attribute	Direct Shipment	Cross-docking (CD)	Inventory of Warehouses
Risk Pooling	Not viable	Not likely	Takes advantage of CD
Transportation Costs	Tend to be higher	Reduced inbound costs	Reduced inbound costs
Holding Costs	No warehouse costs	No holding costs	Increased holding costs
Allocation Decision	Made earlier	Delayed	Delayed

Source: Designing & Managing the Supply Chain, Levi & Kaminsky, Chapter 7, page 240.

Choosing the right distribution strategy also requires a logistics master plan. This distribution strategic plan should examine the following:
- The mission of the distribution/logistics function
- Freight and transportation modes and methods/options
- The inventory level and deployment strategy (and carrying costs)

- Sales growth projections and forecasts
- Production and warehouse capacities
- Customer ordering patterns, demand and variability
- Required customer service levels for in-stock availability and on-time delivery
- Customer delivery windows and delivery frequency
- Industry trends
- A complete review of infrastructure (number and location of all points of distribution).

After the careful examination of these data, you will surely conclude that there is usually no single strategy that fulfills all the requirements of the network and customers. Most supply chain networks have small nuisances that cause a modification to any one strategy. For the most part, the distribution strategy must be fluid and adaptable such that it changes and evolves over time. The key is to constantly review your distribution strategy and tweak it through continuous improvement efforts.

Freight and Transportation Management

One of the most often overlooked parts of the supply chain is inbound and outbound freight, including the transportation and delivery to customers. Simply stated, this part of the business is not considered sexy. However, globalization has caused delivery system economics to be an integral part of overall business strategy. Procuring supply globally is both an art and a science, requiring intimate knowledge of culture, customs, duties, intermodal freight, and the concept of total landed costs. This need for an expanded and vast amount of knowledge has lifted the role of the logistics manager into one of more prominence within progressively run organizations.

Freight and transportation includes the following topics:
- Inbound freight from suppliers
- Outbound freight to plants and distribution centers
- Customer deliveries
- Import/Export management (customs, duties, port management, etc.)

- Mode management (rail, ocean, truck, air freight)
- Freight carrier management
- Freight rates and surcharges
- Private fleet or third party shipping management and costs.

This list of topics reveals the complicated nature of managing freight and transportation. The most important areas that will be explored here are general freight, including inbound freight from suppliers, mode selection and rate management, and private fleet versus third party delivery.

General Freight

According to the national atlas. gov, logistics contributes about 9% of the GDP, or about $1 trillion dollars/year. The domestic transportation system in the United States ships almost four trillion ton miles of freight shipped by more than six million businesses. Rail and ocean freight account for over 40% of the tonnage, although freight is shipped by a variety of additional methods. In addition, transportation accounts for approximately 20% of household spending and is second only to housing.

According to Wikipedia, the largest percentage of US freight (as measured by total percent hauled) is carried by trucks, followed by pipelines, rail, ocean, and finally air. Other modes of transportation, such as parcels and intermodal freight account for about 3% of the remainder. As measured by ton-miles, rail leads the way, followed by truck. Of course, these data are quite different when considering global freight as ocean plays a much more significant role in international shipping. Air

Exhibit 8.6 Freight Ton-Miles

Mode of intercity freight transport	Ton-miles (millions)	Percent
Air	15,731	0. 35%
Truck	1,293,326	28. 50%
Railroad	1,733,777	38. 21%
Domestic water transportation	591,276	13. 03%
Pipeline	903,811	19. 92%

Source: The Bureau of Transportation Statistics.

freight is commonly used only for perishables and premium express shipments. Trucks exceed trains in the percentage of freight hauled category, while trains surpass trucks in the ton-miles category due to the long distances they travel carrying large amounts of freight.

Freight Terms

To understand freight, a review of the most common freight terms is in order. YRC, a premier freight carrier, published this excellent alphabetical glossary of terms.

Accessorial Charges (also called "Assessorial Charges")
Charges made for performing services beyond normal pickup and delivery, such as inside delivery or storage charges.

Air Freight Forwarder
An air freight forwarder provides pickup and delivery service under its own tariff, consolidates shipments into larger units, prepares shipping documentation and tenders shipments to the airlines. Air freight forwarders do not generally operate their own aircraft and may therefore be called "indirect air carriers." Because the air freight forwarder tenders the shipment, the airlines consider the forwarder to be the shipper.

Air Waybill
An air waybill is a shipping document airlines use. Similar to a bill of lading, the air waybill is a contract between the shipper and airline that states the terms and conditions of transportation. The air waybill also contains shipping instructions, product descriptions, and transportation charges.

Articles of Extraordinary Value
Carriers are not liable for "documents, coin money, or articles of extraordinary value" unless the items are specifically rated in published classifications or tariffs. Exceptions may be made by special agreement. If an agreement is made, the stipulated value of the articles must be endorsed on the bill of lading. Articles may include precious stones, jewels and currency. Many tariffs include restrictions on goods with values in excess of a specified amount.

Bill of Lading (BOL or B/L)
A bill of lading is a binding contract that serves three main purposes:
1. A receipt for the goods delivered to the transportation provider for shipment
2. A definition or description of the goods
3. Evidence of title to the relative goods, if negotiable.

Bill of Lading Exceptions
The terms and conditions of most bills of lading release transportation providers from liability for loss or damage arising from:
- An Act of God,
- A public enemy
- The authority of law
- The act or default of the shipper.

In addition, except in the case of negligence, a transportation provider will not be liable for loss, damage, or delay caused by:
- The property being stopped and held in transit at the request of the shipper, owner or party entitled to make such request
- Lack of capacity of a highway, bridge or ferry
- A defect or vice in the property
- Riots or strikes.

Bonded Carrier
A transportation provider by U. S. Customs to carry Customs-controlled merchandise between Customs points.

Break bulk
A break bulk separates parts of a load into individual shipments for routing to different destinations.

Break Bulk Terminal
A consolidation and distribution center. A terminal in the network that unloads and consolidates shipments received from its smaller terminals and from other breakbulks. This terminal may have its own city operation.

Broker
A broker is an independent contractor paid to arrange motor carrier transportation. A broker may work on the carrier or shipper's behalf.

Carmack
An industry term regarding loss or damage of goods. Carmack is governed by 49 U. S. C 14706, which states that a motor carrier must
- Issue the Bill of Lading
- Pay the actual loss or injury to the property.

However, carriers limit their liability for release value products, and can limit their damages to $25 per pound or $100,000 per shipment.

Cartage Agent
A carrier that performs pickup or delivery in areas where your carrier does not serve.
- Cartage agents use their own paperwork while transporting the shipment
- No tracking of the shipment while it is in the cartage agent's possession
- When your carrier gives a shipment to a cartage agent for delivery, the shipment is considered to be "delivered" in your carrier's tracking tool.

Claim (Cargo)
A *Cargo Claim* is a demand made on a transportation company for payment for goods allegedly lost or damaged while the shipment was in the transportation provider's possession. Pursuant to the National Motor Freight Classification (NMFC) Uniform Bill of Lading, all cargo claims must be filed within nine months.

Overcharge/Undercharge
Overcharge or undercharge claims are demands on a transportation company for a refund of an overcharge from the erroneous application of rates, weights and/or assessment of freight charges.

COD
A shipment for which the transportation provider is responsible for collecting the sale price of the goods shipped before delivery.

Commodity
Any article of commerce. Goods shipped.

Common Carrier
Company that provides transportation services to the public in return for compensation.

Concealed Loss
Shortage or damage not evident at delivery.

Consignee
The person or place where a shipment will be transferred for the last time (destination); the individual or organization to whom the goods are addressed.

Deck Trailers
Trailers with rows of tracking on each sidewall and deck load bars. The load bars fit into the tracks to form temporary "decks" on which goods can be loaded. Decks allow more goods to be loaded in the trailer, reduce damage, and speed loading and unloading.

Delivery Receipt
Document a consignee or its agent dates and signs at delivery, stating the condition of the goods at delivery. The driver takes the signed delivery receipt to the terminal for retention. The customer retains the remaining copy.

Dispatch
The act of sending a driver on his/her assigned route with instructions and required shipping papers. YRC Freight maintains contact with drivers throughout the day by phone, pager, radio, satellite communication or cellular phone.

Dock
A platform, generally the same height as the trailer floor, where trucks are loaded and unloaded.

Dolly
Converter that provides an extra axle and fifth wheel and is used to connect multiple trailers.

Doubles
Vehicle configuration in which a tractor pulls two trailers connected by a dolly or jifflox.

Drayage
Also known as connecting road haulage.
1. The hauling of a load by a cart with detachable sides (dray)
2. Road transportation between the nearest railway terminal and the stuffing place.

Electronic Data Interchange (EDI)
The electronic transmission of routine business documents, such as purchase orders, invoices and bills of lading, between computers in a standard format. The data formats, or transaction sets, are usually sent between mainframe computers. Learn more in the EDI Resource Center.

Exceptions
An exception is any delivery in which the receiver or driver notes a problem on the delivery receipt before signing it. Typically, exceptions concern shortage and/or damage.

Exclusive Use
A shipper pays a premium rate for the sole use of the trailer. The trailer will be sealed at loading, and the seal number is recorded on the manifest. The seal number is verified before the trailer is unloaded at destination. When a shipper requests an exclusive-use trailer, no other freight may be added to the unit even if space permits.

Exempt Product
Products that are exempt from federal regulation, such as agricultural and forestry products.

Free Along Side (FAS)
A basis of pricing meaning the price of goods alongside a transport vessel at a specified location. The buyer is responsible for loading the goods onto the transport vessel and paying all the cost of shipping beyond that location.

Free On Board (FOB)
An acronym for "free on board" when used in a sales contract. The seller agrees to deliver merchandise, free of all transportation expense, to the place specified by the contract. After delivery is complete, the title to all the goods and the risk of damage become the buyer's.

FOB Origin
Title and risk pass to the buyer at the moment the seller delivers the goods to the carrier. The parties may agree to have title and risk pass at a different time or to allocate shipping charges by a written agreement.

FOB Destination
Under this arrangement, title and risk remain with the seller until it has delivered the goods to the location specified in the contract.

Freight
Any product being transported.

Freight Bill
Shipping document the carrier prepares to confirm shipment delivery and indicate payment terms (prepaid or collect). The document describes the shipment, its weight, the amount of charges and taxes and whether the bill is collect or prepaid. If the bill is prepaid, the shipper pays the shipping charges. If the bill is collect, the consignee pays the shipping charges.

Freight Broker
Any person who sells transportation without actually providing it. The term usually refers to an agent for truckload shipments, matching small shippers with carriers. Freight brokers often do not accept any responsibility for their shipments.

Freight Forwarder
A freight forwarder combines less-than-truckload (LTL) or less-than-carload (LCL) shipments into carload or truckload lots. Freight forwarders are designated as common carriers. They also issue bills of lading and accept responsibility for goods. The term may also refer to the company that fills railroad trains with trailers.

Gross Vehicle Weight (GVW)
The combined weight of the vehicle (tractor and trailers) and its goods.

Hazardous Material
Hazardous materials are defined by the U. S. Department of Transportation in accordance with the Federal Hazardous Material Law. A substance or material may be designated as hazardous if the transportation of the material in a particular amount and form poses an unreasonable risk to health and safety or property. Hazardous material may include: an explosive, radioactive material, etiologic agent, flammable or combustible liquid or solid, poison, oxidizing or corrosive material, and compressed gas. For more general information, go to the U. S. DoT website at http://www. phmsa. dot. gov/hazmat.

In Bond
Shipments move under bond from point of entry to an interior U. S. destination for clearance or to another border location for clearance.

Intermodal (also called Multimodal)
Shipment moves by more than one mode of transportation (ground, air, rail or ocean).

Less-Than-Truckload (LTL)
Goods weighing less than 10,000 pounds from several shippers loaded onto one trailer. For example, YRC Freight is primarily an LTL carrier, using a nationwide network to efficiently move goods from origin to destination.

Line-haul
Movement of goods between cities or between terminals, particularly between origin terminal and destination terminal (excluding pickup and delivery service).

Minimum Charge
The lowest charge for which a shipment will be handled after discount and/or adjustment.

Multimodal Transportation (also called Intermodal)
Shipment moves by more than one mode of transportation (ground, air, rail or ocean).

National Motor Freight Classification (NMFC)
Industry standard tariff published by motor carriers containing rules, descriptions and rating on all products moving in commerce; used to classify goods for the purpose of rating the freight bill. You can obtain more information about shipment classes and the NMFC at www. nmfta. org.

Non-vessel operating common carriers (NVOCC)
A type of ocean freight forwarder. NVOCCs books space in large quantities for a reduced rate, then sells space to shippers in lesser amounts. NVOCCs consolidate smaller shipments into a container load that ships under one bill of lading.

Order Notify (also called Negotiable Bill of lading)
A shipment requiring the consignee to surrender the original endorsed bill of lading at the time of delivery. A shipper may use this method to guarantee payment for goods shipped. It's most commonly used with truckload shipments.

Origin
Site where the shipment first enters the system.

Overage
Number of units received is in excess of the quantity shown on shipping documents. Overages should not be delivered to a customer. They're returned to the terminal unless the terminal receives more information while the driver is making pickups and deliveries.

Overcharge Claims
The payer of the shipping charges files an overcharge claim to dispute a discrepancy in charges that can stem from overpayment, weight or description corrections, *etc.*

Payment Terms
Generally, the shipper is responsible for payment for prepaid shipments, and the consignee is responsible for payment for collect shipments unless a third party is indicated as payer on the shipping papers.

PRO
An acronym for progressive rotating order; it is a ten-digit number assigned to each shipment and serves as a tracking number and a freight invoice number.

Pickup and Delivery (P&D)
Local movement of goods between the shipper (or pickup point) and the origin terminal or between the destination terminal and the consignee (or delivery point).

Shipper's Agent
A Shipper's Agent is not a carrier, freight forwarder, or broker. Shipper's agents generally arrange for truckload or container load shipment transportation. Shipper's agents commonly provide services related to warehousing or loading and unloading.

Shipping Documents
Papers accompanying a shipment as it moves through the carrier's system, including bills of lading (PDF), packing slips (PDF), Customs paperwork, manifests and shipment bills.

Shortage
The number of units received is less than the quantity shown on shipping documents. The outstanding units may be delivered later.

Tariff
A Tariff is a document setting forth applicable rules, rates and charges to move goods. A tariff sets forth a contract for the shipper, the consignee and the carrier. Motor carriers are no longer required to publish tariffs. However, in accordance with federal law, tariffs must be provided to a shipper on request.

Terminal
Building and grounds where shipments are prepared for local delivery or transportation to other terminals.

Third-Party
A party other than the shipper or consignee that is ultimately responsible for paying the shipment charges.

Truckload (TL)
Large-volume shipment from a single customer that weighs more than 10,000 pounds or takes up all the trailer space so no other shipment can be loaded.

Truck Tonnage
The weight (in tons) of a shipment transported by truck.

UN Number
An internationally accepted four-digit number used to identify hazardous material.

Waybill

A waybill is a non-negotiable document prepared by or on behalf of the carrier at origin. The document shows origin point, destination, route, consignor, consignee, shipment description and amount charged for the transportation service.

Source: YRC Website – Freight Glossary of Terms. All Rights Reserved.

Inbound Freight

One of the never-ending debates within supply chain management is the question of whether or not you should control inbound freight from suppliers or just buy raw materials and goods on a delivered-price basis. Most pure purchasing managers tend to want to simplify things and purchase goods on a delivered price basis. This method does simplify the administrative burden (no need to manage freight carriers) and makes the Finance team happy as title to inventory doesn't normally transfer until it hits your dock.

However, in most cases, it is usually better to control the freight from suppliers by choosing your own carriers and negotiating lower freight rates. In most cases, there is a 10-15% reduction in freight costs when you change the terms to FOB origin (versus destination). Of course, inventory title transfer and the administrative burden associated with managing fright must be taken into consideration. At a minimum, have all suppliers separately delineate freight on invoices so you can spot check the rates and ensure you are getting the best deal in that specific freight lane.

Mode Selection

When it comes to freight management, mode selection and rate negotiations is at the top of the list of the critical decision factors that impact transportation costs. Freight modes include:
- Truck (less than truckload and truckload)
- Air
- Rail
- Ocean (water)
- Pipeline

A secondary mode is also the Internet, as more and more ecommerce firms use virtual businesses to quickly ship goods to consumers. As of this writing, some ecommerce firms are even considering "drones" to air freight goods to individual consumers.

Each mode has advantages and disadvantages, which are revealed in exhibit 8.5. But first, let's quickly explore each mode to gain a better understanding of each method of transportation.

Less than truckload (a. k. a., LTL)
Represents the majority of freight moves and the majority of business-to-business (B2B) shipments. LTL shipments are generally less than 10,000 pounds. The average single piece of LTL freight is about 1,200 pounds and the size of a standard pallet. Heavier and bulkier freight is subject to additional surcharges.

Truckload freight
Truckload shipments are generally heavier than 10,000 pounds. Truckload freight is used when capacity dictates the need for an exclusive trailer. It is usually wise to consolidate LTL shipments into fewer truckload shipments, assuming customer lead times allow for such consolidation.

For perspective, the total weight of a loaded truck (tractor/trailer) cannot exceed 80,000 pounds, with the exception of special permits in certain states. In most cases, long-haul rigs will weigh no more than 35,000 pounds combined (tractor, trailer, etc.), leaving about 45,000 pounds for freight. There are some other factors that may limit this tare weight (such as the number of axles, using a liftgate or a dolly). A freight load is also limited to the capacity inside the trailer. In general, trailers are 53 feet long, 102 inches wide, 105 inches tall (inside height) and 13 feet 6 inches high (measured from the ground) overall. Of course, there are many trailer configurations in terms of varying heights, widths, and lengths. Most companies strive to use the longest, widest, and tallest trailers they can in order to maximize payload and reduce the number of loads required.

To this end, you can compute the theoretical capacity for a fleet of trailers by multiplying the length, width, and height of a trailer. After deducting, let's say 15% for air space and pallets, you can calculate the cubic capacity of an entire fleet of trailers. Wherever possible inbound and outbound loads should be consolidated to reduce the number of overall shipments. The keys to freight management are:
- Reduce miles
- Reduce loads
- Consolidate shipments
- Reduce frequency of delivery.

Air freight

Air freight shipments are similar to less than truckload movements in terms of size and weight. However, air freight loads typically need to "be-there" sooner, moving at much faster speeds. Air freight shipments can be booked directly with air freight carriers, through freight forwarders or brokers, or through online freight services. FedEx™ has popularized air freight shipments for both B2B and B2C movements.

Shipments that have a low weight-to-value ratio and faster speed requirement are ideal for air freight. When the value of goods is high yet lightweight in nature, the cost of air freight is generally acceptable. Although air freight is one of the least used shipping modes overall, globalization and delivery speed and flexibility have increased the need for this mode of freight.

Rail

Rail shipments are generally used when speed is relatively unimportant and when the freight is bulky and weight is considerably high. The domestic railroad system has been expanding the number of lines and enhancing the configuration and design of the trains in order to accommodate multi-modal solutions to freight management. Rail carriers have been aggressively improving service and reliability in an attempt to increase capacity.

Ocean (water)
Water based freight represents approximately 13% of ton-miles. When speed of delivery is less critical and the shipment weight-to-value ratio is high, ocean freight is preferred. Ocean rates are generally viewed as one of the lowest overall ton-mile cost modes. The geographic expansion of supply chains globally has caused ocean freight to become a critical element within freight management. Dealing with the total landed cost of freight, including customs, duties, fees, tariffs, quotas, etc. make this mode of transport and art and a science.

Pipeline
Pipeline transport is the transportation of goods through a pipe. Liquids and gases are primarily sent through this mode of transport, although pneumatic tubes using compressed air can also transport solid capsules.

Any chemically stable substance can be sent through a pipeline. Therefore sewage, water, or even beer pipelines exist today; but arguably, the most valuable pipelines are those transporting crude and refined petroleum products including fuel, oil, natural gas, and biofuels.

Exhibit 8.7 – Comparison of Major International Modes

Table 12-4 Comparision of Major International Transportation Modes

Mode	Reliability	Cost	Speed	Accessability	Capatability	Ease of Tracing
Rail	Average	Average	Average	High	High	Low
Water	Low	Low	Slow	Low	High	Low
Truck	High	Varies	Fast	High	High	High
Air	High	High	Fast	Low	Moderate	High
Pipeline	High	Low	Slow	Low	Low	Moderate
Internet	High	Low	Moderate to Fast	Moderate; Increasing	Low	High

Source: Global Marketing, Warren J. KeeganMark C. Green, Pearson Education, Chapter 12.

Selecting the Right Mode

Selecting the right mode of transport requires an evaluation of the key factors that drive shipping costs. These factors include:
- Speed of delivery requirement
- The weight of the average shipment

- The need for traceability
- The dimensions of the average shipment
- The value of the average shipment
- The available capacity of each mode
- The inherent pros and cons associated with each mode (exhibit 8.8)

Exhibit 8.8 - Pros and Cons of Freight Modes.

Primary Freight Mode	Pros	Cons
Truck	• Flexibility of Delivery • Reliability • Good balance between cost and speed	• Relatively expensive • Slow • Dependency on fuel
Air	• Fastest Mode • Can be linked to truck (multi-modal)	• The most expensive mode
Rail	• Cost effective when freight is bulky • Can be linked to highway	• Limited availability (locations) • Expensive when value to weight ratio is high
Water	• Highly cost effective for bulky items • Global in nature	• Slow • Lack of traceability • Lack of reliability

Exhibits 8.7 and 8.8 will provide the theoretical background to use when choosing a transportation mode. An example of how to compare freight modes is shown in exhibit 8.9.

Exhibit 8.9 - Choosing a Freight Mode (example of shipping from Los Angeles, CA to St. Louis, Missouri – 1,826 miles and 3,000 pounds).

MODE	SPEED	COST
Truck (LTL)	3-4 days	$798
Rail	7-10 days	$3,645
Air	Same day	$11,385

A Word about Freight Rates

An LTL shipper may realize savings by utilizing a freight broker or an online marketplace such as freightquote. com instead of dealing directly with a freight company. Freight brokers can shop the marketplace and obtain the lowest rates in a given lane. Intermediaries typically receive 50-70% discounts from published rates, where a small shipper may only be offered a 10-30% discount by the carrier. Truckload (TL) carriers usually charge a rate per mile. The rate varies depending on the distance, geographic location of the delivery, the type of goods being shipped, the equipment type desired, and the service times required.

The best way to manage rates and optimize service is to sample rates from several carriers, brokers and online marketplaces. Often times an RFQ (request for quote) is used to gather freight rate information. When obtaining rates from different providers, shippers may find quite a wide range in the pricing offered. Most companies focus on their most popular shipping lanes when it comes to negotiating and establishing rates but it is the outliers or remote lanes that drive freight costs.

A few other freight rate considerations include:

1. Managing fuel surcharges. Don't assume that fuel surcharges are fixed. Many companies are overpaying for fuel surcharges.

2. Reviewing and auditing freight bills. The industry standard is a 3-5% error rate; meaning, freight is billed (invoiced) incorrectly about 4% of the time.

3. Managing freight claims such as damage or lost shipments. This takes a considerable amount of time to manage.

4. Accessorial charges, such as lumper, corrugated, pickup charges, etc. Make sure you get a published list of accessorial charges from each and every freight carrier.

Private Fleet Management

One of the debates that has ostensibly been going on forever is whether or not a company should use a private fleet or utilize the services of a third-party carrier to deliver goods. A private fleet is whereby a company uses its own trucks and drivers to pick up materials and/or to deliver finished goods to customers. For example, Wal-Mart employs a private fleet to deliver products from its distribution centers to the retail stores. Other forms choose to use third-party carriers to perform the same services. Private fleets pertain primarily to trucking, although there are some private fleets in the other modes of transportation.

Exhibit 8.10 reveals the major advantages and disadvantages associated with private fleets.

Exhibit 8.10 - Advantages and Disadvantages of a Private Fleet.

Advantages of a Private Fleet	Disadvantages of a Private Fleet
Tighter controls and increased flexibility	Possible lane imbalances
Improved service to customers	Driver turnover
May provide slightly lower costs	Volume required to reach economies of scale

Advantages of a Private Fleet	Disadvantages of a Private Fleet
Low barriers of entry	Capital requirements and cost of money
Improved company image (company graphics)	Low return on investment
Can provide specialized services	Overhead/administrative burden

When to use a private fleet

The decision to utilize a private fleet usually hinges on the need for specialized equipment or unusually difficult customer requirements. Fleet managers can reposition fleet assets to accommodate changes within the supply chain more quickly than when using a third-party. The key to making this in-house versus third party transportation decision is to eliminate all the emotional hogwash that normally enters the picture and stick to performing a detailed evaluation of which service provides the lowest cost at the highest level of service. Exhibit 4.5 in Chapter 4 can be a useful tool when performing this private fleet analysis. Some of the questions that must be answered when deciding on transportation alternatives include:

1. Should I buy (ownership) or lease (or finance) fleet assets?
2. How long should I keep the fleet assets (life cycle costing)?
3. Should I perform in-house or third-party maintenance on trucks?
4. Can we backhaul materials from suppliers to reduce costs?
5. Do we have the capability to hire and train drivers?
6. Do we have the capital to constantly invest in technology to drive down costs?
7. Do we have the staff necessary to meet all Federal and State compliance requirements?
8. Can we employ customer pickup or supplier drop-ship arrangements to reduce requirements?

As far as the equipment acquisition strategy (buy or lease), this is usually a function of the internal cost of capital. As of this writing, most companies use a 10% discount rate when comparing these two alternatives. If an organization values its cash at 10% (meaning, the minimum return required to use internal working capital), it is normally a good idea to consider leasing or financing as an alternative to ownership. When considering leasing, be sure to work with your Finance team to ensure meeting all internal balance sheet and FASB requirements.

The major types of leases include:

Full Service Leasing, which is an all-encompassing financing and maintenance agreement whereby the lessor owns the asset and leases (off balance sheet) the vehicle over a certain time period to a organization. Full service leasing reduces the administrative burden associated with fleet management and provides maintenance, compliance, legal and regulatory services, safety, and training where required. Full service leasing is turn-key and one-stop shopping that removes the need to manage the asset. Full service leases meet the need for off-balance sheet financing.

TRAC Leases (terminal rental adjustment clause), which is typically an off balance sheet operating lease whereby the lessee guarantees the residual value at the end of the lease term. Normally, the residual value at lease end is approximately 20% of the original acquisition value of the truck. Your finance team will need to "test" the lease to ensure it meets all FASB requirements for an off-balance sheet lease. In a TRAC lease, at lease term, if the asset is worth more than the residual value, the lessee benefits; conversely, if the asset is worth less than the pegged residual value, the lessee will owe the difference.

Operating Leases, also known as fair market value leases, are also used due to the attractive nature of the walk-away design, which removes the residual value risk at the end of the lease term. Operating leases also eliminate the taxable event that occurs upon the sale of the vehicle. In order for an operating lease to meet the off-balance sheet criteria, it must meet all FASB requirements. Again, it is wise to have your Finance team test the lease. Remember, while this lease is attractive, when you remove the residual value risk, your monthly lease rate will surely increase as the lessor is now taking the risk. There is no free lunch here.

Capital Leases, which do not meet the off-balance sheet criteria, are listed as a company asset and gets depreciated over a specific period of time. The depreciation expense is recognized on the company income statement. At lease term, ownership is transferred at a fixed price. This type of lease is similar to a simple loan.

Life Cycle Costing

Regardless of whether you decide to buy or lease, there does need to be a formal life cycle policy in place for each equipment type. Exhibit 8.11 reveals the typical "optimal vehicle retention cycle" by equipment type. A life cycle costing model should be used to pinpoint the exact point in which the fixed and variable costs associated with the asset intersect. Normally, just past this intersection point is the most likely replacement point. Exhibit 8.12 shows the theoretical life cycle approach for most fleet assets.

Exhibit 8.11 - Life Cycle Portfolio Matrix

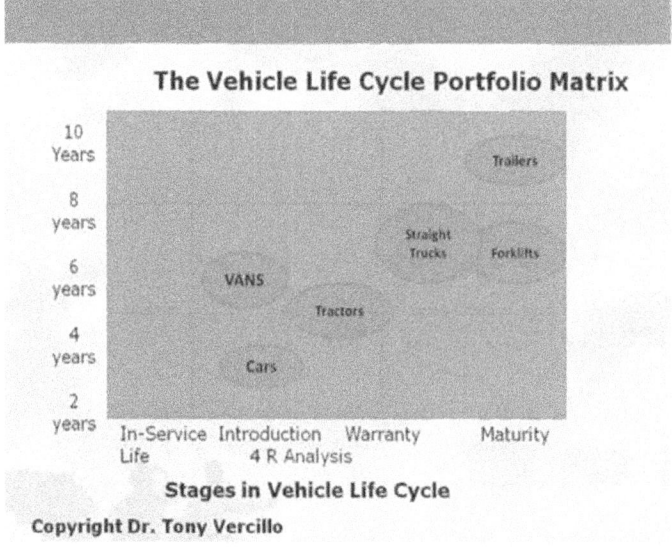

Copyright Dr. Tony Vercillo

Exhibit 8.12 - Life Cycle Replacement Theory

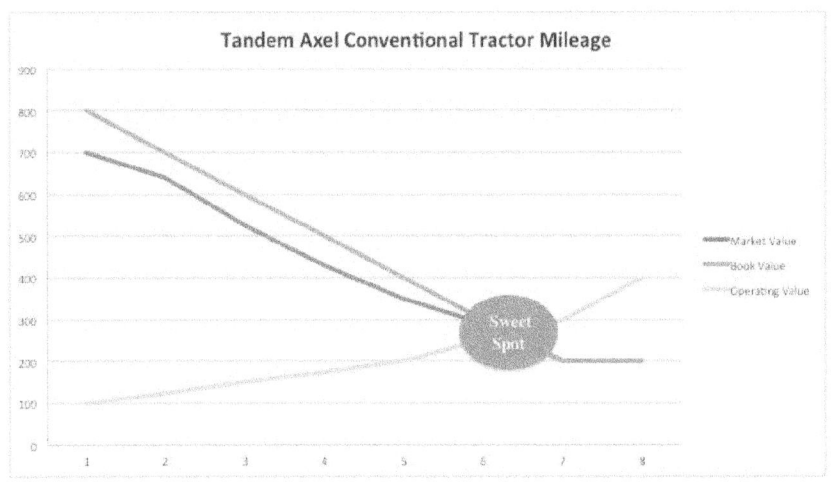

The other question that always comes up is how to perform maintenance on a private fleet of vehicles? There are a few alternatives, including:

- In-House, whereby a company has its own fleet repair shops and employs mechanics to perform all the vehicle repairs. A recent study revealed that in-house fleet mechanics are only turning wrenches 55% of the time. The rest of the time is spent performing nugatory services, usually mandated by the senior management. In-house repairs also require a fleet management information system to track all repairs and services.

- Contract Maintenance, whereby a third-party firm provides all maintenance services under a guaranteed contract at a predetermined fixed and variable rate. The third-party also manages all warranty repairs.

- Independent Repair Network, whereby a firm utilizes a number of local repair facilities to get the work done. These networks will usually discount parts and labor and will accept purchase orders. Typically, drivers can call a toll-free number and be advised where to take the vehicle for repairs.

- Dealer Supplied Network, whereby a company brings vehicles back to the dealer (similar to how you get your personal car repaired, especially while under warranty) to get repair work. The issue here is dealer accessibility and the labor rate charged to perform routine maintenance services.

- There is no right or wrong answer here. The focus should be on providing the highest level of service; who owns and/or repairs the asset should be irrelevant. The other factor is implementing a formal vehicle replacement strategy whereby assets are replaced at the optimal life cycle period (e. g. five years for tractors).

A Word about Reverse Logistics

When setting up your distribution network, be sure to keep in mind the cost of reverse logistics. Returns, damage, overages and shortages, etc. are costly mistakes. In fact, some companies simply tell customers to keep or throw away damaged product due to the cost of returns. Every time the warehouse needs to take back a product, there are many steps required to ultimately resolve one simple return. Managing reverse logistics should be part of your overall distribution plan.

Conclusion

This chapter has explained the criticality of understanding and managing logistics, freight, and distribution, affectionately called the backend of the business. Simply stated, logistics and distribution can be the difference between a mediocre or high degree of profitability. If managed properly, the total logistics function can increase inventory velocity, compress time to market, and enhance customer service. Logistics and distribution helps reduce the overall number of touches within the supply chain. Distribution interfaces with each and every function within a firm and should be held in high esteem. A formal distribution master plan should be developed and implemented, including key performance indicators as outlined in Chapter 10. Total order visibility and traceability should be the ultimate goal. In addition, your distribution prowess should be the *reason* customers choose you over the competition. This is when you truly know your logistics network is adding significant value.

Chapter Summary

- Logistics is the efficient and integrated inbound, outbound and reverse flow of goods, services, and information from the point of origin to the final destination for the purpose of meeting or exceeding customer expectations.

- Logistics includes order processing, inventory control, freight and transportation, and customer service.

- A basic distribution system consists of four (4) major dependencies – suppliers, production, distribution centers, and customers.

- There are two (2) primary approaches to physical distribution; direct shipment and the inventory storage method.

- There are two (2) approaches to distribution that can be followed to achieve a balanced inventory and the appropriate level of safety stock, namely a push, or pull system.

- Choosing the right distribution strategy requires a logistics master plan.

- Managing inbound and outbound freight, including mode selection and rate negotiations can lower total supply chain costs.

- When setting up your distribution network, be sure to keep in mind the cost of reverse logistics such as returns.

Exploratory Questions

1. What are the basic elements of a distribution master plan?

2. What is the difference between a push versus pull inventory system?

3. Why is eliminating "touches" within the supply chain so important?

4. Why should a firm consider managing inbound freight from suppliers?

5. What are the key factors to consider when choosing a freight mode?

6. How does logistics add bottom line (profitability) value?

7. What are the advantages and disadvantages of employing a private fleet?

Case Study and Questions

CWT is a waste water technology company located in Southern California. CWT is an innovator in the field of wastewater treatment. CWT focuses on improving the technology for the waste water industry. They specialize in solutions for the *primary* treatment of water. CWT has offices in North and South America and in Mexico.

CWT was experiencing customer complaints associated with shipping costs. A large customer was concerned about the freight costs of the chemistry product shipped to them from the CWT distributor located in Alabama. The product is used in the water treatment system provided to customers by CWT. Product can be shipped from the CWT Los Angeles facility or from a distributor located in Alabama.

An analysis of the existing freight costs was conducted, including the packaging/crating associated with each shipment. The large customer, located in Iowa was used as the primary source of information. The map reveals the two shipping options.

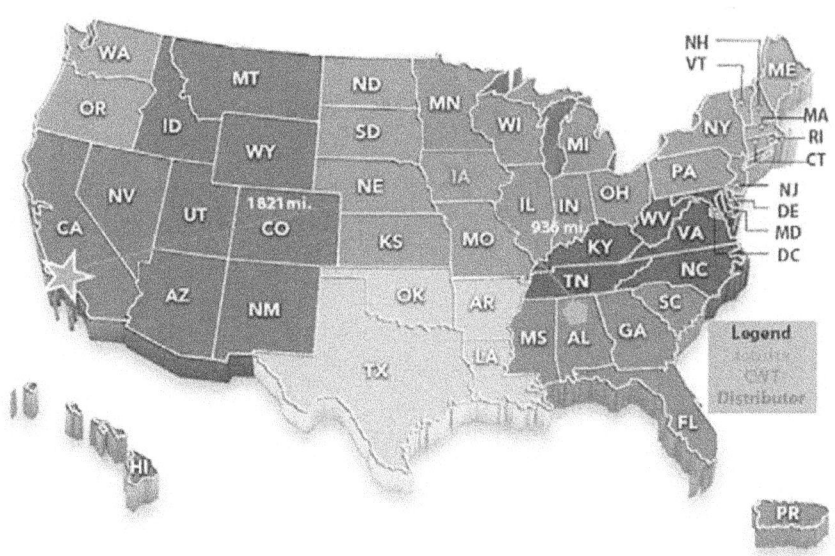

The freight cost/pallet and the corresponding lead time (from order to delivery in days) from each facility were analyzed.

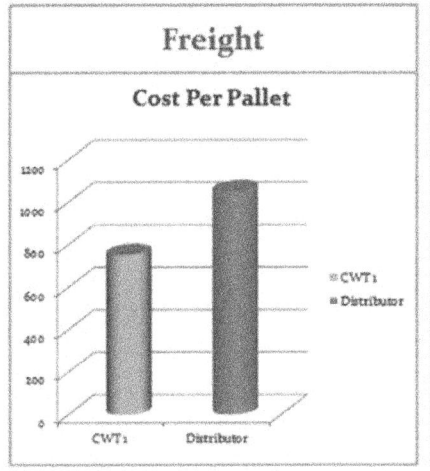

Then freight quotes were requested from a number of carriers. Different transit times were also considered.

Carrier	Mode	Transit Time	Distance (AL-IA)	Freight Quote
Carrier #1	LTL	2	936 miles	$1,067
Carrier #2	LTL	2	936 miles	$1,314
Carrier #3	LTL	4	936 miles	$1,329
Carrier #4	LTL	3	936 miles	$1,390
Carrier #1	LTL	6	1,821 miles	$877
Carrier #2	LTL	4	1,821 miles	$910
Carrier #3	LTL	4	1,821 miles	$1,068
Carrier #4	LTL	5	1,821 miles	$1,192

Source: Introduction to Supply Chain Management Group Project: Jonathan Salazar, Betty Thompson, Joel Llanes, Vivian Chao.

The data revealed that although the Alabama distributor was closer in proximity to the customer, it actually made more sense to ship product from the LA facility due to the increased competition and traffic in that freight lane. The freight cost per shipment to customers could be reduced significantly, but customers must be willing to wait a few more days for each shipment. Therefore, even though Alabama seemed to make more sense, Los Angeles was chosen as the origin point to reduce freight costs. In this case, customers were willing to wait a few more days in order to reduce freight costs by almost 20%.

Case Study Questions:

1. How should CWT communicate the freight rate reduction, considering the fact that total lead time increases significantly?

2. What other freight alternatives should CWT consider?

3. Should CWT ever consider air freight for these deliveries?

4. Do you think CWT should charge customers for faster transit times?

9. WAREHOUSING AND MATERIAL HANDLING

"Desire increases when fulfillment is postponed."
PierreCorneille

Since we covered distribution strategy in Chapter 8, this chapter is devoted to more pure warehousing concepts. Of course, there will be some overlap as warehousing is an integral part of overall distribution strategy. Warehousing has historically been viewed as a bunch of buildings where goods sit idle in storage, taking up valuable space and tying up precious company capital. This view has changed today as warehousing now plays an integral role in controlling infrastructure and inventory costs. In fact, warehousing has become a strategic supply chain initiative, taking on a much broader role in overall business operations.

The purpose of this chapter is to define warehousing, explain its role within the supply chain, and provide some insight into not only how to improve warehouse operations, but also the emerging trends within the industry. The topics covered in this chapter include:
- The definition of warehousing
- The role of warehousing within the supply chain
- The functions within warehousing

- Static and dynamic storage
- Space, layout and design
- Material handling
- Reducing distribution costs
- Warehouse information systems
- Tips to improve warehouse operations
- Emerging trends within warehousing

Definition of Warehousing

Warehousing is defined as any operation that stores, stages, picks, sorts, packages, coordinates or centralizes raw materials or finished goods. Warehousing is used to strategically position goods closer to supply and demand. Proper warehousing techniques results in reduced inventory levels, shorter lead times, improved supply chain flexibility, better response times, and lower freight and distribution costs.

As so aptly put by Brian Hudock, partner at Tompkins Associates, a premier warehouse consulting firm, "the lines between manufacturing, the warehouse, the distribution center, and the customer have all blurred. Operations typically performed in the manufacturing plant are now conducted much further down the supply chain. At the same time, some operations normally reserved for the surge warehouses, have now moved further upstream."

The Role of the Warehouse

The warehouse plays an integral role within any supply chain and has become much more important in recent times due to the pressure on improving service and increasing inventory velocity. The role of warehousing includes:
1. The balancing of production schedules with demand.
2. The storage of inventory.
3. Raw material and product consolidation.
4. Customer demand positioning.
5. The creation of shorter delivery routes.

The Functions within the Warehouse

There are five major functions within a warehouse including receiving, storing, picking, loading, and shipping. In addition, some warehouses also perform kitting, packaging, and customization. These functions are defined as follows:

Receiving is the activity associated with the receipt of raw materials, supplies, and goods. Receiving also entails count verification to ensure that goods received are in the correct quantity.

Storing consists of holding goods in anticipation of demand. After receiving goods, the putaway activity places the items into storage.

Picking removes items from inventory to ultimately stage for delivery.

Loading provides the physical placement of materials and goods within a container, truck, or trailer.

Shipping entails verifying order accuracy, packing goods into the appropriate container or box, weighing and measuring orders, and distributing goods to customers.

Secondary Functions *include:*

Kitting involves minor assembly and the combining of sub-assemblies or components to build a final product. Kitting can be done sequentially, in batch form, or via zone.

Packaging gets the finished product ready for shipment.

Customization is whereby the warehouse provides value-added and special services to create product uniqueness.

These functions, when performed correctly, can add significant value to the customer experience. In addition, when these major warehouse

functions are managed well, inventory accuracy improves. In particular, when receiving is performed correctly, inventory accuracy improves significantly. This is important as receiving can account for as much as 25% of total inventory inaccuracy. Therefore, sound receiving principles must be used to ensure the safe unloading of inbound carriers, the accuracy of receipts, and the fulfilling of orders. Receiving procedures must be established for the following activities:
- Pre-receiving of all materials and goods
- Dock management (assigning docks to carriers at specific times)
- Advance shipping notices (ASN's)
- Unloading practices
- Putaway procedures
- Carrier routing guides
- Verifying receipts, including matching against packing slips
- Documenting overages, shortages, and damages (OS&D).

The keys to sound receiving include cubing and/or weighing goods upon receipt, eliminating time and motion associated with putaway, and ensuring the appropriate use of bar-coding, RFID tags, and labeling. In addition, as simple as this may sound, it is also crucial that all suppliers utilize the same naming convention for all raw materials, packaging, and finished goods. This simple technique may instantly cause an increase in inventory accuracy.

Order Picking and Slotting

Order picking is the choosing of the correct product in the right quantity in order to meet customer demand requirements. There are four (4) types of order picking, including:
- Case picking (picking full cases from inventory)
- Layer picking (picking full layer of goods off pallets)
- Broken or split case picking (picking individual items or inner cartons within a master case)
- Pallet picking (picking full pallets of products)

The decision of which pick method to use is contingent upon the use of automated versus manual picking procedures, the use of zone, batch, or wave picking methods, and whether or not you have a sophisticated or rudimentary warehouse management system (WMS). That being said, there are still some fundamental principles that should be followed. These principles include:

1. Use the 80/20 rule. In most cases, 20% of your inventory items represent the overwhelming majority of customer orders. These items need to be placed closest to the dock and shipping area for ease of access. These fast moving items should also be the focal point for pick accuracy.

2. Implement detailed picking instructions and train all warehouse employees on the importance of picking and its impact on inventory accuracy. In fact, be sure to prominently post a scorecard of picking errors by shift such that all pickers can see how their shift is performing. Another important consideration here is holding the entire warehouse accountable for picking accuracy. In some cases, an incentive system can be used to create excitement around the picking process.

3. Use an automated stock location system that easily reveals the precise location of all inventory items. If the warehouse employees can't find it, they can't pick it! Minimize warehouse travel time wherever possible by grouping together the 20% of your SKU's that make up 80% of your orders.

4. Match inbound packaging with the typical outbound order size. The more you eliminate broken or split case picking, the higher the accuracy. Choose only two or three standard shipping boxes to eliminate confusion.

5. Implement a redundant picking approval process, whereby each pick gets re-checked to ensure accuracy. Of course, this can be automated through the use of technology.

6. Implement cycle counting that includes error identification and root causes. When picking errors are noted, resolve the

errors immediately and put into place procedural fixes that prevent future incidents.

7. Sequence your orders by pick path, making sure you batch together same zone orders, single lines, and the most difficult picks (i. e., non-conveyor items).

8. Slot your fastest-moving SKUs in the waist-to-shoulder or "wheelhouse" area of your storage media.

9. Implement an incentive program for picking accuracy. Reward the pick crew for a high degree of accuracy and be sure to post the results.

10. Implement enhanced bard-code and/or RFID tags to increase efficiency and reduce human interference.

Order Picking Methods

Batch Picking, whereby a picker selects a group of orders at the same time. When a product appears on multiple orders, all the goods required to fulfill all the current orders are picked simultaneously.

Zone Picking is accomplished when the entire picking area within the warehouse is segmented into zones. Pickers select all the SKU's required to fulfill current orders within each zone. Zone picks are then usually consolidated in another area to complete customer orders prior to shipping. Zone picking can be performed sequentially (one zone at a time) or simultaneously (selecting from all applicable zones).

Discrete Picking is used when it is critical to pick one order, one line at a time. Typically, this method is used when order selection is performed throughout the day. This is the simplest form or order picking and is used by many organizations due to its ease of understanding. This method is also utilized when a less robust WMS (warehouse management system) is in place. Better stated, this method is often used when a firm is operating under the spreadsheets"R"us banner.

Wave Picking is similar to discrete picking with the exception that this picking method is scheduled, by shift, at specific times of the day. Wave picking is used in an attempt to better coordinate with the shipping function.

There are also combination methods, whereby a warehouse may use more than one form of pick method. This normally has to do with order sizes, shipping method, and functional coordination throughout the supply chain. In addition, many organizations will choose a more complex combination pick method when employee a highly sophisticated WMS that includes advanced technology.

Types of Picks

Picking labor is driven by selection. Pick selection can come in a variety of forms, including:

- Picker-to-Location, which is the way most warehouses function. Most important here is the use of an automated inventory location system so pickers do not spend an inordinate amount of time searching for product within the warehouse. Individual items usually get picked this way. The opposite pick method, *location-to-picker*, utilizes carousels or automated retrievals systems to bring product to the picker. This can dramatically improve productivity. Both vertical and horizontal carousels can be used.

- Picker-to-Pallet, whereby the operator utilizes a pallet jack or a forklift to move pallets throughout the warehouse. Case picking is normally performed using this pick method.

- Picker-to-Conveyor, whereby the picker gets assigned to a specific zone of the conveyor system. Normally used for broken case or split case picking and where flow rack storage is utilized.

- Picker-to-Cart utilizes a manual or powered cart (radio frequency) to perform picks. This form of picking is used when the majority of inventory is at floor level.

Automated Picking

Wherever possible, automated picking should be considered. Automated picking will increase cases/hour, improve picking accuracy, and eliminate employee industrial accidents and injury concerns. The idea here is to use computer aided putaway and retrieval (AS/RS) to eliminate the possibility of human error. There are pick-to-light systems that lead the picker to the assigned zone, carousel, or flow rack. There are also radio frequency controlled systems that tell the picker exactly what to do. Both on-board and hand-held devices can be used to literally control warehouse productivity and labor using real-time information to drive results. This technology will be further explored in Chapter 11.

Automated pick systems use computer-driven commands to receive line-by-line instructions for each order then retrieve the correct quantity of goods without any human intervention. There are a number of automated systems that can be used, including:
- Unit Load AS/RS Systems
- Horizontal and vertical case flow systems
- Cylindrical item dispensers
- Robotics

Picking is an art and a science. When deciding on whether to use manual or automated picking, the true measure of success should be picking performance as defined by:
- Pickers/Order
- Line Items/Pick
- Picks/Hour

Comparing the manual versus automated approach in this way allows for the numbers to tell the story. If the automated system improves productivity and has a decent ROI (return on investment), by all means, go automated. Automation and technology will be further explored in Chapter 11.

Slotting

Slotting is another critical procedure within any warehouse. Proper product slotting increases space efficiency and reduces material handling by locating goods in the optimal picking sequence within the warehouse. Slotting is all about the proper placement of goods within the facility. Proper placement of goods reduces material handling travel time, which typically represents more than 50% of warehouse labor costs. Slotting will also increase picking accuracy by separating similar products, thereby reducing proximity picking errors. Slotting will ensure that the heaviest products are picked first and the fastest moving items are closest to the shipping dock. Slotting also organizes products by family group and reduces sorting.

Static and Dynamic Storage

Static Storage consists primarily of racks or shelving, or a combination of both. Static storage can be an effective way to putaway and pick products within a warehouse. It is imperative that products be stored in a way that the most popular items are more easily picked. Racks are normally used for larger products while shelving is used for smaller, less dense items. The main issue here is productivity. Putaway, pick, and travel times must be considered when using pallet racks or shelving as time and motion can be the death knell of warehouse productivity.

Dynamic Storage is used to improve pick efficiency whereby a flow-rack (pallet or carton) design is employed to create a more streamlined and gravity-fed approach. Conveyors and/or air flotation rails are used to move product more efficiently to a pick location. Normally, a carton flow rack is used for individual item picking whereas a pallet flow rack is used for full case picking. When it comes to making the decision surrounding static versus dynamic storage, it comes down to the measurement cost per cubic foot stored. The investment in dynamic storage needs to return lower labor costs and less overall pick time in order to be justified.

Space, Layout and Design

Warehouse capacity, space utilization, and design layout should be part of an overall supply chain strategic plan. In a supply chain survey we conducted, when asking more than 150 warehouse professionals what their biggest single problem was, a majority responded by saying "a lack of space. " In fact, many companies face this lack of space and address the issue inappropriately by:
- Unnecessarily using outside storage
- Storing product in mobile trailers or storage units
- Using temporary structures to handle storage overflow
- Using a second warehouse in close proximity to the primary warehouse.

Most of the time, the problem associated with lack of space could have been addressed during the supply chain planning process. Warehouse capacity planning should include:
- Receiving volume forecast for three years
- Dock requirements and schedule planning (number and configuration of docks)
- Shipping detail and forecast for three years (average load, expected number outbound loads)
- Product dimension planning – current versus future (cubic foot requirements)
- Product weights
- Product and pallet space requirements and stackability
- Changes to product classifications (i. e. hazardous).

As mentioned in Chapter 6 on Forecasting, most future sales estimates are wrong. Therefore, when projecting warehouse space and capacity, it is important to select the most representative product SKU's that make up 80% of all volume. The key to warehouse space planning is the detailed understanding of the frequency of activities, including:
- Number and frequency of inbound loads from suppliers
- Number of receiving trucks needed to accommodate receipts
- Average load and unload time by trailer/container type
- Average outbound loads shipped, including frequency

- Matching inbound and outbound trucks requirements with dock count/need
- Dock labor availability and scheduling times.

Warehouse space planning includes estimating:
1. Dock and receiving space.
2. Staging area.
3. Storage space.
4. Shipping and dispatch area.
5. Administrative areas.

Exhibit 9.1 – Typical Warehouse Layout

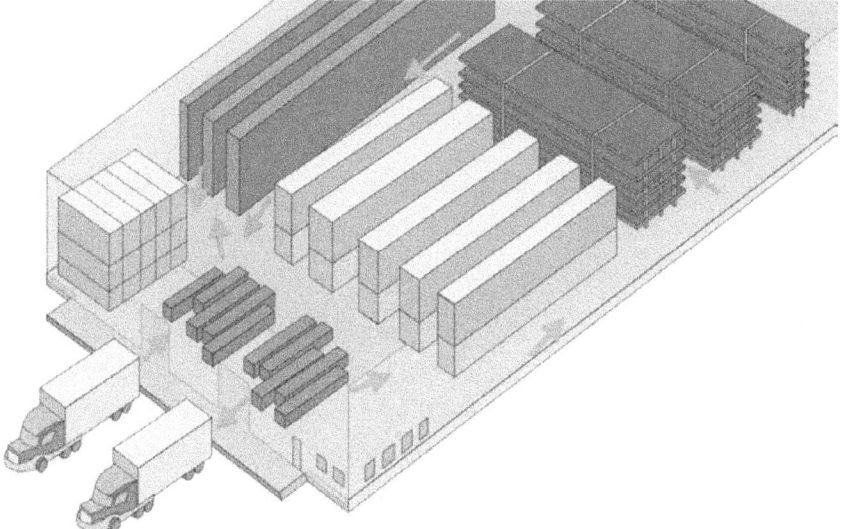

Source: Typical warehouse layout - warehouse-layoutdesigns. blogspot. com

Reviewing historical trends associated with receiving and dock utilization will help to better understand future requirements. It is also important to know the variability associated with receiving and dock utilization. Do carriers randomly show-up at the warehouse dock, or are ASN's (advanced shipping notices) used to reduce variability and schedule carrier and dock times? There are modeling and simulation tools that can be used to assist with this part of the planning process. Regardless of how this modeling is performed, the key to success is the data analysis associated with cubic capacity requirements.

The number of docks required to handle today and the next three to five years is the starting point. The next step is to understand the requirement associated with the staging of products. The staging area within the warehouse is the central repository post receiving. Staging is used to quickly unload carriers or in-house fleets in order to avoid delay charges. Determining the amount of space required for staging is a function of historical receiving activity and pattern identification. The more precisely scheduled inbound loads are, the more likely you can limit the size of the staging area. Generally speaking, one truckload of goods per dock bay is considered appropriate for staging purposes. Therefore, the staging area at each dock should have lanes that are sized for a typical load.

All of this is easier said than done. Even with sophisticated technology and simulation tools, sizing the dock and staging areas is still an arduous task. Some form of projecting and/or guessing is often used to estimate this important aspect of warehousing. After the number of docks (and receiving area) and staging area are calculated, the next space requirement is storage. Storage takes up the overwhelming majority of space requirements within a warehouse. This is one area where you do not want to under or over estimate. Too little space causes lousy productivity and a high degree of human error, while too much space is simply too costly.

In addition to the data already gathered to calculate the staging area, to calculate the storage area, the average inventory on-hand, including the minimum and maximum allowable levels by SKU (the min/max number of units) must also be collected. After current inventory levels are gathered, a projection for future inventory requirements should be established. Inventory can be collected and converted to required pallet positions and/or cubic feet of space. Then, a small amount of safety stock can be added to complete the inventory storage requirement. Putaway must then be considered as either fixed or random location methods can be employed. Fixed location storage selects a specific area for each SKU whereby that inventory item can only be found in that one (1) area. This is the easiest storage method to implement. Using a fixed storage approach will improve accuracy over time as item location doesn't change. However, the fixed storage method may cause poor space utilization as it does not allow for flexibility of SKU location.

The other method is random location storage. This method, when used in conjunction with a good location identification system, will reduce space requirements assuming some sort of FIFO (first in, first out) picking method is used. Even if random storage is chosen, the fastest moving items should be closest to the shipping area while the slowest moving SKU's should be placed in the most remote areas within the warehouse. Random storage will result in better space utilization and generally requires less than 50% of the space needed for the fixed location method. This does not mean that random storage should always be used. The tradeoff associated with ease of accessibility and improved accuracy must be pitted against the high cost of additional space. Some companies, especially those with extremely high cost items such as Rolex™ watches, may decide to employ the fixed location method to ensure a low level of inventory loss.

The ultimate goal is to figure out the warehouse "footprint" required to accommodate the number of pallet positions (space) needed to receive, stage, and store goods. Of course, the number of storage levels within the warehouse and the type of racking, etc. will somewhat dictate the footprint. The warehouse space calculation should result in a total square foot requirement to handle all raw materials and finished goods (including a small amount of safety stock), administrative areas, all warehouses related processes, and an accommodation for growth.

Layout Planning

Warehouse layout should be included in the Supply Chain Strategic (master) Plan. The layout planning process should include specific goals and objectives for the following areas:
- Space utilization and efficiency.
- Material handling effectiveness.
- Storage capacity.
- Safety and cleanliness.
- Projections for growth.

The warehouse layout process should also consider and carefully evaluate a few alternatives before choosing a final design. There are seven major steps to the warehouse layout process, including:

1. Calculate the useable warehouse square footage by major process area.

2. Identify the existing warehouse constraints (building columns, heating/ac, etc.).

3. Calculate the remaining warehouse space minus all constraints.

4. Choose the receiving and shipping locations to optimize efficiency (considering rail access, flow-through design, and dock efficiency).

5. Identify your storage area, including aisle widths and heights/levels that maximize material handling usage.

6. Generate layout alternatives that consider varying aisle widths and heights (levels), and a few alternative configurations.

7. Evaluate each alternative layout using the following criteria:
   - Senior management acceptance
   - Impact on productivity (fastest moving items located at point of use)
   - Effect on time and motion (overall travel time within the warehouse)
   - Impact on picking and putaway (labor hours)
   - Material and inventory accessibility
   - Cost to implement
   - Impact on housekeeping.

A simple ranking system (on a scale of 1-5, with five being excellent) that compares each alternative against pre-determined selection criteria (such as cost) should be used to provide some level of objectivity to the selection of the appropriate layout. The decision matrix provided in Chapter 3 can be used to conduct this analysis.

Material Handling

Let's face it, conveyors, racking, forklifts, and pallet jacks are simply not sexy. As such, this part of the warehouse planning process is often neglected. Intense domestic and global competition, however, has made the need for sophisticated material handling equipment and automation a necessity, not a luxury.

Material handling includes:
- Pallets and materials to secure goods
- Industrial lift trucks and pallet jacks
- Fixed equipment such as conveyors, carousels, and racking (see Exhibit 9.1)
- Robotics and artificial intelligence (AI)
- Control systems that help to integrate information throughout the warehouse.

Exhibit 9.2 - Typical material handling rack/shelving with bar coding

For a detailed look at fixed equipment, including carousels, conveyors, guidance systems, automated storage and retrieval systems, and

USING YOUR SUPPLY CHAIN AS A COMPETITIVE WEAPON | 195

sortation equipment, the excellent work, *The Supply Chain Handbook* by James H. Thompkins, Ph. D and Dale Harmelink is a must-read. Material handling control systems and technology will be explained in Chapter 11. The other two (2) major topics associated with material handling; specifically, pallets, industrial trucks and jacks will be covered here.

Pallets

A pallet, or a skid as it is often called (although technically this is inaccurate as a skid has no bottom deck boards), is a primarily wooden or plastic transport structure that supports and stabilizes goods while being hoisted by a forklift, pallet jack, or other lifting device. A pallet is the structural foundation of a unit load which results in improved handling and storage efficiency. Goods are usually placed on a pallet then secured with strapping, stretch wrap, or shrink wrap to secure the load. This readies the load for shipment.

Most pallets are wooden, but depending upon the industry being served and the sustainability or "green" efforts in place, can also be made of plastic, metal, or even recycled materials.

Exhibit 9.3 - Standard Wooden Pallet

Courtesy Shoppas Material Handling.

Most pallets can support a load of approximately 2,200 pounds (1,000 KG). According to Wikipedia, there are more than 500 million pallets produced each year and an estimated 2 billion pallets in use within the United States alone. Besides stabilizing the load, standard pallets are used to reduce the overall cost for handling and storage.

Pallets allow for ease of movement and increased velocity throughout the warehouse. Not all organizations use pallets, as it is dependent upon the dimensions and weight of the goods being stored.

One of the problems caused by increased globalization is that there isn't a single standard for pallet size. The lack of an international pallet standard causes inefficiencies and added costs. A single standard is difficult because of the wide variety of conditions a standard pallet would need to address (i. e. fitting through different door widths). In fact, it is estimated that there are more than 100 different pallet sizes being used worldwide.

Although pallets do have a finite life (especially wooden pallets), more and more companies are using pallet pooling and reusable pallets with internal tracking devices built in to control pallet expense. There a number of third-party pallet management firms available to minimize the administrative burden associated with pallet control.

Pallet Dimensions

Wooden pallets are measured in "stringer" and "deckboard" lengths. The stringer is the length while the deckboard designates the width. There are two-way (two entry points) and 4-way (entry points on all sides with more durability) pallets. The standard pallet used throughout North American, or GMA pallet, is 40 x 48 inches. The GMA pallet represents approximately 25-35% of the current pallets in use. However, the International Organization for Standardization (ISO) identifies six pallet dimensions,

Dimensions, (W × L in inches)	Region most used in
40.00 × 48.00	North America
39.37 × 47.24	Europe, Asia
45.9 × 45.9	Australia
42.00 × 42.00	North America, Europe, Asia
43.30 × 43.30	Asia
31.50 × 47.24	Europe

Exhibit 9.4 - Pallets being used in a warehouse

Paper or eco-friendly pallets, are often used for light loads, but are increasing in use due to the variety of "go-green" efforts being implemented. Paper pallets are also used where recycling and easy disposal is important. Plastic pallets, made of HDPE or recycled PET (drinking/beverage bottles) are also being used primarily where a highly durable, weather resistant, and improved bio-safety approach is required. The use of plastic pallets is increasing as more and more organizations seek to reduce cost and waste while increasing health and safety.

Exhibit 9.5 - Standard Plastic Pallet

Courtesy Shoppas Material Handling.

Steel or metal pallets are used for heavy and high-stacking loads but make up a very small percent of the overall pallet market. The advantages of metal pallets include:
- Insect free
- Improved safety (reduces splinters)
- Improved cleanliness
- Can be recycled/reused
- More durable

The disadvantages include:
- Higher initial cost
- Increased weight
- May rust
- Slippery surface

Using plastic or metal pallets needs to be analyzed over the long term as the initial higher cost may be offset by durability.

Industrial Trucks/Jacks

A forklift (aka, a fork or lift truck) is a powered industrial truck used to hoist and move goods throughout a warehouse, primarily over short distances. The industrial truck industry is estimated to be more than $30 billion worldwide. More than 1.1 million industrial trucks are sold every year. Forklifts are load rated for a specific maximum weight and a forward center of gravity. Loads must not exceed these ratings as overloading will create an increase in safety hazards. Forklifts are highly unstable and require a trained operator to drive them. A forklift should never negotiate a turn at high speed with a raised load, as this can cause an industrial accident.

Exhibit 9.6 – Typical Forklift

Source: Wikipedia.

As can be seen on the accompanying exhibits, forklifts are available in many configurations and load ratings (capacity). Most forklifts have load capacities between 1-5 tons. Larger forklifts are usually reserved for extremely heavy loads such as overseas shipping containers.

These configurations include:
- 3 and 4-wheel forklifts
- Scissor lifts
- Reach-style lift trucks, designed for narrow aisles
- Side-loader lift trucks
- Towing trucks
- Truck mounted forklifts

There are also, for certain configurations, stand-on end, stand-on center, and sit-down center style units available. Speak to your local material handling supplier to get a recommendation on which style lift would best suit your needs. Each style and configuration serves a very specific purpose within the warehouse such as picking, stacking, towing, etc. The warehouse layout, the type of racking/shelving, the height required to lift, the use of automation, and the width of the aisles all play a role is choosing the appropriate lift truck. Ask your local material handling dealer to conduct a material handling audit to assist with the selection process.

Exhibit 9.7 - Typical 3-Wheel Forklift

Courtesy Shoppas Material Handling

Exhibit 9.8 - Typical 4-Wheel Forklift

Courtesy Shoppas Material Handling

Exhibit 9.9 - Typical Reach Truck

Courtesy Shoppas Material Handling.

Exhibit 9.10 - Typical Side Loader Truck

Courtesy Shoppas Material Handling

Exhibit 9.11 - Truck Mounted Forklift

Source: www. hiabus. com

When it comes to powering a lift truck, there is electric, propane, gasoline, natural gas, diesel, hydrogen, and even hybrid powered equipment available (depending about the style, configuration, and environment). Of course, not all power/fuel types are available in all forklift categories. The type of power is dictated by the following:
- Inside or outside use
- The load and power rating required
- The local climate
- Refrigerated or dry inside environment
- The company stance on emissions.

Pallet Jacks

A pallet jack, also known as a pallet truck, is a piece of equipment used to lift and move pallets throughout the warehouse. Just like with forklifts, there are a number of styles and configurations available depending upon the required utility. The primary configurations include:
- Manual pallet jack, which is hand-powered
- Electric powered pallet jacks, propelled by batteries

Powered pallet jacks, also known as walkies and power jacks, are motorized to allow picking, lifting and moving of pallets. Some jacks contain a rider platform for the operator to stand on while moving pallets.

There is some standardization of pallet jacks throughout North America, and generally speaking, fork lengths are between 36 - 48 inches.

Exhibit 9.12 - Manual Pallet Jack

Courtesy Shoppas Material Handling.

Exhibit 9.13 - Electric Pallet Jack

Courtesy Shoppas Material Handling.

Exhibit 9.14 Walkie/Rider Pallet Jack

Courtesy Shoppas Material Handling.

Cost

The most common forklifts are typically electric powered and have a capacity of about 2.5 tons. The cost of these units is between $20,000-$35,000, depending upon brand, model, type of power, and load rating. Of course, there are larger and more heavy-duty lift trucks available that can cost more than $100,000. Standard forklifts can also be leased for about $400-$700/month.

Pallet jacks are less expensive. Manual jacks cost between $300-$1,000. Electric jacks, depending upon capacity and configuration (walkie, rider, etc.) can run between $3,000-$12,000. Again, these units can also be leased for a few hundred dollars/month, although, since pallet jacks are typically held for extended periods of time, most companies normally option to purchase them, then eventually salvage this type of equipment.

Industrial Truck Acquisition and Life Cycle Life Strategy

When securing industrial trucks and jacks, there a few central questions that must be answered.

These questions include:
- What acquisition strategy should we employ (purchase outright, finance, or lease)?
- How long should we retain our industrial equipment (three years, five years, or longer?).

As mentioned previously, the decision to own or lease should be a function of:
1. Best use of company capital dollars (is it wise to use company funds to buy a forklift?).
2. The cost of capital (internal hurdle rate as compared to the lease interest rate).
3. The holding period (lease companies prefer shorter lives).
4. Annual operating hours (the higher the usage, the more ownership makes sense).

In terms of how long industrial trucks should be retained, a formal life cycle analysis should be conducted to pinpoint the optimal life. Life cycle costing should include a detailed evaluation of:
- Initial purchase price
- Resale value
- Cost for fuel
- Cost of maintenance

This should be viewed over at least a ten-year period to determine the total cost of ownership (approximately two "cycles").

As with other fleet assets such as tractors, forklifts and pallet jacks should have a prescribed "optimal" life. That is, a defined retention period that dictates the replacement strategy. Most organizations hold on to their material handling equipment way too long. Based upon their annual operating hours and rigor of use (and abuse!), most material handling equipment (mainly forklifts and electric pallet jacks) should be replaced after 5 or 6 years (at 2,000 hours/year). A range of four to eight years is the generally accepted rule of thumb (see Chapter 8 – exhibit 8.11).

The decision to replace should be based upon the following criteria:
- Annual operating hours (higher the use, the shorter the term)
- The environment (abuse, weight being carried, etc.)
- The predicted resale value for each year in use
- Technological obsolescence (new technology).

Maintenance Control

Regardless of whether you decide to own or lease, the key to material handling equipment longevity is preventive maintenance. To lower the overall cost per hour to operate, material handling equipment should be routinely inspected every two to four months or 200-400 running (also known as pedal or key-on time) hours, whichever comes first. Make sure your PM (preventive maintenance) schedule meets all OSHA requirements. Many OEM's (original equipment manufacturer) provide full service maintenance to eliminate the headache associated with maintenance. Many material handling dealers will also provide on-site preventive maintenance at a reduced rate. Alternatively, you can perform the maintenance in-house or through a network of material handling dealers. At a minimum, be sure to negotiate a preferred rate for preventive maintenance.

Two additional and important maintenance considerations when using electric lift trucks and pallet jacks are the battery charging and fill procedures. In fact, in many cases, the over or under charging of the lift truck battery and/or the lack of a formal water fill procedure are the causes of premature battery failure. Follow these simple steps to prolong battery life:

Charging:

- Charge a battery when it reaches 80% depth of discharge, not before. Generally speaking, an electric forklift battery will last between 6-8 hours, depending upon use.

- Charge only when required. Just like with your cell phone battery, this will improve lift truck battery life.

- Select the appropriate charging designation such as "weekend," "equalize," or "weekly" (depending on your brand of charger) approximately every five to ten cycles to keep the battery performing at peak efficiency. Speak to your material handling supplier about the best way to charge your particular type of battery. Most new batteries are designed to provide at least 1,500- 1,750 charge cycles.

- Post a formal battery charging procedure and train the operators on the need to adhere to strict compliance to the program.

Watering:

- New batteries require water approximately every 10 charges.

- Check 2 or 3 pilot cells every 4-6 charges to see that the water level is slightly above the perforated element protector.

- Add only enough water to cover the element protector by about ¼. " The space is necessary for expansion while gassing at the end of the charge.

    Of course, there are some sealed batteries in many cases that do not require water.

Reducing Distribution Costs through Warehousing

Warehousing can impact overall distribution costs in many ways. Besides making sure that inventory is deployed in the "right" distribution center to reduce inter-DC transfer shipments, the three most commonly deployed cost reduction strategies are consolidation, cross-docking (which was explained in Chapter 8), and utilizing a hub-and-spoke system. Another popular cost saving technique is postponement.

Consolidation involves pulling together smaller shipments from various sources and combining them into larger shipments. Warehouse consolidation, as shown in exhibit 9.14, attempts to combine plant or carrier shipments to gain economies of scale.

Exhibit 9.15 -Warehouse Consolidation

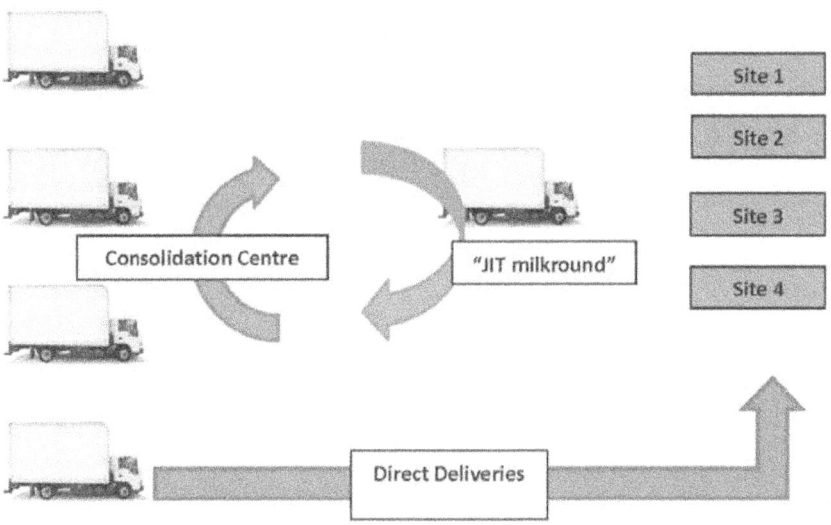

Source: constructionexcellence. org

Cross-Docking

Cross-docking is the logistical practice of accepting mainly larger shipments, holding them for less than twenty-four hours, and turning these shipments into smaller loads that go to individual stores or customers. Cross-docking reduces material handling and inventory carrying costs. A manufacturer may use cross docking to break-up large rail shipments into smaller outbound loads. This is typically called a break-bulk operation. Retailers also use cross docking to receive goods from numerous suppliers, then sort and ship products to individual stores.

Hub and Spoke Design

A hub and spoke warehousing system attempts to combine the benefits of both consolidation and cross docking. The hubs are used as primary sorting and transfer stations and are usually strategically located in high traffic locations. The spokes are the routes serving the destinations associated with the hubs. The hubs typically do not hold any inventory. Large freight carriers use this hub and spoke design to be closer to the customer and to consolidate and break-bulk shipments. Exhibit 9.2 shows a hub and spoke network.

Exhibit 9.16 - Example of a Hub and Spoke Network

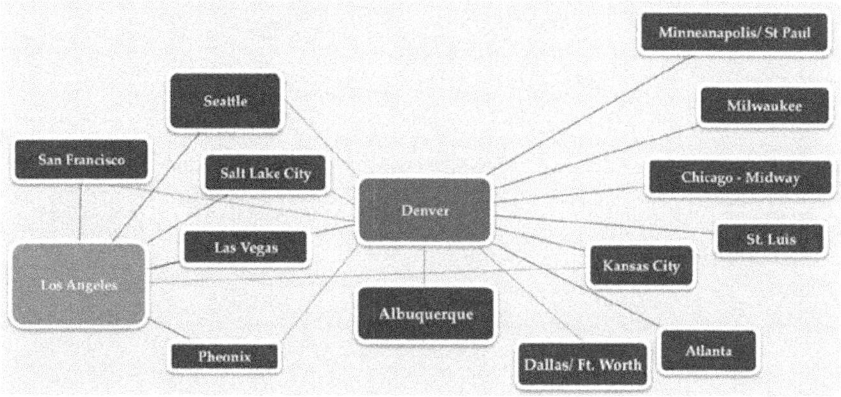

Copyright NextGenCr8vs.com. Image by Marcus B Hernandez

The hub-and-spoke distribution model is a system of connections arranged like a wheel, in which all traffic moves along *spokes* connected to the *hub* at the center. The model is commonly used in airlines, freight and transport, and telecommunications.

Pros of using Hub and Spoke
- Less routes are required to connect spokes as compared to a point-to-point network.

- More efficient use of transportation resources.

- Complicated activities such as sorting can be carried out at the hub, rather than at every spoke.

- Spokes can be set-up quickly.

Cons of using Hub and Spoke
- Because a hub and spoke network is centralized in design, it lacks flexibility and is not very nimble.

- Route scheduling is complicated in a hub and spoke system. Detailed traffic pattern analysis and precise timing are required to keep the hub operating efficiently.

- Downstream impact when there is a problem at the hub. Delays at the hub can result in delays throughout the entire network.

- Longer overall delivery times as most freight must pass through the hub before reaching its destination. This is undesirable for time sensitive freight.

Postponement Warehousing

A postponement strategy delays final assembly or packaging until the last possible moment. Postponement combines warehousing with light production activities in order to create flexibility and lower inbound freight costs. For example, an overseas supplier may ship in bulk (to reduce freight expense) to a postponement facility which, in turn, creates a more customer friendly package and individual shipments to retailers. The supplier saves money on freight while the postponement warehouse can wait until final customer requirements are received prior to shipping. Postponement, when used correctly, is a win-win for supplier and distributor.

Warehouse Alternatives

As a side note, there are alternatives to in-house warehousing. A company can use the services of a third-party logistics firm (or 4PL which includes technology) which can supply warehousing and fulfillment services, or they can use public storage, or even mobile storage trailers. Of course, the cost and productivity difference between in-house warehousing versus a third party alternative needs to be carefully evaluated as outlined in Chapter 4. Most companies should, at a minimum, consider using outside (third-party) warehousing for surge and seasonality purposes. It is usually cheaper to temporarily rent space for short periods of time rather than incur the fixed cost of long-term ownership of buildings that are filled only partially throughout the year.

Shipping Tenets

Shipping normally entails the staging, consolidating, and loading of outbound orders. Shipping is a labor intensive operation that requires a significant amount of space to accomplish effectively. Manual loading using forklifts and/or pallet jacks requires a large amount of manpower. Where possible, the use of automated material handling equipment should be considered. These devices feed directly into the trailers to be loaded, eliminating the manual loading labor involved in the process.

In addition to direct loading, there are a few other shipping principles that should be employed. These tenets include:
- Using ASN's to assist with improving dock management
- Utilizing reusable, returnable, and where appropriate, plastic pallets and/or collapsible totes
- Consider using slip sheets to improve space utilization
- Securing all cartons internally (foam, peanuts, bubble wrap)
- Securing all pallets using shrink wrapping or pallet tie downs
- Securing all loads within trailers using bulkheads or tie-bars
- Using automated dispatch and OBC's (on-board computers) to eliminate driver paperwork.

Every load being transported should follow these three (3) simple principles of shipping:
1. The load should be Secure.
2. The load should be Safe.
3. The load should ship via the Lowest Cost shipping alternative.

Exhibit 9.16 - Critical KPI's (key performance indicators tracked by a typical WMS).

> Cases/Hour
> Cost as % of Sales
> Picks per hour
> Returns management

How to Select a Warehouse Management Systems

Warehouse management systems (WMS) are used to manage the handling, movement and information flow associated with the storage of materials within a warehouse. As shown in exhibit 9.16, a WMS is also used to track key performance indicators that drive warehouse performance. There are three levels of WMS software: Tier 3, Tier 2, and Tier 1. Tier 3 warehouse management systems are the least robust in functionality and are the least expensive. Tier 3 WMS provide the basic requirements to manage a warehouse and is generally used by smaller firms. Tier 2 WMS have more functionality and wider application than Tier 3 systems, but does not contain all of the features and benefits of a Tier 1 WMS. Warehouse management systems are used in large-scale or high-volume warehousing environments. Common features and functionality of a WMS include storage location management, automated picking and order selection, inventory control, and the tracking of receiving and shipping. Exhibit 9.17 reveals the cost and functionality for each type of system.

Exhibit 9.17 - Tiers 1-3 WMS Cost and Functionality

WMS Type	Range of Cost	Functionality
Tier 3	$20,000 - $150,000	• PC based • Create work orders • Print shipping labels • Zone picking • Inventory control

Tier 2	$150,000 - $500,000	• PC/Mainframe • Automated wave planning • Cross docking • System directed replenishment • Load planning • Real time data • Partial Integration
Tier 1	$500,000 - $2,500,000	• Mainframe or web based • Voice activated • RFID Tagging • Wireless communication • Full integration with ERP

Steps to Selecting a WMS

There are seven (7) major steps to take when considering a WMS:

1. Process map all the major activities within the warehouse. Process mapping will help identify all the tasks required to get the job done.

2. Define your specific WMS requirements. Be sure to identify requirements in all the major areas associated with warehousing including: receiving, putaway, picking, storage, inventory, staging, loading, and shipping. Use this simple fill in the blank to get you started: The WMS must be able to... (For each area of the warehouse).

3. Identify the top 3 warehousing goals that the WMS must help track and meet (such as exceeding customer requirements, achieving labor productivity targets, and improving inventory accuracy and control.

4. Evaluate a minimum of 3 WMS then choose the system that best fits your needs based upon steps number 2-3. Be sure to minimize customization requirements to keep costs reasonable.

5. Develop a formal implementation and transition plan with key timing milestones.

6. Run a test of the new WMS by entering actual data. Run the new system in parallel with the existing manual or low-level system for the first 30 days to work out the "bugs."

7. Train the warehouse staff on the new WMS. Do not underestimate the need for training. When in doubt, train more!

Tips to Improve Warehousing

The top ten tips to improve warehouse operations include:

1. **Eliminate time and motion**. Profile your orders to identify the fastest moving inventory items then placed them closest to the shipping dock to reduce travel time. Re-slot your warehouse frequently to ensure pick and putaway times are minimized. In fact, perform a time and motion study of each and every route taken by forklift and pallet jack operators. While studying each path, determine ways to reduce travel time wherever possible. Sometimes all it takes is removing some obstruction to significantly reduce dock travel time.

2. **Analyze your picking methodology**. Whether you choose single order, multi-order, batch picking, or zone picking, the correct picking methodology is critical for optimizing productivity. Analyze the efficiency and productivity of your picking methods. If employing order-picking of cartons from pallets, for example, a good trick to decrease labor is to have the forklift operators rotate the pallets 180 degrees each day to allow operators ease of access to cartons. Maximize the use of ergonomic picking with the use of proper height picking zones. You do not want pickers needing to reach or get on their knees to pick goods.

3. **Choose the appropriate material handling and warehouse equipment.** The key here is to be 100 percent sure that the appropriate type of racking/shelving, conveyors, etc. is being used. In addition, have a material handling expert review the configuration of all forklifts and pallet jacks to make sure you are utilizing the highest efficiency type of units. Vertical storage systems will also allow for increased cube and efficiency.

4. **Choose the minimum number of package designs and shipping containers.** To decrease packaging and shipping material costs and reduce freight expenses, limit your container sizes to three or four. This allows shipping personnel to pack orders more quickly and efficiently. It will also reduce the cost of materials.

5. **Create an incentive for warehouse personnel.** Studies show that incentives for the warehouse work! Incent warehouse employees for improving picking accuracy, cases/hour, and for lowering warehouse costs through productivity improvements.

6. **Use cycle counting to increase inventory accuracy.** Forget annual physical counting. As discussed in Chapter 7 on inventory, cycle count frequently. Eventually, eliminate the need for an annual physical count.

7. **Carefully evaluate your receiving process.** A significant amount of inventory and putaway/picking problems can be averted if proper receiving techniques are employed. Wherever possible, use technology and automation to reduce human error. In addition, integrate supplier inventory naming convention to ensure accuracy. Supplier receipts must also be carefully scrutinized.

8. **Label everything.** Use bar-coding, RFID, and basic labeling on pallets, shelving, etc. When in doubt, label it. Each product should have a unique identifier.

9. ***Use automation and other technology to drive results.*** Use WMS software to properly sequence orders. Sequencing your orders by pick path, and batching together same-zone orders and difficult picks, such as non-conveyable items, saves a tremendous amount of time. Multi-level pick towers also save travel time. There is a number of technologies that can be employed to increase efficiency, including pick-to-light, voice activation, and 3D bar coding and printing.

10. ***Create a three-year plan to reduce warehousing cost as % of sales while increasing cases/hour.*** Tracking these two critical KPI's and implementing specific tactical initiatives to improve productivity and lower costs will help to make warehousing a more crucial function within the business.

Emerging Trends in Warehousing

There are a few trends that will continue to shape the warehousing industry. These trends are driven by an increase in globalization, an increase in the speed of technology and computers, and the growing implementation of robotics and AI (artificial intelligence). Paying attention to these trends will ensure business sustainability over the long term.

Trend 1: The warehouse will play a more integral role in the overall supply chain.

The warehouse will be seen as a way to create a point of difference with customers. Increased inventory velocity, improved fill rates and on-time delivery, and a reduction in backorders will raise awareness about the strategic importance of warehousing.

Trend 2: Go green efforts will intensify as firms attempt to become more environmentally responsible.

Suppliers, shippers, and third-party service providers will be expected to reuse, recycle, and properly dispose of anything that potentially hurts the environment. Reducing corporate carbon-footprint or greenhouse gas emissions will be commonplace. Social consciousness will become part of corporate strategy.

Trend 3: Cost to Serve Modeling will become a central analysis tool.

The days of delivering to a demanding customer *anything they want* are over! Companies will be forced to look at each customer based upon their particular ordering pattern, the specific demands upon the warehouse, and the actual cost to deliver the expected service level. The objective is to implement supply chain policies that turn unprofitable customers into profitable ones. Exhibit 7.6 in Chapter 7 is an example of a cost to serve model.

Trend 4: There will be an increase in demand for Value-Added Services.

There seems to be no end in sight as it relates to customers demanding additional services from the supply chain. Kitting, customization, packaging, international support, and assembly are going to increase in demand. It will be critical, however, to apply a menu-driven pricing model to ensure customers pay for these additional services

Trend 5: Focus on Total Landed Costs.

With the advent of globalization, sourcing outside the United States has become the norm. Historically, sourcing strategies were largely based upon unit pricing. It is important to consider all of the costs associated with materials and finished goods purchased abroad. Best in Class companies incorporate total-landed-cost analysis into their procurement decisions. Total landed costs are based upon a holistic view of cost, including:
- Unit price
- Customs, duties, and taxes
- Expediting costs
- Freight costs, including ocean and inland transportation
- Inventory carrying costs

- The cost of quality (e. g. comparison of defects/1,000 units)
- Product rework and damage costs
- Reverse logistics costs

Trend 6: Warehouses will be expected to compress space and time.

Customer demands for faster but less expensive service will continue to increase. Internet retailers using delivery drones to deliver products within 2 hours after ordering will be the norm. Post-recession inventory levels will also become the normal practice as the days of "bloating" are over. Inventories will remain in-check as forecasting becomes even more of a daunting a task due to the lack of order predictability. Technology will be the driving force behind time and space compression.

Trend 7: Differentiation becomes a core business strategy.

Demand signals now come from a variety of channels and customers. At the same time, customers are becoming increasingly more impatient and even more demanding, often expecting Nordstrom™ type service levels. To that end, companies are going to need to create a point of difference; a real reason why a customer should do business with you as opposed to the competition. Customers will have different replenishment requirements, based upon the service required, the volume and the profitability of that customer, and the channel used to support the business.

Conclusion

Chapter 9 explained the ever-changing role and function of warehousing and material handling. These two functions have been transformed into strategic weapons due to increased technology and mobility. The warehouse and material handling aspects of a business have become the main way to create a point of difference, thereby increasing customer satisfaction. Warehousing truly impacts productivity, process, and supply chain infrastructure costs. The warehouse should no longer be viewed as a dirty old building that holds inventory, but instead, a vertical storage facility that uses technology and the seamless flow of information to speed products to the marketplace. Material handling has now become an important initiative to compress time and space in an attempt to rush "perfect orders" to customers. When managed aggressively, warehousing and material handling can dramatically reduce overall supply chain costs as a percent of revenue. In addition, sound warehousing principles will increase inventory velocity and cases/hour. This can have a significant impact on the company balance sheet.

Chapter Summary

- Warehousing is defined as any operation that stores, stages, picks, sorts, packages, coordinates or centralizes raw materials or finished goods.

- The primary role of the warehouse is to balance production schedules with demand while properly storing inventory.

- The main functions within a warehouse include receiving, picking, storing, loading, and shipping.

- Order picking is the choosing of the correct product in the right quantity in order to meet customer demand requirements.

- Proper product slotting increases space efficiency and reduces material handling by locating goods in the optimal picking sequence within the warehouse.

- There are two kinds of storage; static and dynamic.

- Warehouse design and layout should be part of the Supply Chain Strategic Plan.

- Material handling includes pallets and materials, industrial trucks, racking/shelving and conveyors.

- The three most commonly deployed cost reduction warehousing strategies are consolidation, cross-docking, and utilizing a hub-and-spoke system.

- There are three (3) levels of warehouse management systems: Tier 1, Tier 2, and Tier 3.

Exploratory Questions

1. What are the main KPI's (key performance indicators) to track to improve warehousing?

2. Why is the receiving function within a warehouse so important to overall inventory control?

3. What are the main types of picking methods used in warehousing?

4. What are the major steps to warehouse planning and layout?

5. Why is choosing the "right" WMS (warehouse management system) so important?

6. What is meant by the expression "focus on total landed costs?"

Case Study and Questions

SF Foods is a broadline food distributor located in California. They had three warehouses that were serviced by more than 350 suppliers. The warehouses, in turn, distributed to four separate business units across the United States. The existing warehouse network was fraught with a number of supply chain issues, including:
- Decentralized order processing with a 8% error rate
- Lack of adherence to minimum order quantities
- Duplication of effort in invoicing and payments
- Significant number of LTL movements
- Large degree of safety stock throughout the network

USING YOUR SUPPLY CHAIN AS A COMPETITIVE WEAPON | 221

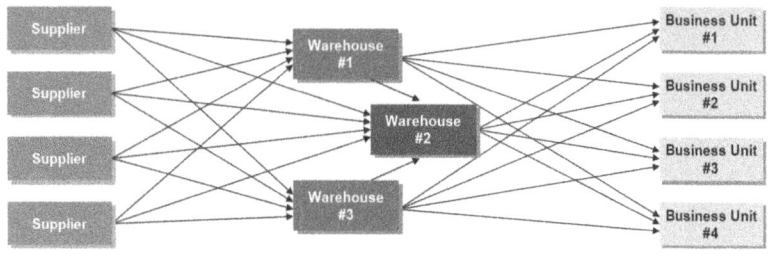

Current State has inefficient links between Suppliers and Business Units

- Multiple orders flowing from different Business Units
- Separate invoices and payments (duplication of effort)
- Duplication of safety stock across system
- Lack of freight consolidation
- Minimum order quantities often ignored

SF wished to evaluate the cost/benefit of implementing a consolidated warehouse strategy, or RDC (regional distribution center). The suppliers and the VP's of the business units were highly skeptical of this change as they were accustomed to perishables going to one warehouse and dry goods going to the other two. At the start of the project, it was difficult to garner support from anyone. Every department within the supply chain, especially the warehousing group, voiced objections.

The main question being asked was:

Can one warehouse take the place of three? Although you would think this was a network optimization study, it wasn't. The focus was on improving warehouse processes and gaining efficiencies through redistribution. The following steps were taken:

1. Process mapping of every procedure within each of the existing 3 warehouses.
2. Gathering of inventory levels, including safety stock.
3. Collecting details surrounding purchase orders, invoices, and payments.

4. Identifying ordering patterns from each business unit.
5. Profiling of all shipments to and from each warehouse (load size, cost, etc.).
6. Current fixed cost and labor expense determination for the 3 warehouses.

Since this was not an optimization study whereby we would analyze the "optimal" number and location of the warehouse, the analysis was restricted to determining whether or not major efficiencies in process and fixed cost could be realized by using a centralized RDC network. After 120 days of data collection and careful analysis of the pre and post impact of a redistribution center, SF made the strategic decision to move forward with the plan to consolidate to one center.

The results were quite impressive. Besides saving millions of dollars in fixed costs, inventory, and freight, SF experienced a dramatic improvement in the processing of orders and the disbursement of purchase orders and invoices.

> **Re-distribution** is the process of aggregating demand for products across business units by determining the lowest possible cost path for each product

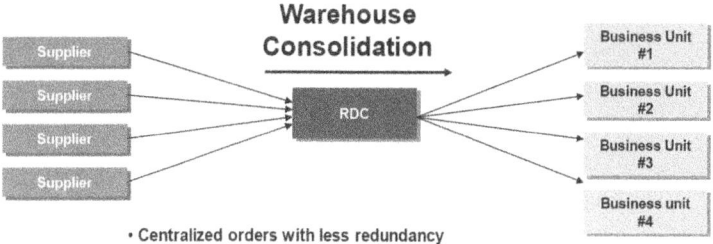

- Centralized orders with less redundancy
- Less destinations fro suppliers; less prone to error
- Reduction in the number of invoices and payments
- Decrease in safety stock
- Increase in truckload shipments through consolidation
- Increase in the number of pallet quantity orders

Case Study Questions:

1. Why do you think the suppliers and business unit VP's were so against the project?

2. What are the pros and cons of warehouse centralization?

3. What key metrics should SF use to track productivity and costs?

4. Which departments should be considered stakeholders in the consolidation project?

5. What kind of follow up can SF senior management employ to ensure that the business units remain satisfied?

10 SUPPLY CHAIN METRICS AND MONITORING

"If you don't know where you're going, you might wind up someplace else?"

Yogi Berra

When I conduct a supply chain diagnostic assessment of a company, I always start by asking the management team this question, *"At the end of the day, how do you know you did really well?"* You would be surprised how many times I hear, "if sales, my boss, or any customers are not screaming at me, I assume we had a good day. " The second question I ask is "What are the key measures that drive your supply chain?" Sure, occasionally I get some decent attempts at key performance measures (KPI's), but for the most part, 80% of the companies I provide consulting services to, at least initially, are measuring some key ratios that are insignificant in the big scheme of things.

Simply stated, the design and selection of the appropriate metrics will literally dictate the actual performance of your supply chain. As the old saying goes, you cannot manage what you do not measure. If you are not monitoring and aggressively managing metrics focused on reducing the cost of warehousing or logistics, the initiatives and logistical practices will follow suit. If the measures are in sync with the initiatives it is logical to assume that initiatives will drive significant results.

The purpose of this chapter is to provide insight into the following concepts:
- Selecting and measuring the right metrics
- Key measures that truly make a difference
- Balancing the cost, service, and quality tradeoffs
- Performing a Supply Chain GAP analysis
- Developing a EIS (executive information summary) Report
- Using key metrics to rally the troops.

One reason why many organizations do not measure supply chain prowess is the fundamental belief that functions such as order processing, warehousing, and logistics do not materially impact profitability. A recent study we conducted concluded that the majority of CEO's involved in the study believe that supply chain activities barely make a difference to company profitability.

Exhibit 10.1 Does Supply Chain Management Improve Profitability?

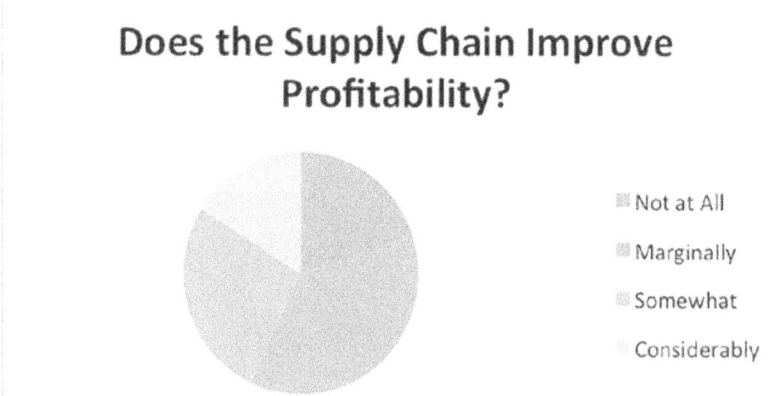

Source: IFMC study of 218 CEO's across 6 industries.

Another reason why many companies do not track supply chain metrics is the basic belief that "our company is unique, our business model is different, and many of the standard measures do not apply. " I hear this everywhere I go. The reality is, *80% of all supply chain activities are identical regardless of the product being delivered.* Therefore, most supply chains will benefit from a standard framework of metrics that are designed to drive costs lower, improve service and enhance quality. Just imagine a sporting event without a scoreboard that is keeping track of either the score or individual performance! The same can be said for a company; that is, if you are not keeping score of the key measures that increase profitability, improve service, reduce the time in the supply chain, or drive quality, you will wander around in the dark spinning your wheels going nowhere. A supply chain should be measured against the competition and held to the same level of financial scrutiny as any other part of the business.

In addition, it is imperative that a single-point of accountability be used to ensure performance continuity and responsibility. We will discuss this further at the end of this chapter.

Selecting and Measuring the Right Things

In order to properly select a measure, you must first understand the definition of a metric. A business metric is any type of measurement used to gauge some quantifiable component of a company's performance, such as return on investment (ROI).[1]

Supply chain measurement can be broken down into categories, including:
- Cost and Financial Measures
- Productivity and Time Measures
- Service Measures
- Quality Measures
- Process Measures

The graphic below reflects the tried and true Balanced Scorecard approach to performance measurement. Although using a balanced scorecard is definitely a good start, they often ignore some of the more supply chain oriented measures that will drive results.

---

(1) Source: Whatis. com.

Exhibit 10.2 Balanced Scorecard

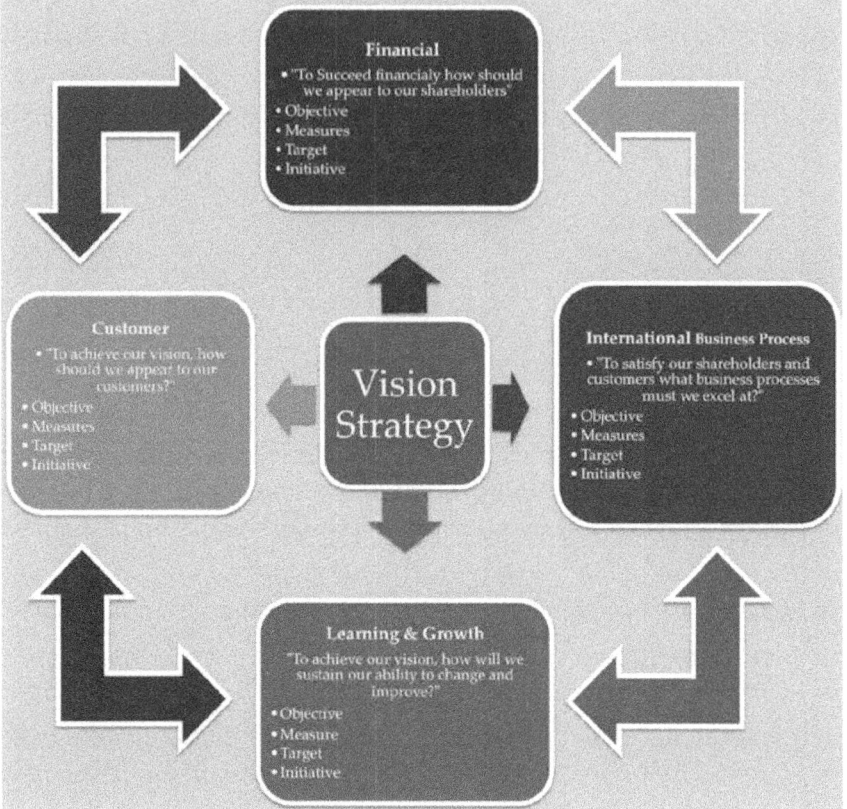

Source: Balanced Scorecard Institute

The idea here is to track quantitative measures that reveal performance to ultimately provide a *Gap Analysis* of comparison against like-firms[2]. These measures will also indicate the financial opportunity that may result through the implementation of supply chain best practices. In addition, when choosing supply chain measures, it is essential that you consider the following:
- Measurement Alignment with Corporate Objectives
- Metrics that truly drive the RIGHT results.

---

(2) Since 80% of all supply chain activities are the same regardless of the product, we can certainly benchmark our performance against firms with similar operating characteristics as well as the direct competition. The Gap Analysis reveals the delta between your company performance and that of the like firm or competitor.

When selecting supply chain measures, the following process steps should be followed:

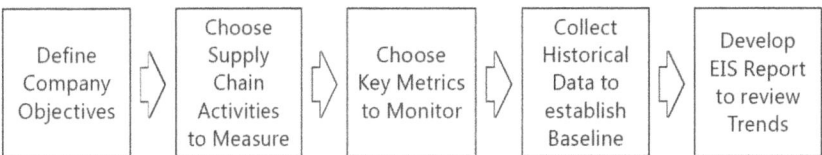

Step 1: Define Company Strategic Objectives.
Step 2: Choose the Supply-Chain functions to be measured (i. e., warehousing, distribution).
Step 3: Choose supply-chain metrics within each category and align them with company goals.
Step 4: Collect historical data for the key measures and set 3-year targets.
Step 5: Develop an Executive Information Summary report (EIS) that tracks each measure.

Note: Aligning measures with company objectives means ensuring that each metric adds-value in an area that is important to the corporate mission. For example, if the main company goal is to improve profitability by 5% for the following year, each measure should be focused on reducing costs or improving margin/profit.

Sample EIS Report

Category/ Function	Measure/Metric	Last Year's Performance	Plan Year Target (3 year goals)
Order Processing	# orders/hour		
	TOCT (total order cycle time in days)		
	Cost/Order		
	Perfect Order %		
Warehousing	Cost/Hour		
	Cases/Hour		
	Damage %		
	Cost/Piece or Case		
Inventory Control	% Accuracy by SKU		
	Carrying Cost		

	% Obsolete		
	Turnover Rate		
	Forecast Accuracy %		
Transportation/ Freight	Cost as % Sales		
	Cost/Unit or Case		
	Cost/CWT or Pound		
	Cost/Load		
	On-Time Delivery %		
Supply/ Purchasing	COGS as % Sales		
	Cost/PO		
	Cost/Unit		
Customer Service	# CS Calls		
	% Returns		
	Satisfaction %		
	% In Stock or Fill Rate		

To accommodate the more senior-level executives in the firm, there are several higher-level metrics that you should consider tracking, including:

Return on Supply Chain Assets (ROSCA): Defined as the ratio of company profit to supply chain asset value. Supply chain asset value is computed as the current worth of deployed assets within the supply chain such as warehouses, trucks, and material handling equipment.

ROSCA = Profit/Supply Chain Assets

Supply Chain Asset Turnover (SCAT): Defined as the ratio of company revenue to the overall investment in supply chain assets. This metric measures the utilization of supply chain assets.

SCAT = Revenue/Supply Chain Assets

Total Supply Chain Cost as a % of Revenue: Defined as the ratio of the total supply chain costs (for warehousing, transportation, order processing, etc.) to total revenue. This metric should be used to monitor the supply chain spending trend while sales and revenue are fluctuating. This metric reveals how the supply chain is reacting to changing business conditions (i. e. a change in the product mix which causes increased warehousing or distribution costs).

SCC%R = Supply Chain Costs/Total Revenue

The graph below reveals some of the industry specific supply chain costs as a percent of revenue. You can find this data by contacting your respective industry association. For example, in the food service distribution business, one industry association, IFDA (International Foodservice Distributors Association) publishes an industry benchmark study every year that highlights the various key ratios highlighted in this chapter. Go to www. ifdaonline. org for more details.

Exhibit 10.3 Supply Chain Costs by Industry

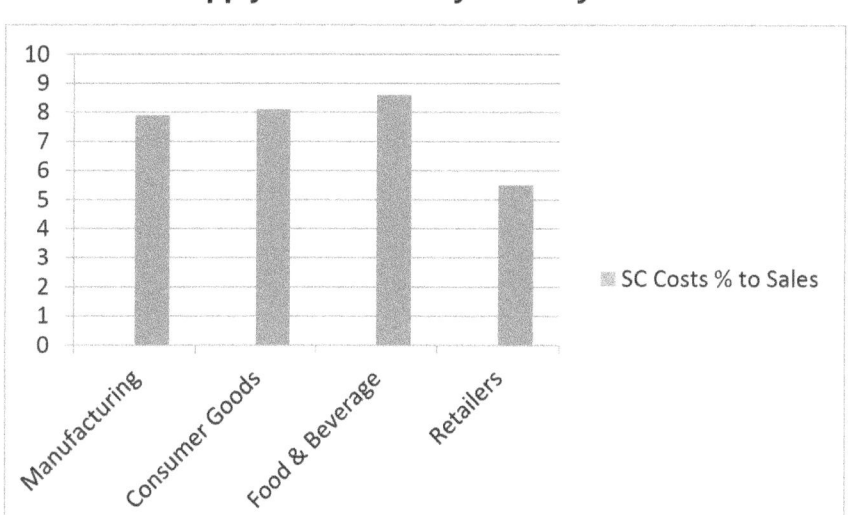

Source: Ifdaonline. Com

When creating your EIS Report, it is imperative that the appropriate baseline of information is documented to ensure metric integrity. Some of the baseline information that should be reviewed includes:

- Sales by Channel – as % of total sales (product "mix")
- Average Weight/Unit or Case
- Average Order Size
- Cases/Pallet (pieces per pallet)
- Total Sales Volume compared to Prior Year and Current Year Plan (% increase/decrease).

This baseline establishment will help to explain changes in the business that may be dictating subtle increases in supply chain expenses independent of any actual rise in costs (e. g. increase in warehouse labor costs due to an annual increase in wages). For example, in the beverage industry (soft drinks), if the product mix shifts from two-liter plastic bottles to twelve-ounce cans, the corresponding impact on the supply chain is an increase in distribution costs due to the higher weight associated with a pallet of cans as compared to a pallet of bottles.

The next step to the metric implementation process is to perform a Gap Analysis of results.

Performing a supply chain GAP Analysis

After developing your key metrics, reach out to your industry association or research benchmark data that may be available via the Internet. Two sources for this are:

www. brs-seattle. com
www. best-in-class. com

It is usually less daunting to compare only two or three of the most critical measures against either the competition or like firms. However, it is of the utmost importance to make sure that the measures being compared are precisely defined on an apples-to-apples basis. You then placed initiatives against the measure in question in an attempt to improve the metric. For example, if you are comparing warehouse case/hour (throughput), it might look like this:

Metric	Current Performance	Like Firm Performance	GAP	Initiatives
Warehouse Cases/Hour	120 cases/hour	135 cases/hour	15 cases/hour or 12.5%	• Reduce warehouse labor through improved picking procedure • Increase efficiency through automated putaway-process. • Increase material handling effectiveness through a time-motion study.

The final consideration is to make sure that each metric has been scrutinized for completeness and specificity. When setting goals for each measure, use the SMART[3] approach to setting targets.

Specific
Measurable
Attainable
Realistic
Timely

Specific –Each target must be specific as a precise goal has a greater chance of being accomplished than a generic goal. To set a specific goal you must answer these questions:
*Who: Who is involved?
*What: What do I wish to accomplish?
*Where: Where does the data reside?

---
(3) Source: Dr. Edwin Locke.

*When: Establish a specific time-frame.
*Which: What's stopping us? Are there any constraints?
*Why: Specific benefits of accomplishing the goal.

EXAMPLE: A generic goal would be, "Reduce delivery costs. " A specific goal would be, "Reduce delivery costs 4% by October of this fiscal year through the reduction of overtime."

- -

Measurable –Each metric must have in place a mechanism to ensure progress toward the attainment of each target. The question you should ask is: How will I know when the goal has been accomplished?

- -

Attainable–Your supply chain goals should be a stretch, but attainable such that you get buy-in from the troops. There is nothing worse than a senior level executive setting a goal for the organization that is unattainable and unrealistic. This type of approach will completely demoralize the team.

- -

Realistic - Your goal is probably realistic if you truly *believe* that it can be accomplished. Additional ways to know if your goal is realistic is to determine if you have accomplished anything similar in the past or ask yourself what conditions would have to exist to accomplish this goal.

- -

Timely - A goal must have a specific time frame. Without a time constraint there will be no sense of urgency. You can attain most any goal you set when you plan your steps wisely and establish a time frame that allows you to carry out those steps.

- -

Balancing the cost, service, and quality tradeoffs

One of the objections I usually hear from my clients is "supply chain metrics must maintain customer service levels. " While I fully support providing an appropriate level of customer service, using the Nordstrom "customer service regardless of the costs" approach may not be the most cost effective business model. For perspective, Frito-Lay, the premier global snack food company, carefully measures their customer in-stock % such that they will allow for low-level stock-outs if the cost/service tradeoff dictates the decision. Ninety-seven percent customer service may simply be good enough. The chart below shows the incremental cost associated with 98-100% customer service. The industry standard for this is for every 1% increase in customer service above 95%, your supply chain costs increase approximately 15%.

Exhibit 10.4

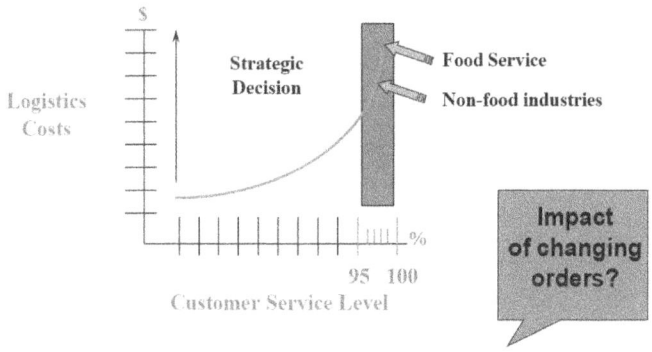

Relationship Issues: The Customer Service/Logistics Tradeoff

Struggle may exist due to food service logistics mandates.
Seemingly ridiculous logistics decisions would be questioned by any third-party provider.
Intense customer focus and high switching cost probability creates higher delivery costs.
Other industries often question the extreme cost of marginally incremental customer service.
The company is desperately attempting to cope with this paradigm shift.
The customer service issue is clearly causing the majority of the frustration.

Using Key Metrics to Rally the Troops

As mentioned earlier in the chapter, it is imperative that a single-point of accountability be used to ensure performance continuity and responsibility. A metric-champion, someone who has total responsibility for the proper and timely reporting of the metrics and EIS Report, is an essential aspect of supply chain performance monitoring.

The supply chain metric process can be an invaluable tool to rally your team around a cause and provide some directional purpose for the group. To motivate your supply chain department, be sure to:

- Solicit input from all levels of the supply chain department before deciding on measures.

- Place the supply chain EIS Report on the company Intranet Portal for all to see.

- Post the monthly results in break rooms, the dispatch office, company bulletin boards, etc. to showcase the effort.

- Provide employees with business cards that have the Supply Chain Vision, Mission, and Key Metrics listed on the back.

Conclusion

The development and monitoring of critical supply chain metrics will make an immediate impact on your company's overall financial performance. The key here is to measure metrics that, when cost savings initiatives are placed against them, the results can be clearly demonstrated and realized. Supply chain metrics can be the means to obtaining increased customer value which is at the core of business strategy. Metrics that reveal critical customer data such as product availability, the status of orders, and expected delivery times is quickly becoming an essential capability. In addition, supply chain metrics can provide customers with keen insight into your distribution prowess and a new method of interaction. Supply chain metrics can also be used to predict trends that may impact overall business strategy. These trends should influence the company's future business model by providing quantitative data that highlights areas that require immediate attention.

Chapter Summary

- A business metric is any type of measurement used to gauge some quantifiable component of a company's performance.

- Metrics should be considered in the areas of cost, productivity and time, service, quality, and process.

- Developing the right supply chain metrics starts with the understanding and aligning with overall company objectives.

- The development of an EIS (Executive Information Summary) Report is crucial to overall supply chain success.

- A Gap Analysis of the current state compared to the desired (future) state as compared to like companies or competitors will ensure continuity of effort.

- The SMART method of setting goals/targets places each objective into definable and measureable terms.

- When designing your supply-chain, the true cost of customer service must be established and measured. Remember, there is a tradeoff associated with Nordstrom's level customer service.

- Every member of the supply team should be able to articulate the goals, key measures, and targets.

Exploratory Questions

1. What supply chain measures does your company currently track?

2. Does your Supply Chain department have an overall mission?

3. Is there a supply chain champion responsible for the success of the department?

4. Have you benchmarked your performance against like firms via a Gap Analysis of measures?

5. Do you know the true cost of customer service at your company?

6. Are you monitoring the right measures?

7. Do you conduct quarterly reviews of supply chain performance?

8. Have you involved all levels of the organization in the supply chain goals?

9. Does the top management truly understand the criticality of the supply chain effort?

10. Do you have a three-year plan for improving the supply chain?

Case Study – MF Foods

MFI is a privately held company in Del Mar, California. They distribute snacks and frozen entrees throughout the United States through retail/grocery stores. MFI's two divisions were fragmented in terms of supply chain measurement. The CFO requested a diagnostic health check of their company, with special emphasis to be placed on the development of supply chain metrics that would make a difference in the area of cost reduction.

During the assessment, we uncovered the need for an overall EIS Report that integrated the two divisions from a supply chain performance standpoint. In addition, we wanted to track a few measures that would ultimately drive cost reduction. At the conclusion of the consulting engagement, we suggested the following measures:

Order Processing
- Cost/Order
- Total Order Cycle Time (in days)

Warehousing
- Cases/Hour
- Cost/Case
- Cost/Pallet

Freight
- Cost/CWT
- Cost/Load
- Cost/Case
- Cost as % Sales

Inventory Control
- Inventory Accuracy %
- Turnover Rate

Customer Service
- On-time delivery %
- In-Stock %

Note: Each measure was first tracked in their respective division (i. e. Frozen Entrees), then combined into a total company performance "look."

Eighteen months after the conclusion of the study, MFI reported the following results:
- A reduction of inventory of 27%
- A reduction of cost/order of 32%
- A reduction of cost/case in freight of 13%
- A reduction of 16% in warehousing
- A 7% improvement in on-time delivery.

Case Study Questions:

1. Why are key performance metrics so critical to long-term business success?

2. Why do you think so many companies are not monitoring critical measures of performance?

3. Why do you think so many firms look to an outside consultant for advice?

11. THE APPLICATION OF TECHNOLOGY WITHIN THE SUPPLY-CHAIN

"If GM had kept up with technology like the computer industry has, we would all be driving $25 cars that got 1000 MPG."
                                                            Bill Gates

Technology changes so rapidly that I considered not even including this chapter within this book. Between the rapid pace of change, the ever-expanding nature of the Internet and Social Media platforms, and the shrinking nature of the global economy, this chapter posed a significant challenge; that is, how to explain the application of systems and information within the supply chain without risking technological obsolescence. Due to this, this chapter is designed to be a high-level look at the supply chain technologies available today along with a glimpse into the future. In fact, the approach taken in this chapter was to summarize technology, in general, and provide some rudimentary thoughts on the kinds of systems and software organizations are using to improve productivity, enhance process control, and lower costs.

USING YOUR SUPPLY CHAIN AS A COMPETITIVE WEAPON

The purpose of this chapter is to provide key insight into the types of technology available today along with some commentary about the importance of integration and total order visibility. The topics covered include:
- The definition of technology
- Product life cycle logistics
- The criticality of integration
- The organizational levels of technology
- Functional application of technology
- Evaluating new technology
- The top ten supply chain technologies
- The future of supply chain technology

Definition of Technology

Merriam-Webster defines technology as:

"The use of science in industry, engineering, etc. to invent useful things or to solve problems."

As it relates to Supply Chain Management, technology is any equipment, machine, robot, artificial intelligence, system, application, or even software that helps to improve process and/or labor efficiency. Technology is generally broken down into five (5) distinct categories:
1. Tangible technologies, such as proto-types, models, blueprints.
2. Intangible technologies, such as training methods.
3. High, such as automated or intelligent technologies such as robots.
4. Intermediate, such as semi-automated or partially intelligent technologies.
5. Low, such as labor intensive assembly lines.

Source: Businessdictionary.com

Technology can be applied to dramatically improve the numerous methods being used within a supply chain by looking at any process

holistically and then applying process value analysis in an attempt to do one of three things with each process:
- Eliminate it
- Simplify it
- Optimize it.

Product Life Cycle Logistics

The application of technology needs to be viewed across the entire supply chain as so many companies still employ as many as five (5) disparate systems that do not "talk" to each other which results in spreadsheets"R"us. A few organizations, however, are using total product life cycle logistics to improve the entire business from beginning to end of the supply chain. Total product life cycle logistics attempts to link functional areas together cohesively in order to make smarter and better supply chain decisions. Product life cycle logistics uses technology and information systems to improve:
- Packaging
- Manufacturing Processes
- Returns and Reverse Logistics Management
- Freight and Distribution
- Warehousing and Fulfillment

Product life cycle logistics (PLC) helps to eliminate all the "paper" within an organization by replacing it with an improved system, technology, or application. The application of PLC begins at the early developmental stages of product introduction (R&D). PLC fundamentally asks the question, "How can we use technology, from cradle to grave, in order to reduce human intervention?" PLC uses cross functional teams that brainstorm about improving process, product, or efficiency.

The Criticality of Integration

In order for technology to be effective and provide a competitive advantage, it must be:
1. Seamless.
2. Connected.
3. Holistic, and cut across the entire enterprise.

The more integrated your supply chain technology is, the more responsive it is. Tightly integrated supply chains increase operational flexibility by allowing management to quickly respond to changes in the market or moves made by the competition. A supply chain that can rapidly source products from overseas, for example, will be in a better competitive position. Technology integration helps to improve inventory control by increasing supply and order visibility throughout the chain. Retailers can adjust their forecasts in real-time with technology integration. This improves in-stock availability and reduces total order cycle time. Integration ultimately improves profit margins. At a minimum, a simple data bridge that passes information between the various systems should be employed to push customer orders seamlessly throughout the supply chain. In addition, a data bridge that provides daily feedback which gets fed into the front-end part of your ERP, should be used to develop a historical view of each day's events. Essentially, what you are attempting to do is gain total order visibility throughout the entire supply chain. At any point within the chain, you should be able to "see" the status of all orders, production, inventory, shipping, and invoicing. Integration of technology must be a strategic imperative fully supported by the senior management of an organization. In fact, a technology plan, including the integration timeline, should be put into place and supported either internally or through external outside resources.

Exhibit 11.1 reveals a simple, but integrated use of technology – information is seamlessly connected.

Exhibit 11.1 - Technology Nirvana.

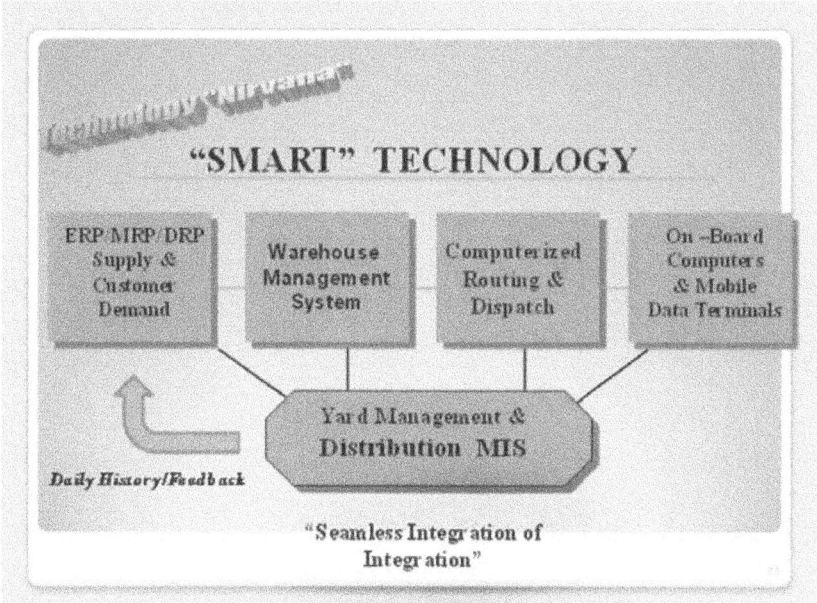

Levels of Technology

Technological Nirvana starts with an ERP (enterprise resource planning) tool, either via an on-site or a cloud-enabled and mobile based system. The ERP is the brain behind the distribution of information providing the planning, coordination, and communication between outside influences (i. e., suppliers) and the functional areas within a company.

Generally speaking, there are three levels of technology used to run an organization. These levels are reflected in Exhibit 11.2. These levels include:
- Enterprise Resource Planning Tools
- Facility Management Tools
- Distribution Management Tools

Exhibit 11.2 - Major Supply Chain Technologies

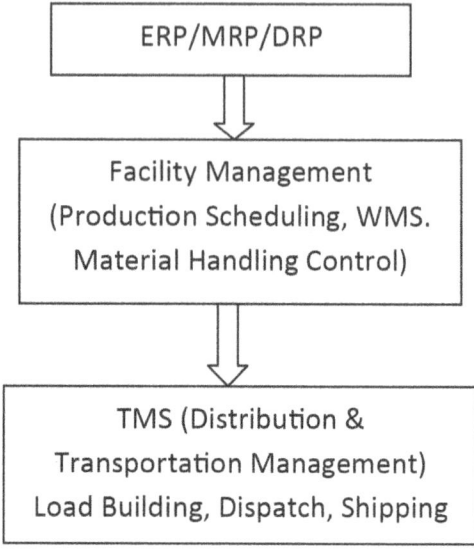

Functional Application of Technology

Within the supply chain, there are a number of technologies that can be used to improve productivity, enhance process control, and lower infrastructure and operational costs. These technologies are used in three (3) primary areas:
- Warehousing
- Material Handling
- Distribution/Transportation

We will explore the main technologies being used within each of these functional areas. But, as mentioned earlier, since technology changes so rapidly, I highly suggest you contact a few supply chain technology providers to determine what is new and exciting. Exhibit 11.3 reveals the major technologies being used by "best-in-class" companies to drive significant results.

Exhibit 11.3 Functional Techologies

Functional Area	Technology	Primary Benefit
Warehouse/Material Handling	Automated Dock Management	Improves dock usage Reduces carrier wait time
	Automated putaway/selection	Enhances aisle management and product placement
	Automated sortation systems	Reduces labor
	Voice Recognition/Activation	Improves picking
	AGV (automated guided vehicles)	Eliminates "touches"
	Robotics and AI	Eliminates human error
	Automated Receiving – RF & ASN's	Improves inventory control and in-stock %
	RFID/Remote Asset Tracking	Makes crates/containers intelligent; improves remote inventory control
	Impact/Shock Manager	Decreases phantom damage on forklifts
	Forklifts using AGV Technology	Reduces human error
Distribution/Transportation	Computerized Routing/Dispatch	Reduces miles Reduces driver/truck resources
	GPS/Locator Systems	Improves backhaul potential; provides real time dispatch "on-the-fly"
	Load Building	Optimizes trailer loading Increases loading efficiency
	On-Board Truck Computers & Telematics	Reduces driver delay time Increases MPG Reduces trip times
	Yard Management	Improves trailer utilization and optimizes dock scheduling

Evaluating New Technology

Fifty percent of new technology implementations fail. Eighty percent of the time it has nothing to do with the technology that was chosen. Most of the time, the failure is due to poor planning or ineffective implementation. These technology failures can be avoided by putting together a simple technology plan. The plan should include:
- Process mapping of the existing technology
- User's needs assessment, which includes interviewing all users and management
- Description of the proposed technology, including:
  - Must have's
  - Nice to have's
  - Wish list items.
- Project Objectives and Goals with key milestones and timelines
- Technology Evaluation using key criteria:
  - Cost & Estimated ROI (return on investment)
  - User friendliness and ease of use
  - Features and benefits analysis and comparison
  - Client references
  - Support and maintenance.
- Implementation plan
  - Run in parallel
  - Timeline
  - Key dates
  - Roles and responsibilities
  - Training plan.
- Success Measures.
  - Key performance metrics.

Top Ten Supply Chain Technologies

There are a number of other technologies being discussed and analyzed today in an attempt to further integrate supply chain activities and speed up the processing of information. The purpose of these technologies is to provide a seamless flow of information from customer order (start to finish) to the store-shelf. In addition, these technologies are being used to increase the velocity of information throughout the chain and ultimately produce the key performance metrics that drive the business.

The top ten (10) technologies being considered are:

1. Comprehensive connectivity technologies such as improved wireless LAN, enhanced cellular networks, and supply chain related Bluetooth technology, all attempting to untether workers from existing hard-wired forms of technology.

2. Speech recognition and enhanced voice recognition technology which will reduce computer keystroke errors once these systems are perfected. Remember, on average, for every 300 keystrokes on a computer, a human error occurs! This technology has application in order processing, warehousing, material handling, and shipping.

3. Three dimensional bar coding technology which can hold 100 times more information than a two dimensional bar code. This helps to keep better track of inventory.

4. Digital imaging (On-board cameras) which will help to create a safer workplace and more compliance and accident free distribution and material handling.

5. Portable and 3D printing which will improve R&D (research and development), package design, and prototyping.

6. Supplier portals that drive down material costs, provide process improvement of the procurement cycle, and provide inbound order visibility to reduce or eliminate out-of-stock conditions.

7. E-auctions whereby supplier negotiations are conducted via an online platform.

8. Remote asset management and real-time location technology that will provide instantaneous information surrounding "where are my materials or shipments" and provide a detailed understanding of remote inventory levels. You will be able to see into containers or boxes and determine off-site or remote inventory without needing to physically go there with a truck.

9. *Wireless and device security technology* that will reduce the likelihood of hackers stealing information off your servers.

10. *Holistic and convergence technology* that eliminates the need for stand-alone technologies for warehousing, material handling, and distribution. Eventually all technologies will converge onto one platform, probably in some sort of virtual or hand-held device.

The Future of Supply Chain Technology

If we look out ten to twenty years, the future of supply chain technology looks quite promising. The smart money is on three main technologies; that is Bluetooth, virtual reality/artificial intelligence, and enhanced cell phone technology. As Stephen Hawking, the world famous theoretical physicist stated in *A Brief History of Time*, "There will be a *Grand Theory* that encompasses all theories and helps to explain the Universe. " The same will be said for supply chain technology. A holistic, virtual, and even thought-controlled warehouse with driverless trucks is not out of the question. This will help to consolidate technologies into one major platform that provides total order visibility with real time tracking of goods and orders.

There are ten (10) major areas that will be impacted by technology, including:

- **Telecommunications**
  Pocket sized cell phones with lightning fast computing power and a standard global frequency will be the norm. No more SIM cards, global phones, or paying ridiculously high roaming charges while traveling abroad. In fact, your supply chain will be managed remotely using nothing but a cell phone.

- **Computers**
  Computer clock speed will see a quantum leap over the next ten years as new super chips take hold. Trillions of instructions per second will speed-up information throughout the supply chain as key performance metrics gets communicated each and every minute. You will be able to manage your business from anywhere in the world without leaving the comfort of your home.

- **Travel**
  Hypersonic, scram-jet technology will dramatically increase the speed of air freight and human transport. Travel from Los Angeles to New York will drop from five hours to one. Globalization will become the standard practice for most companies as the world continues to shrink. Rail will also speed up and it is highly likely that a new form of human transport will surface (most likely an air turbine tunnel that "swooshes" travelers from Los Angeles to San Francisco in fifteen minutes).

- **Global Focus**
  Research and development and new products will be focused on the global marketplace from inception. Packaging, language, size, and pricing will be driven by the global nature of the economy. 3D design, enhanced CAD, and virtual package design will be the norm.

- **Monetary Systems Consolidation**
  Further collapse and consolidation of the global monetary systems will cause trade to speed up between nations. It is likely that North America will collapse into one monetary system just like the EU. Trade barriers will be eradicated and political structures will consolidate. This will cause the concept of a "global supply chain" to take-on new meaning. Technology will be forced to include real-time traceability from points all over the globe. Remote asset tracking of inventory and freight will be commonplace.

- **Standard Metrics Worldwide**
  Fuel, Bar-coding, RF, and RFID will finally see a worldwide standard for key metrics. The USA will adopt liters, meters, etc. and worldwide electrical systems will finally converge (no more silly electrical adaptors carried in your briefcase as you travel around the world). This will allow a global product to quickly move throughout the supply chain and gain acceptance worldwide in weeks versus months.

- **Driverless Trucks**
  Yes, driverless trucks and operator less forklifts. Humans will be replaced by technology and freight will move at three times the current speed without the need to adhere to hours of service restrictions.

- **People-less Warehousing**
  People will be replaced with AGV's, robots, and artificial intelligence. Vertical warehouses that take up less space will be run by only a few humans. Eventually we will see most warehouses adopt automated putaway, picking, loading, etc. in an attempt to remain competitive.

- **Alternative fuel vehicles including electric cars that can travel 1000 miles**
  Electric cars and trucks will finally have batteries that allow for long distance travel. Hydrogen powered and other forms of alternative fuels will finally gain acceptance worldwide. Fuel consumption of gasoline and diesel will plummet as more and more global corporations strive for improved sustainability efforts.

- **Delivery**
  Every mode of transportation will witness a dramatic increase in speed and efficiency. Drones delivering products to individual customers will take the place of standard delivery. Ocean freight will see the most dramatic change as new technology and lighter weight materials will speed up boat travel. Zero emission, carbon-fiber trucks getting fifteen miles to the gallon will be commonplace.

Each of these technologies will spill over into the supply chain increasing efficiency and productivity by reducing human touches while increasing inventory and order velocity. The end result will be total order visibility with two-hour delivery to customers. Ordering will be done through interactive devices, even tablet driven television, by global customers who experience customer service in their own language and the ability to return products no matter where the origin. Exciting stuff!

Conclusion

Technology will radically change the course of supply chain management. Global supply chain managers will be able to use their thoughts to drive computers and virtual reality. Robots and AI will dominate the warehousing and material handling industries. Speed to market and customers will create differentiation between competitors. And finally, seamless integration across entire supply chains will permeate throughout the globe. This rapid pace of technological change will modify the way we approach supply chain management; that is, information will drive the business, not the other way around. Key metrics will be reported instantaneously causing businesses to react much faster than ever before. In summary, technology will continue to drive the evolution of global trade and will be the catalyst for quantum leaps in supply chain performance.

Chapter Summary

- Supply Chain Management, technology is any equipment, machine, robot, artificial intelligence, system, application, or even software that helps to improve process and/or labor efficiency.

- Technology is broken down into five (5) distinct categories: tangible, intangible, high, intermediate, and low.

- Total product life cycle logistics attempts to link functional areas together cohesively in order to make smarter and better supply chain decisions.

- In order for technology to be effective, it needs to be seamless, connected, and holistic in design.

- There are three (3) levels of technology used to run a business: enterprise resource planning software, facility management systems, and distribution management tools.

- A technology plan should be documented, including a detailed evaluation method for new technology.

Exploratory Questions

1. Why do so many technologies fail?

2. What should be the main goals for any new technology?

3. Why is a technology plan so important?

4. Why do you think so many people are afraid of new technology?

5. Why is supply chain technology integration so critical?

Case Study and Questions

SB is a supermarket chain with more than 150 stores. SB was struggling with numerous distribution related problems, including:
- Late deliveries to stores
- Excessive fuel consumption
- An increase in delivery costs as a percent of sales
- Increase in inbound (from suppliers) freight expense.

The management at SB decided they needed to stop the bleeding and get serious about becoming the "low-cost" provider of high quality service to the stores. At the same time, the management was seriously considering outsourcing the delivery system to a third-party, even though that might entail gross layoffs which the company has historical avoided.

We were asked to evaluate the current delivery system and to recommend any technological solutions we deemed appropriate for the SB culture and environment. During our evaluation, we uncovered the following data:

- On time delivery to stores was tracking at 82%, on average, for the recent 6 months
- On time delivery was being tracked incorrectly as the measure being monitored was on time dispatch
- The actual on time performance was 69% during the same 6 months when calculated correctly
- Fuel consumption was 6% higher than the expected fuel economy given the truck/engine type
- There was no monitoring or governing of vehicle road speed
- No standard trip times per route were being tracked
- Driver wages had climbed an average of 12% in the most recent 3 years
- Inbound freight expense was up 6% as compared to the previous year
- Delivery expense as a percent of sales had also increased 10% over the past 3 years.

This data, while alarming, could easily be fixed using technology. We were asked to evaluate various technological solutions. After careful consideration and much debate, we made the recommendation to employ two types of technologies; computerized routing/dispatch (territory planning) and OBC's (on board computers for trucks). By integrating these technologies through a simple data bridge, SB would be able to develop standard trips times per route and feedback daily historical data such as:

- Cases delivered per hour
- Departure and arrival times by store
- Stops per hour and day by driver
- Delay time by reason code
- Actual trip time versus planned time by route
- Actual miles by route compared to plan
- Speeding events by driver for every route
- Average speed by driver

- Average miles per gallon by truck and driver (ranked highest to lowest)
- Driving habits by driver
- GPS location of every truck and trailer.

The systems were run in parallel with the manual dispatch process for the first thirty days. There was some driver resistance at first as the technologies were being viewed as "watch-dogs." By posting individual route performance (best to worst) in the dispatch office and creating an incentive program for the best performing drivers, the drivers policed themselves. Nobody wanted to be at the bottom of the list. After six months of tweaking both systems, SB realized the following:

- MPG increase of 7%
- On time delivery soared to 92%
- Backhaul revenue increased 18%
- Resource requirements dropped 10% (trucks and drivers)
- Cases per hour and stops/day also increased.

The distribution group went from goats to heroes. In fact, the distribution group was recognized at the annual sales meeting for the first time in the history of the company.

Case Study Questions:

1. Why do you think SB wasn't able to clearly identify the problem?

2. Who do you believe is at fault here; management or drivers?

3. What might be the ancillary benefits associated with reducing mileage and road speed?

4. Why is tracking on time delivery to stores more important than monitoring on time dispatch?

5. What other technology may have been employed to further increase productivity and reduce paperwork?

12 SUPPLY-CHAIN NETWORK DESIGN AND OPTIMIZATION

"A camel is a horse designed by a committee."
Sir Alec Issigonis

Supply chain design and optimization (SCDO) involves modeling the entire network in order to minimize infrastructure costs while maximizing service. The ability to optimize inventory across the entire chain using minimal infrastructure will lead to significant efficiencies and improved customer satisfaction. SCDO also involves long-tail analysis of product families to help identify low volume, low margin, and high variability products that might be leading to increased operational costs. Analyzing product families, optimizing inventory, and minimizing infrastructure costs is all part of network planning and design. Network planning and optimization is the overall goal of SCDO.

The purpose of this chapter is to provide a high-level understanding of the key tenets surrounding SCDO. The primary goal here is to present the major steps to take in order to establish the current network design and costs, and then compare it to a redesign of the network that minimizes the number of buildings and the inventory required to satisfy sales. This chapter includes the following:

USING YOUR SUPPLY CHAIN AS A COMPETITIVE WEAPON

- Definition of supply chain design and optimization
- Why bother with SCDO?
- Understanding supply chain complexity
- The importance of supply chain segmentation
- Designing the optimal operational strategy
- The Hierarchy of SCDO Planning\
- Network Planning
- The SCDO Modeling Approach
- SCDO Gap Analysis
- The Future of SCDO

Definition of SCDO

The physical supply chain consists of suppliers, plants, warehouses, distribution centers and depots, and customers. This infrastructure holds raw materials, WIP inventory (work in process), and finished goods. These materials and goods flow between facilities and get shipped in order to ultimately meet customer demand. SCDO attempts to find the right balance between costs and service in the configuration of the supply chain network.

The definition of supply chain design and optimization is *"a holistic approach to network planning that optimizes service while minimizing costs."* SCDO has three (3) main goals:
1. Correctly positioning the appropriate and minimal amount of inventory to satisfy demand.
2. Utilizing the minimal amount of effective resources and infrastructure to get the job done.
3. Matching supply and demand in an uncertain environment.

Why Bother with SCDO

SCDO is hard work. It requires a ton of data collection, detailed modeling and analysis, and even a little change management. So, why bother with SCDO? The reason is simple; SCDO delivers best-in-class performance at minimal cost. SCDO attempts to answer the following questions:

1. What is the appropriate (minimal) number of facilities?
2. Where should the facilities be located?
3. What should be the size and capacity of each facility?
4. Where should inventory be best positioned?
5. What customers should be serviced by which facility?
6. What resources level is needed to accommodate the infrastructure?
7. What should be the delivery frequency and service level to each customer?
8. Which transportation methods should be employed?

SCDO also allows organizations to analyze "what if" scenarios that question the likely outcomes associated with facility consolidation, route re-engineering, and inventory redeployment.

SCDO has become important due to product mix changes, constant changes to demand patterns, and the seemingly never-ending mergers and acquisitions that continue to cause industry consolidation.

Understanding Supply Chain Complexity

Network planning is a complex process that involves infrastructure design, inventory positioning, and resource allocation. Supply chain design and optimization is further complicated by product specifications, delivery methods, and the need to align the customer value proposition with your network strategy. In addition, the supply chain is affected by many outside influences, including:
- Geographic shifts in demand
- The legal and regulatory environment
- The volatile price of fuel
- Intense service level requirements
- Product life cycle expectations
- Domestic rivalry and global competition
- The general economy
- Knockoffs and intellectual property infringement

These factors exacerbate the complexity associated with managing a global supply chain. Needless to say, supply chain management is now a critical part of overall business strategy.

Importance of Supply Chain Segmentation

Another important aspect of supply chain design and optimization is the idea of segmentation. Supply chain segmentation starts with the understanding of the customer value proposition. The customer value proposition defines how each end-user utilizes and interacts with your product. When designing and optimizing a supply chain, it is critical to start with the customer in mind. The basic question you must ask is, *"how can our supply chain provide a unique customer experience such that it results in a sustainable competitive advantage?"*

Supply chain segmentation consists of five (5) steps, including:

- **Define the customer value proposition.** The value proposition includes an understanding of the types of customers you best serve, the markets you best compete in, and an explanation of your unique product/service offering.

- **Align the customer value proposition with your supply chain strategy.** As can be seen in Exhibit 12.1, major firms such as Amazon and Wal-Mart carefully define their company value proposition then align their supply chain strategy around this value statement.

- **Evaluate the product or service portfolio.** The point here is to analyze customer demand, lead times, delivery frequencies, and each and every SKU (stock keeping unit) to determine poor performing products, and unnecessary and/or unusually stringent service levels. A cost to serve model as described in Chapter 7 on inventory control should be used to ferret-out underperforming products and/or unprofitable customers.

- **Leverage opportunities across the supply chain.** Look for synergies, consolidation opportunities, and process simplification throughout the supply chain by modeling the baseline cost and performance then performing "what-if" analysis to determine areas of improvement. The main areas to analyze include product design, sourcing and procurement, warehousing, and distribution and logistics.

- **Employ key metrics that support the strategy and value proposition.** After you have carefully identified areas of opportunity within the supply chain, it is important to monitor the key initiatives by employing sound performance metrics to ensure success. Chapter 10 details many of the measures that should be used to track supply chain performance. A few of those measures include:
  - Warehouse expense as a percent of sales
  - Distribution expense as a percent of sales
  - Cases/Hour (warehouse and delivery)
  - Cost/Order (to process orders)
  - Cost/PO (procurement)

Source: Adapted from the article, Supply Chain Optimization, OPS Rules. All rights reserved.

Exhibit 12.1 - Customer Value Proposition and Operations Strategy

Customer Value Proposition	Example	Operations Strategy
High fashion content at a reasonable price	Zara	Speed to Market
Everyday low pricing	Wal-Mart	Cost Efficiency
Product selection and availability	Amazon	Efficient and Reliable Order Fulfillment
Product innovation	Apple	Efficiency through Outsourced Manufacturing and Logistics
Customer experience	Dell Direct	Responsiveness to Configure to Order

Source: Ops Rules Management Consultants. All rights reserved.

Designing the Optimal Operational Strategy

The supply chain network strategy must be fundamentally based upon demand and customer location. The optimal operational strategy attempts to configure the logistics network in a way that minimizes total system-wide costs, including:
- Fixed facility costs
- Storage and handling (inventory carrying) costs
- Transportation and freight expenses
- Sourcing and purchasing costs
- The cost of customer service (in-stock availability, on-time delivery, etc.).

The operational strategy should include a detailed look at the following:
1. The number of suppliers being used.
2. The overall sourcing strategy (where suppliers are located).
3. The number of production facilities.
4. The number of and size (capacity) of warehouses and depots.
5. The amount of inventory being held at each facility (and where it is being held).
6. The number of trucks or carriers used to deliver product.
7. Which warehouse should service each customer?

The key here is minimization. The supply chain should employ the *minimum* number of facilities, inventory, and overall infrastructure to meet customer requirements. It is a fine balancing act that requires a complete understanding of the tradeoff between cost and service. Historically, the adage "the customer is always right" drove many companies to add infrastructure in an attempt to be closer to the customer. Big box retailers demanded stringent service levels that required an increase in inventory levels and fast and reliable transportation. Essentially, if a customer demanded one case to be delivered on a Sunday at an unusual time, supply chains all over North America responded by over-reacting and over-spending to keep customers happy. Those days are gone! Today, it is smarter to collaborate with key suppliers and customers to minimize costs while adhering to reasonable yet aggressive service levels. Before adding a new warehouse or an additional route to the network, supply chain managers must ensure that there are no other alternatives. Adding infrastructure should be the last resort.

Hierarchy of SCDO Planning

SCDO and network planning should be conducted at a number of planning levels. These levels include Strategic, Tactical, and Operational. Exhibit 12.2 reveals the various types of planning and the corresponding time horizon.

Exhibit 12.2 - Levels of Planning

Planning Level	Purpose	Time Horizon
Strategic	To identify overall company goals and objectives, including plans for growth and new products. To define the SCDO approach including resource allocation and infrastructure requirements.	3-5 years
Operational	Defines the resources (labor, capital, and technology) required in order to meet strategic goals.	1-3 years
Tactical	Layouts specific initiatives that will help accomplish the operational and strategic goals.	6-12 months but revisited each and every year in order to modify or add more tactics

At the strategic level, SCDO attempts to meet all of the edicts and overall mission/vision of the firm. The strategic level deals with accommodating growth and expansion (both new products and new markets). The strategic level also delves into legal and regulatory issues and any geographical shifts in demand.

The operational planning level of SCDO incorporates the directional aspects of the strategic level and the timing of the events within the tactical level. The operational planning level should include workload scheduling, vehicle utilization and scheduling, inbound and outbound freight considerations, and the technology requirements that will assist in meeting overall company goals.

The tactical level is where the everyday tasks get identified. Tactical initiatives should be identified that will allow the supply chain function to fulfill all the operational and strategic targets laid out in the other planning levels.

Network Planning

Network planning and design has a long-term impact on a firm's profitability and sustainability. Network planning and design determines the physical configuration and the amount of infrastructure within a supply chain. Network planning helps to provide customers with the right product, in the right amount, at the right time, in the right place; all at a reasonable cost.

Strategic network planning takes a look at overall infrastructure costs and weighs the tradeoffs between three (3) critical cost variables: facility/fixed costs, inventory, and transportation in order to pinpoint total overall supply chain costs. Exhibit 12.3 shows the cost relationship between these variables. As the number of warehouses increase, inventory costs rise while transportation cost/unit (not necessarily in total dollars) decreases. Of course, the more warehouses, the higher the fixed building expense. The key to network planning is to find that delicate balance between warehouse and inventory costs and transportation expense.

Exhibit 12.3 - Total Supply Chain Infrastructure Cost Tradeoffs.

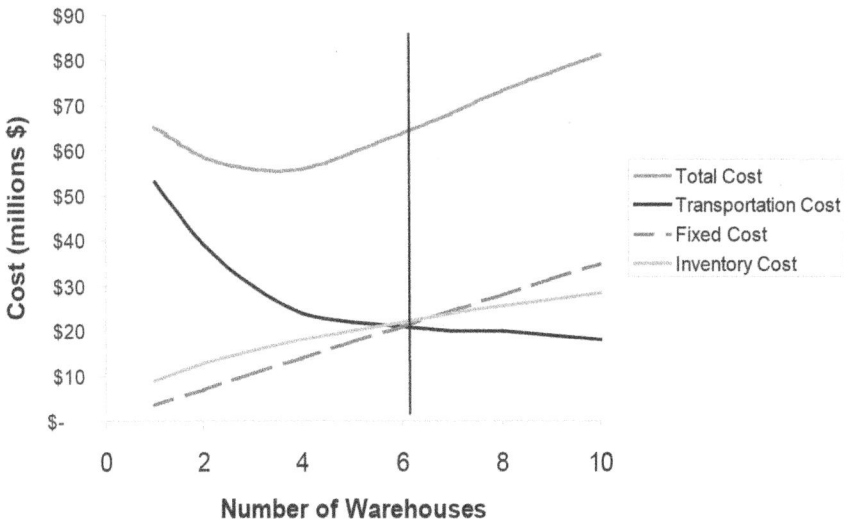

Network planning attempts to design the supply chain infrastructure in a way that minimizes cost while maximizing customer service. Network planning increases profits and optimizes service. There are a number of factors that influence network planning including:
- Globalization and foreign sourcing and production
- Geographical shifts in demand
- Demographic shifts in the population
- New market entries
- Escalation in energy and sustainability (go green) costs
- Government regulations and changes in the legal environment
- International product life cycle shifts
- Global competition
- Real estate prices
- The general economy.

Network planning is a detailed process that requires continual updating. It should be conducted at least every two years. At the highest level, network planning consists of:
1. Documenting the existing network configuration.
2. Establishing the baseline costs of the existing network.

USING YOUR SUPPLY CHAIN AS A COMPETITIVE WEAPON | 265

3. Identifying the current distribution patterns and customer service requirements.
4. Modeling of annual operating costs of the existing network.
5. Evaluating alternative solutions and configurations to determine the impact on cost and service.

There are three (3) hierarchical steps to the network planning process:

Exhibit 12.4 Network Planning Hierarchy

Network Design
- Number, locations and size of manufacturing plants and warehouses
- Assignment of retail outlets to warehouses
- Major sourcing decisions
- Typlical planning horizon is a few years

Inventory positioning:
- Identifying stocking points
- Selecting facilities that will produce to stuck and thus keep inventory
- Facilities that will produce to order and hence keep no inventory
- Related to the inventory management strategies

Resource allocation:
- Determine whether production and packaging of different products is done right at the facility
- What should be the plants sourcing strategies?
- How much capacity should each plant have to meet seasonal demand?

Source: Designing and Managing the Supply Chain,
Chapter 3, Simchi-Levi and Kaminsky.

Network planning is part of overall supply chain design and optimization. A more detailed approach to supply chain design and optimization follows.

SCDO Modeling Approach

Supply chain design and optimization takes network planning to the next level. SCDO is an all encompassing approach to implementing business strategy. It helps to explain exactly how you intend to execute your distribution strategy. SCDO is about modeling various infrastructure scenarios to determine which design best accomplishes the company mission while maximizing profits and service. As mentioned in Chapter 1, SCDO is a quantitative and qualitative approach that uses quantitative and qualitative methods to minimize infrastructure, process, and delivery costs while maintaining service levels. SCDO is a methodical approach to minimizing total delivery system economics. SCDO has two (2) primary objectives:

a) To identify the cost of the existing infrastructure.
b) To develop alternative infrastructure ideas to reduce cost while improving service.

Here are the sixteen (16) steps to the SCDO process:

1. Define the SCDO project scope and objectives. Scope should include business units and divisions to be involved, product categories that will be included or excluded, and the time horizon. The project should include some high-level objectives such as percentage reduction in supply chain costs.

2. Establish the design assumptions. Assumptions should be developed for factors such as sales growth, labor costs, the price of fuel, freight rates, etc. A sensitivity analysis that details a range for each assumption should also be included in the data gathering.

3. Complete a SCDO Questionnaire (exhibit 12.5) for the existing network profile.

Exhibit 12.5 - Supply Chain Design Questionnaire

1. Business Description: Describe your industry and business model.

_____
_____
_____
_____

Which best describes your core business (check all that apply):

Shipper ☐ Manufacturer ☐ Raw Material Supplier ☐ Reseller ☐
Freight Forwarder ☐ Transport Provider ☐ Wholesaler ☐

2. What is the main product or service you provide? _____

3. Which business functions do you support?

Distribution ☐   Warehousing ☐   Manufacturing ☐
3rd Party Logistics ☐ Other ☐ (Please describe):_____
Sales ☐   R&D ☐   Finance ☐

4. Describe your competitive advantage:

Customer service ☐   Service Offering ☐   Unique Product ☐
Size ☐   Industry Experience ☐   Location ☐   Financial Strength ☐
Brand Recognition ☐   Market Reach ☐   Other (Please describe): ___

5. Demand Requirements:

Customer demand is geographically: Local ☐   Domestic ☐
                                    International ☐
Customer destinations are: Static ☐   Change Regularly ☐
                                Change Dynamically ☐
Customer order patterns are: Predictable ☐   Unpredictable ☐
Customer order quantities are: Stable ☐   Variable ☐
Customer delivery times are: Flexible ☐   Fixed ☐
                                Very Tight ☐   Loosely defined ☐

Customer territories are: Grouped by city/province ☐
                         Not Used ☐   Other ☐
                         Grouped by sales territory ☐
                         Grouped by postal code ☐
                         Other (describe):_____
Do you offer vendor managed inventory to your customers
                         Yes ☐   No ☐

6. Supply Requirements:

Do you have a choice in suppliers or supplier locations: Yes ☐ No ☐
Do you manage inbound freight of supplier goods: Yes ☐ No ☐
If not, does the cost of the product include freight? Yes ☐ No ☐
Do you participate in Vendor Managed Inventory? Yes ☐ No ☐
Do you utilize forecasting or inventory management tools? Yes ☐ No ☐
Describe any seasonal differences:
   Cost ☐   Supply ☐   Delivery patterns ☐
   Freight methods ☐   Supply locations ☐   Sales Curve ☐

   Other (describe):_____
   Number of inbound suppliers: _____

7. Distribution and Freight Requirements:

Your freight control includes: Inbound ☐   Outbound ☐   Both ☐
Are delivery requirements: Hourly   Daily   Weekly Monthly
Other: (describe):_____
Are returns (packaging, outdated product, damaged product) a component of the transport environment?   Yes ☐ No ☐
If "Yes", is this component integrated:
   With Delivery/ Pickups ☐ Separately ☐

Cross Dock: Yes ☐   No ☐
If "No", is this a strategy for future consideration?   Yes ☐   No ☐

What modes of transport do you currently use or will use in the future:
   Air ☐   Rail ☐   Truckload ☐   LTL ☐   Pipeline ☐
   Ocean Freight ☐   Courier/Express ☐   Private Fleet ☐

Total number of annual miles if private fleet: _____
Does the time associated with border crossing play a significant role in your transport decision? Yes ☐ No ☐
What percent of transport time is attributed to border crossing delays? ___
Do you include customs, tariffs, and duties when calculating freight costs? Yes ☐ No ☐
Do you work with freight forwarders: Yes ☐ No ☐
If you outsource transport, how many carriers are used _____

What areas of transport are you interested in studying:

- Individual customer profitability ☐
- Mode selection by lane, product and customer ☐
- When, where and what to outsource ☐
- What level of service is appropriate given transport options ☐
- Carrier selection or monitoring ☐
- Minimizing transport costs ☐
- Bid evaluation ☐

What percent of overall distribution costs are attributed to inbound freight: ____
What is the warehousing cost as a percent of sales? ____
What is the outbound delivery expense as a percent of sales? ____
What is the overall inventory costs as a percent of sales? ____

What is the TOTAL SUPPLY CHAIN COSTS as a percent of sales? ____

8. Facilities

How many locations?

Suppliers: ____ Plants/Manufacturing: ____ DC/Warehouses: ____
Depots ____ Cross Docks: ____ Other (list): _____

Are all facilities full service (carry or produce all products)? Yes ☐ No ☐

Identify cost components measured:
    Production (e. g. : handling, labor, production, storage)
    Handling
    Storage
    Inventory
    Fixed
    Other (list): _____

Are all facilities owned? Yes ☐ No ☐

If "No", which are not owned: _____

What is the lease payment structure: Per unit ☐   Per Month ☐
                                      Per Square Foot ☐

Other: _____

What percent of distribution costs are attributed to facilities: _____

9. Products

Number of product categories that are delivered: _____

Is it possible to ship all products together? Yes ☐ No ☐
If "No", describe the shipping characteristics of each product group (frozen, hazardous, etc.): _____
_____

Do all products have the same facility costs? Yes No

Unit of measure by Product: Weight ☐   Pallets ☐
                              Cube (Volume) ☐   Boxes ☐
                              Container ☐   Vehicle% ☐
                              Revenue or Product Cost ☐
                              Pieces (units or count) ☐

\# orders/month: _____
\# active SKU's: _____
\# orders/loads shipped per day: _____

10. Shipping Profile:

What is the cycle of shipping: Weekly ☐   Monthly ☐   Daily ☐
Bi-Weekly ☐   Quarterly ☐
Bi-Quarterly ☐   Other: _____
Does this differ by product type or customer: Yes ☐ No ☐
Average demand (volume): _____
Average number of deliveries per customer per time period: _____
Does volume vary by season describe): _____

_____

11. Production:

Is production multi-stage   Yes ☐ No ☐
Do you sell components of manufactured end products: Yes ☐ No ☐
Do you outsource some production: Yes ☐ No ☐
Do end products share components: Yes ☐ No ☐
Do end products share production resources: Yes ☐ No ☐
Are manufacturing costs significantly different by end product:
Yes ☐ No ☐
Is manufacturing time significantly different by end product:
Yes ☐ No ☐
Is inventory a concern in the manufacturing process: Yes ☐ No ☐
Is the market value of different end products significantly different:
Yes ☐ No ☐
Is market demand significantly different by end product: Yes ☐ No ☐
Do you produce to stock or to orders: _____
What percent of distribution cost is manufacturing? _____

12. Measurement Indices

How is customer service measured? _____
_____
_____
_____

List supply chain functional performance indices and KPI's (include warehouse, distribution, etc.):_____

13. Systems and Technology

Please list systems/technology used in operations or planning

- ☐ Computerized Routing_____
- ☐ Inventory Planning_____
- ☐ Demand Forecasting_____
- ☐ Market analysis_____
- ☐ GPS/On-Board Computers_____
- ☐ Financial_____
- ☐ ERP/MRP/DRP_____
- ☐ WMS _____
- ☐ Load planning_____

Other: _____
_____

4. Gather specific network profile data, including:
   - Active Customer addresses (zip plus 4 if available)
   - Customer order size and sales profile data in dollars and units
   - Annual demand by product for each customer location
   - Supplier addresses and volumes/capacity
   - Plant and Warehouse addresses, capacity, and current volumes/throughput
   - Cost/Unit produced, warehoused, and distributed/transported
   - Warehousing costs, including inventory costs, fixed costs, and labor
   - Individual route information, including stops, mileage, and trip times
   - Customer delivery frequency and windows (available delivery times by customer)
   - Order processing costs (cost/order)
   - Transportation rates by mode (cost/unit, cost/mile, and in total dollars/units)
   - Annual fixed and variable costs for leased or private fleet of trucks
   - Annual mileage by vehicle

- Truck/Trailer capacities.

- *Note*: Be sure to develop a standard unit of measure across all functional areas (i. e. convert all measures to cost/unit). When gathering costs data, it is important that all expenses are collected:
    - Purchasing: Cost/PO, labor, administration, supplier volumes
    - Plant: labor, equipment, technology, fixed cost of facility (total cost)
    - Warehousing: labor costs, material handling, fixed cost for buildings (total cost of facility)
    - Inventory: carrying cost, redeployment/transfer expenses
    - Transportation: mileage, fuel, driver labor, carrier (LTL and Truckload), truck expense
    - Order processing: labor, telecommunications, technology
    - Customer Service: labor, telecommunications, technology
    - Current space and capacity for all plants and warehouses
    - Delivery frequencies by customer, delivery windows by customer

5. Geo-code (find latitude and longitude using mapping program) all addresses and develop individual and combination maps for:
    - Supplier locations (Map 1)
    - Plant locations (Map 2)
    - Warehouse locations (Map 3)
    - Customer locations. (Map 4)
    - Supplier and Plant Locations Combined (Map 5)
    - Supplier, Plant, and Warehouse Locations (Map 6)
    - Warehouse and Customer Locations (Map 7)
    - Total Network Map (suppliers, plants, warehouses, and customer – Map 8).

Be sure to include all distribution routing to/from all origins and destinations on each map.

6. Aggregate the customer and product data into zones and clusters to simplify the maps and the costing. By using aggregated data, a clustered set of customers is replaced with one large customer at the center of the cluster. Product aggregation is whereby goods originating from the same source and going to the same destination are grouped into clusters. The maps in exhibit 12.6 reveal customer and product aggregation. In most cases, the difference in costs between aggregated and disaggregated data are negligible.

Exhibit 12.6 - Customer and Product Aggregation

Customer Aggregation based upon 3-digit zip codes

Total Cost: $5,796,000
Total Customers: 18,000

Total Cost: $5,793,000
Total Customers: 800

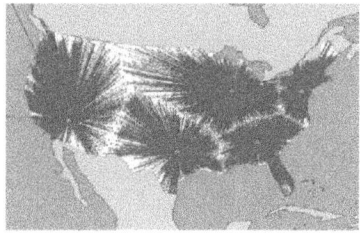
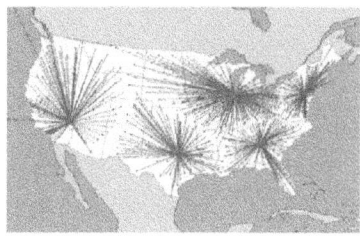

Cost Difference < 0.05%

Product Aggregation

Total Cost: $104,564,000
Total Products: 46

Total Cost: $104,599,000
Total Products: 4

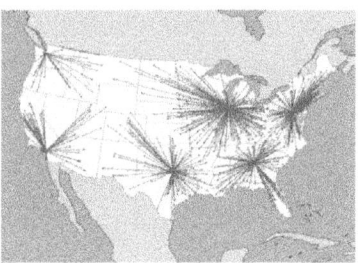
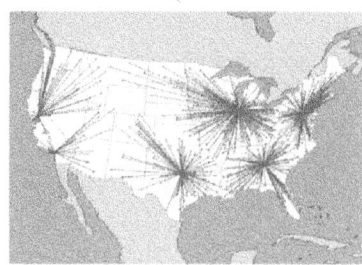

Cost Difference: 0.03%

Source: Designing and Managing the Supply Chain, Chapter 3, Simchi-Levi and Kaminsky.

Note: There are sophisticated modeling tools that do allow for the use of non-aggregated data. Aggregation is normally used when the number of customers and/or products is extremely large.

7. Baseline existing supply chain network costs, calculating the total cost for fixed facilities, inventory, warehousing, and delivery. When dealing with transportation costs, be sure to include both internal fleet costs and external (third-party) transport expenses. Transport rates tend to be linear with distance but not with volume due to increased weight. Compare the output of costs from the model to the firm's accounting information. The objective here is to calculate the total cost of the existing supply chain configuration and gain acceptance that these costs are consistent with what is being reported by Finance.

8. Develop a list of "what if" scenarios. What if scenarios might include:
    a. What if we shut down a warehouse?
    b. What if we move or consolidate production?
    c. What if we redeploy inventory?
    d. What if we service a customer out of a different facility?
    e. What if we direct ship from the plant to the customer?
    f. What is the optimal number of warehouses which results in the lowest cost?
    g. What if we relocate/move a facility to a different location?
    h. What if we add capacity to a plant or a warehouse?

9. Enter all the data into a SCDO modeling tool. Decide on the method for evaluating the outcomes, including:
    a. Using heuristics to find decent solutions but not necessarily the optimal answer. Heuristics are an experienced based educated guess or rule of thumb. An example of a heuristic is the "dart method." After completing the maps, and being able to view the entire network, one of the simplest ways to determine a possible solution for a consolidation or shutdown initiative is to use the dart method. The dart method is simple, but is only used as

a starting point. You basically take the geocentric center of first, the supply volume, and then the demand. After that, you "throw an imaginary dart" into the center of the centroid of the supply and demand. This is usually a nice way to get a sense for what the data are telling you. Heuristics based solutions are used when time is of the essence and when an exhaustive approach is impractical. Exhibit 12.7 shows an example of using the center of demand (dart) method.

Exhibit 12.7 - Heuristic Approach to a Network Consolidation Question

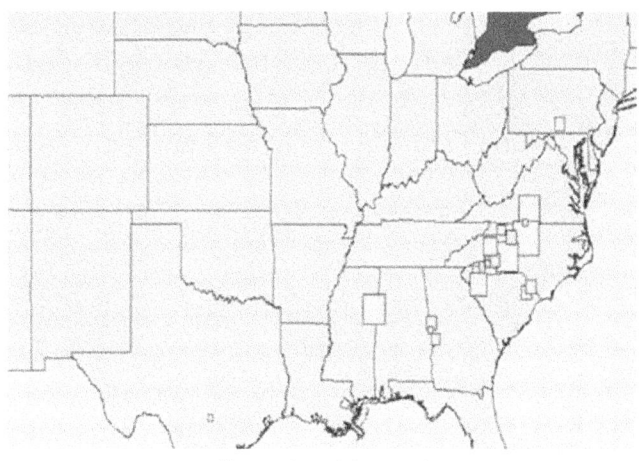

Suppliers sized by Volume

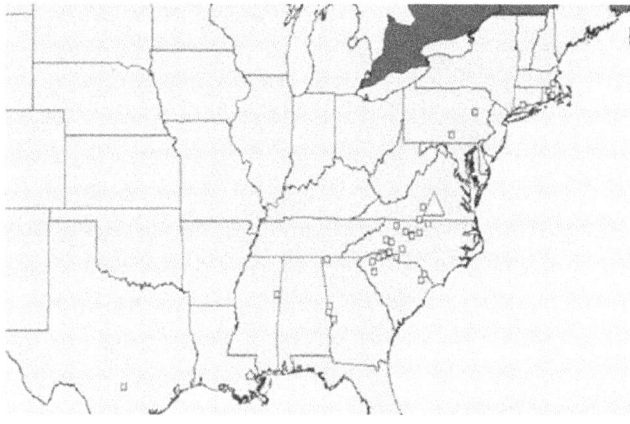

Geographic center of supply

USING YOUR SUPPLY CHAIN AS A COMPETITIVE WEAPON | 277

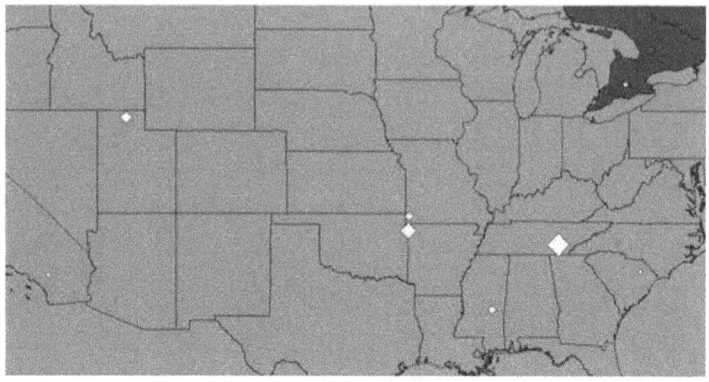

Plants scaled by production volume

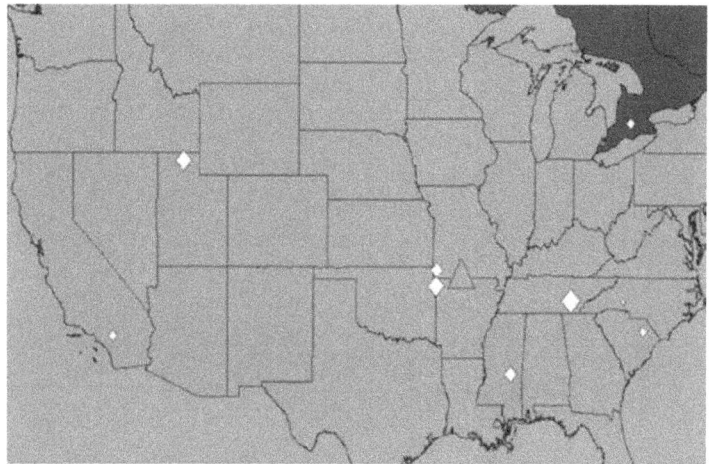

Geocentric center of demand (plants).

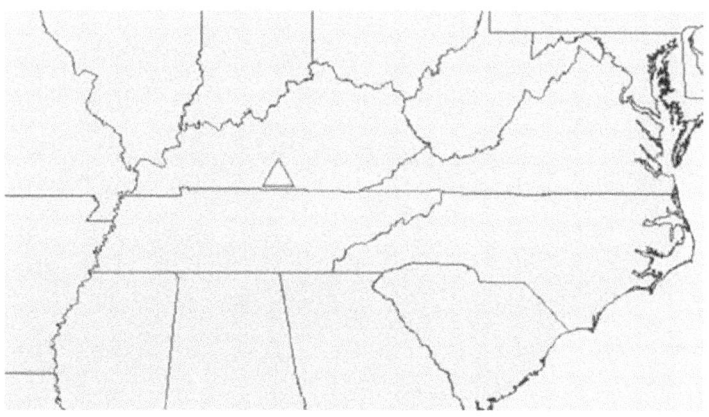

Geocentric center of supply and demand.

a. Using exact mathematical algorithms to find the optimal solution. Most network modeling tools use algorithms and sophisticated mapping software to precisely pinpoint the optimal solution to each what if scenario presented within the model.

b. Using simulation modeling to emulate the existing and newly configured network design. The simulation technique showcases how an alternative network design might behave in terms of cost and service.

10. Run scenarios, usually starting with employing one mega-facility in lieu of numerous warehouses. Another scenario is normally to run an unconstrained optimization that pinpoints a candidate pool of locations It is also usually wise to find the optimal number and location for warehouse facilities, being careful to emphasize the minimum amount of infrastructure. Exhibit 12.8 reveals an unconstrained candidate pool of locations when considering consolidating from three facilities to one centralized location.

Exhibit 12.8 - Unconstrained candidate pool of consolidating to one location

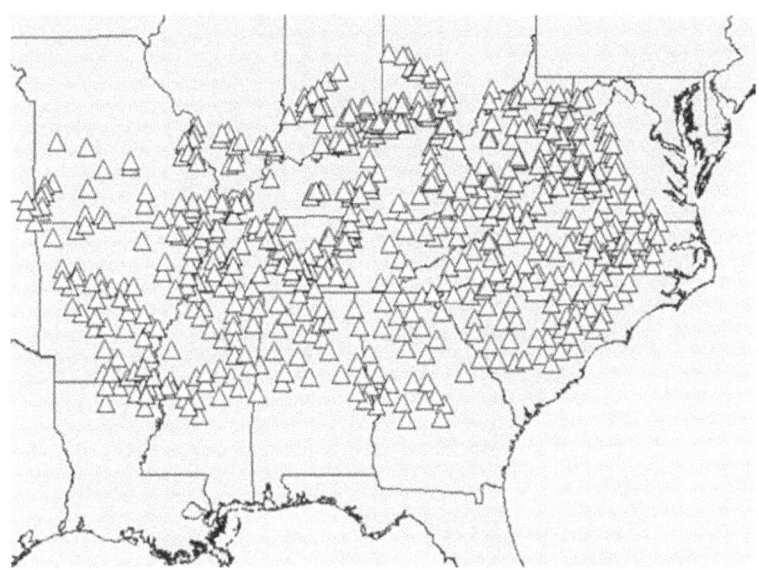

11. Rationalize the scenarios by considering the following cost factors:
    - Optimizing inventory deployment and minimizing inventory levels
    - Freight and Distribution mode optimization and load consolidation
    - Accommodating future sales growth and new product introductions
    - Improving service by ensuring customers are assigned to the correct warehouse

12. Compare scenarios to each other and the baseline in terms of cost and impact on service.

13. Add other considerations such as skilled labor by City, real estate cost/square foot by City, legal and regulatory concerns, human resource issues, transition costs, highway access, rail access, etc. Exhibit 12.9 shows an example of typical rail and highway access.

Exhibit 12.9 - Sample rail and highway access.

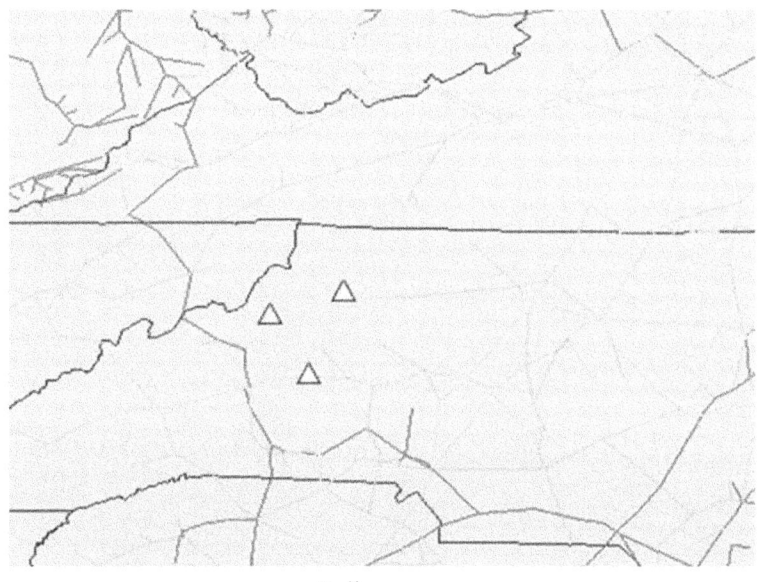

Rail access

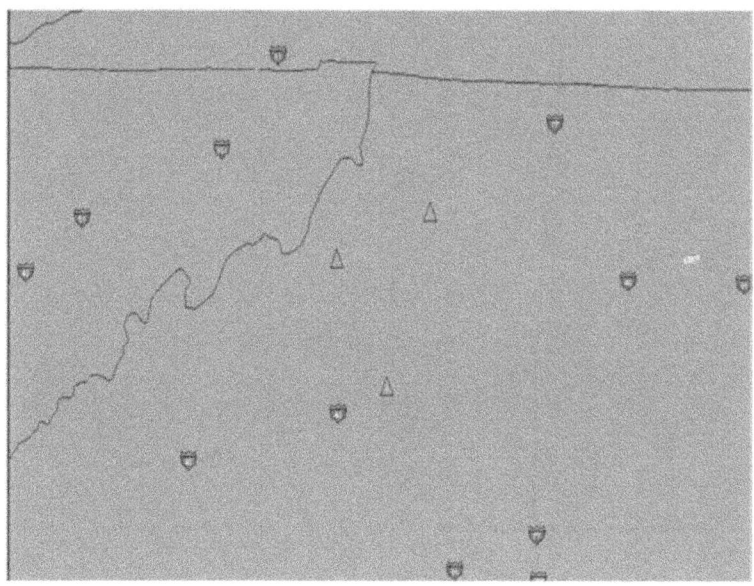

Highway access

Other considerations include:
- National resource availability
- Acceptance by senior management and the general public
- State and local taxes and regulations
- Free trade or federal empowerment/enterprise zone availability
- Federal work opportunity credits
- Sales, use, and real estate tax incentives
- Availability of skilled labor
- Job training and State sponsored programs
- Possibly assigning customers to warehouses based upon maximum allowable distance (and time to service; for example, all customers to be within 150 miles from a distribution center).

Do not underestimate the importance of these factors. It is suboptimal to choose a facility based solely upon the costs/labor associated with the new facility. In many cases, the non-cost factors outweigh the costs when comparing two to three facilities that are close in total cost. In addition, it is fairly common to gain local tax or labor incentives from a particular City that may tilt the analysis in favor of an ostensibly more costly alternative.

14. Choose the optimal solution to the chosen what if scenario based upon costs, service, and the considerations outlined in step 13.

15. Develop estimated cost savings net of transition and severance costs, if applicable. When calculating the alternative facility or a new location of an existing warehouse, it is imperative to include the cost to shut down the old building, any labor/severance expenses, relocation costs, inventory transfer costs, and any new building lease or ownership expenses

16. Develop an implementation and monitoring plan, including key measurements to ensure project success. Typically, cost/unit and cost as a percent of sales are key measures to consider.

SCDO Gap Analysis

Total order cycle time from customer order to delivery is a critical measure that needs to be considered when conducting any SCDO study. Without an understanding of how the alternative network will impact customer service, you might be saving operational dollars at the risk of losing sales. If customer requirements are not included in the SCDO study, a service gap may occur after implementing the newly designed network. To ensure customer satisfaction, a Gap Analysis, which attempts to balance cost and service, should be included prior to implementing the final supply chain design. The gap analysis reveals the impact that the new design has on two (2) major factors; cost and service.

Generally speaking, as total order cycle time increases, profits tend to decrease. The gap analysis chart in exhibit 12.10 shows the tradeoff between days of delivery (waiting time) and costs. A gap analysis attempts to determine the right combination of total distribution costs that will deliver maximum service given the proposed facility.

Exhibit 12.10 - Gap Analysis

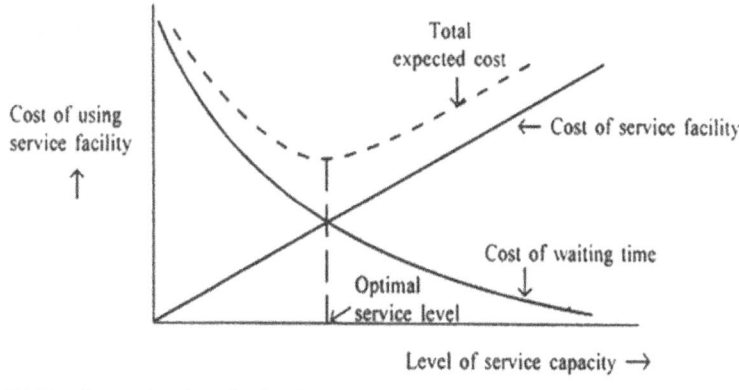

Waiting line cost and service levels

Waiting line cost and service levels
Source: www. transtutors. com

The point here is prior to finalizing your network, a pre and post "days of delivery" and total order cycle time analysis must be conducted. Simply compare the estimated new total order cycle and days of delivery to the current network, then survey the top ten percent of the customer base to query them on the proposed change. Be careful here as many large and demanding customers may threaten moving to the competition if a proposed new facility is situated too far away from the customer's delivery point.

Another aspect of supply chain gap analysis is to develop a set of baseline metrics to compare against known industry benchmarks for superior performance. Exhibit 12.11 provides an example of a supply chain gap analysis that isolates certain key performance indicators and reveals how they compare to industry standards.

Exhibit 12.11 - Supply Chain Performance Gap Analysis

Data Points	Orders/Person Hour	Inventory Turns	PO's/Man Hour	Vehicle Utilization	DC Units/Man-Hour
Volume/Data	300K Orders	$700MM Sales	47K PO's	3.5K Loads	1.2MM Units
Current Performance	40/PH	3 turns/year	22 PO/PH	.82 Utilization	12 Cases/PH
Resources Required	7.5K Hours	$233MM	2.1K PH	4.3K loads	100K PH
World Class Performance	50/PH	5 turns/year	30 PO/PH	.95 Utilization	20 Cases/PH
World Class Resources	6K PH	$140MM	1.6K	3.7K	60K
Estimated Savings	$45K	$28MM	$17K	$1.8MM	$1.0 MM

The analysis reveals the difference or "gap" between world class performance and the current execution. The idea here is to identify the weak areas within the supply chain, then implement specific initiatives to improve the performance to world class level.

The Future of SCDO

The future of supply chain management is quite exciting. Supply chain managers will play a much more significant role in overall business strategy. Global supply chains will become points of competitive difference between rivals. Total global order visibility and complete end-to-end system integration will be the norm. Third party relationships will play a critical role in overall supply chain execution. At the same time, technology will allow supply chain managers to completely control plants, warehouses, and distribution remotely and wirelessly. In summary, supply chain management will become a more valuable part of business strategy. So, what's next? Here is what you have to look forward to when thinking about the future of the exciting world of supply chain management:

1. Service will become a major point of difference. In fact, service differentiation will become more important than the product being delivered.

2. Supply chain management employees will become more global and untethered from traditional corporate structure. Supply chain managers will work remotely and wirelessly from all parts of the world.

3. There will be an accepted and more formal certification process for supply chain managers. Although certification currently exists, the future certification will have the prestige of a doctorate degree.

4. Velocity will become the most critical key performance indicator (KPI). Total order cycle time compression, increased inventory speed, and super-fast delivery will become the norm for best-in-class supply chains.

5. Technology will separate the winners from the losers. Total global order visibility and complete end-to-end systems integration will be commonplace. Technology will create

6. The ability to deliver products in hours not days. The entire supply chain of most companies will be overhauled as artificial intelligence and robotics take the place of most human tasks. Even the trucks of today will look and perform quite differently in the future. For example, consider the WAVE (Wal-Mart's Advanced Vehicle Experience) initiative that Wal-Mart is currently undertaking. According to Wal-Mart, the vehicle runs on a "prototype advanced turbine-powered, range-extending series hybrid powertrain (or microturbine-hybrid powertrain) combined with an electric motor and battery storage system. " This means that the

engine can be powered by many different sources, including diesel, biodiesel, natural gas, "and probably other fuels still to be developed." The carbon-fiber design will dramatically improve fuel economy and drastically reduce greenhouse gas emissions.

Exhibit 12.12 - Wal-Mart WAVE Truck Technology

Courtesy Wal-Mart.

7. Social Media will play a crucial role in supply chain management (customer service). Social media will influence inventory policy, returns management, and pricing strategy.

8. Micro-segmentation will play a major role in the understanding of customer behavior. Target market defining and ethnic diversity will change the course of marketing and distribution. Products will be sourced from all over the world in order to satisfy a changing consumer base.

9. Sustainability and go-green efforts will play a central role in supply chain strategy. Social consciousness surrounding health, recycling, reusability, improving the environment will become part of the strategic planning effort.

10. Virtual businesses will once again become the central approach as more and more firms attempt to completely

eliminate infrastructure and "brick-and-mortar." At my alma-mater, PepsiCo, we used to joke about eliminating all the plants, warehouses, and trucks such that when a consumer turned on a faucet in their home, Pepsi Cola would come out instead of water.

11. Supply chain prowess will become the reason why customers buy from a particular company.

Conclusion

Proper supply chain design and optimization can be the difference between mediocre and superior profitability performance. Proper network planning improves inventory positioning, increases customer satisfaction, and reduces overall infrastructure and distribution costs. Although SCDO is a difficult project to undertake, it is an extremely worthwhile effort that pays significant dividends in the long term. In addition to reducing costs and improving service, SCDO will also help to remove functional barriers and will ultimately improve company teamwork. The whole key to SCDO is to understand the baseline cost of the existing infrastructure as compared to the proposed network. At the same time, significant consideration should be given to the impact that the newly designed network might have on customers. Annual SCDO studies will become the standard practice for progressively run companies as further globalization will continue to complicate network decisions. In fact, supply chain design and optimization specialists will surface as critical players in corporate strategy.

Chapter Summary

- The definition of supply chain design and optimization is *"a holistic approach to network planning that optimizes service while minimizing costs.*

- SCDO has three (3) main goals:
    1. Correctly positioning the appropriate and minimal amount of inventory to satisfy demand.

2. Utilizing the minimal amount of effective resources and infrastructure to get the job done.
3. Matching supply and demand in an uncertain environment.

- Network planning is a complex process that involves infrastructure design, inventory positioning, and resource allocation.

- Supply chain segmentation starts with the understanding of the customer value proposition. The customer value proposition defines how each end-user utilizes and interacts with your product.

- There are three (3) levels of supply chain planning: Strategic, Operational, and Tactical.

- The optimal operational strategy attempts to configure the logistics network in a way that minimizes total system-wide costs

- Network planning and design determines the physical configuration and the amount of infrastructure within a supply chain.

- SCDO is an all-encompassing approach to implementing business strategy.

- Customer and product data aggregation is a way to simplify the SCDO modeling process.

- A supply chain Gap Analysis attempts to balance cost and service and should be conducted prior to implementing the final supply chain design.

Exploratory Questions

1. Why is a SCDO and network planning project so difficult to conduct?

2. What are the five (5) major steps to network planning?

3. What outside factors influence network planning?

4. Who should be involved in a SCDO project (which functions within the company should be represented)?

5. What are the two (2) primary goals of supply chain design and optimization?

6. What is meant by a Supply Chain Gap Analysis? How can a supply chain gap analysis help to improve performance?

Case Study and Questions

DF is a leading food and beverage company with distribution centers located throughout the United States. DF was struggling with the increased cost of distribution within the State of Texas. Senior management was concerned about the recent increase in cost/unit and distribution costs as a percent of sales. At the time of the study, DF had two plants servicing the Texas market, along with trucks domiciled at each location. DF decided to undergo a SCDO Study that would have the following objectives and key goals:

To optimally reconfigure the Texas supply chain infrastructure based upon customer demand requirements and supply chain capacity and resources.

To determine the impact that performing deliveries using a combined single fleet of vehicles would have on customer service and satisfaction.

To identify potential savings from the modification to the supply chain infrastructure.

DF requested a simple SCDO methodology that "would be understood at all levels of the organization." To that end, the team assigned to the project, developed the follow process steps to isolate the key steps to the SCDO study:

1. Develop project goals and objectives and solicit project approval from senior management.
2. Develop the initial set of "what-if" scenarios that clearly identify the business case for the study.
3. Collect data on costs, capacity, resources, and inventory.
4. Aggregate the data to simplify the mapping of the current state.
5. Develop a baseline of the current network costs and service execution.
6. Revisit the what-if scenarios to determine if modification is needed based upon the data.
7. Run scenarios to determine the impact on cost and service.
8. Choose the optimal scenario that properly balances cost and service.
9. Develop an implementation and transition plan.
10. Implement key measures to ensure success of the project.

The team gathered data surrounding fixed costs of the plants, labor, capacity, route-level delivery costs, and customer frequency and delivery windows (including individual stop duration by customer). The data were reviewed first separately by plant, and then combined. The routing and fleet data were key data points. The route level data reviewed included:

- Number of routes from each facility (using an agreed upon fifty hours/week/driver)
- Total time, on average, to deliver a complete route over a two-week period
- Total miles driven
- % Drive Time
- % Unload/Service Time per Stop
- Number of total stops
- Fuel consumed for each route

- Aggregated product and customer data (frequency of delivery, time windows, volumes).

The study quickly uncovered that a combined solution would offer significant costs savings. Consolidating the two plants into one mega-plant and utilizing a central fleet of vehicles would save DF on the order of $2.5 million/year net of transition and severance costs. In addition, the impact on service levels was considered negligible. An additional benefit to the study was that DF could now design the new mega-plant in a way that would improve sustainability efforts, improve productivity through an enhanced layout and design, and reduce the amount of overall material handling "touches."

Case Study Questions:

1. Why is a SCDO study such as the one undertaken by DF "easier said than done?"

2. What other factors do you think DF considered when combining the plants?

3. What human resources issues did DF face when making the decision to combine plants?

4. What type of incentives can be used to bolster employee morale when an organization decides to shut a facility or combine routes?

EPILOGUE

So, there you have it. A practical guide to supply chain management. It is my hope that this work provides you with the major tenets that will drive supply chain success, ultimately providing your firm with a sustainable competitive advantage. As mentioned earlier, the entire point of this book is to get your network to the point that customers choose your company due to your supply chain prowess. Supply chain management will clearly be a function of critical importance to most global firms, creating points of difference between competitors. As we look out in time, supply chain managers will undoubtedly become more educated, more sophisticated, and will be held in higher esteem by multinational firms. Technology will continue to surprise us and provide the critical linkages between supply and demand. In fact, I speculate that there will be another quantum leap in technology to the tune of the creation of the Internet. I simply can't wait.

Supply Chain Exercises

These exercises should be used in a group environment, preferably with members from a variety of departments. You should time each exercise, allowing approximately twenty (20) minutes for each session. In addition, it is usually better to have someone act as a facilitator, pushing the groups to completion.

Exercise One: Make an airplane exercise

Divide the audience into at least two (2) groups. Each group must assign a spokesperson who will share results with the larger group. Instruct the first group that they are to act as design engineers who have been tasked with manufacturing a new commercial jet that transports passengers from Los Angeles, CA to Sydney, Australia. The engineers must keep cost in mind when designing the new plane. They should consider things such as size, speed, and amenities. The second group is instructed that they are consumers and do not need to consider costs. The sky is the limit here. After each team spends 10-15 minutes designing their new airplane, the spokesperson for each group explains their new design.

You will notice that the engineers will design a less than consumer friendly plane with a few decent amenities. The consumer group will ask for the craziest amenities and will demand a design that is totally impractical.

There are two (2) learnings here:
1. Businesses should always listen to the customer.
2. The cost/benefit tradeoff associated with design will clearly impact the supply chain. That is, depending upon the design, functions such as supply, sourcing, inventory, etc. will be impacted in a significant way.

Exercise Two: Glass Egg Packaging

Divide the audience into groups of 5-6 people. Assign a spokesperson for each group and allow 10 minutes for the brainstorming portion of the exercise. Explain that they are to design a package that would allow a glass (or crystal) egg about 10 inches high to be dropped from a two (2) story building such that the egg would not shattered upon impact with the ground. They are allowed to be creative and suggest anything, but must consider the cost to purchase and ship the package they have designed.

There are two (Z2) important concepts to discuss:

1. The impact that upstream functions such as packaging and design have on the backend of the business (shipping/freight).
2. The tradeoff associated with cost and design.

Exercise Three: Network Design

You have been asked by your company to completely review the entire supply chain network, including:
1. Establishing a baseline of costs.
2. Graphically representing the existing network.
3. Deciding the optimal number of DC's.
4. Deciding upon the optimal location of the DC's.

You have been told to 'use a clean-sheet-of-paper' and that there are no resources or monetary constraints.

  a. What people would you put on the project team? Which departments?
  b. What outside people might you add to the team?
  c. What factors must you consider before choosing the optimal locations?
  d. What data might you gather to complete the project?

Exercise Four: Supply Chain Downstream Impact

ABC Company forecasted the following for the upcoming year:
- Sales growth of 6% (but the actual results were a 1% drop in sales
- 2 new product introductions (actually introduced 3 – and all failed)
- Market share increase of 2% (actual performance was no share increase)
- Profit per unit increase of 1% (actual was a 3% reduction in profit per unit)

1. List the downstream effects by individual function (i. e., warehousing, inventory, distribution).

2. How might tight inventory control & improved forecasting somewhat mitigate the losses?

3. How might price & product availability impact this situation?

Exercise Five: Inventory Control

ACME Food Company has the following issues:
- $6 million in inventory
- 2,000 total SKU's
- $500,000 in obsolete inventory
- 350 inactive SKU's
- Average inventory on-hand @ 9 months

1. How might you stratify the inventory?

2. What initiatives would you employ to improve the inventory control and profitability?

Exercise Six: Forecasting

- List the major causes of forecast inaccuracy
- List the challenges associated with forecasting
- List the major benefits of proper forecasting

SUBJECT INDEX

A

application of technology 22, 69, 119, 139, 240–242, 245
automated picking 187, 212

B

backorders 18, 31, 46, 48–49, 53, 56, 95, 100, 117–118, 137, 139–140, 146, 216
balanced scorecard 226–227

C

carrying cost of inventory 23, 31, 46–47, 53, 123, 139, 150
cause and effect diagram 37
cost to serve modeling 119, 126, 217
cross-docking 133, 146, 149–151, 208, 220
customer service policy 77, 84–85, 87, 90–92, 122, 138
customer service tradeoff 79
cycle counting 17, 24, 120, 128, 137–138, 185, 215

D

definition of SCM 76
demand forecasting 100, 272
design and optimization 16, 119, 124, 256–259, 266, 286–288
distribution strategy 142, 151–152, 176, 180, 266
dynamic storage 181, 188–189

E

economic order quantity 23, 46, 53, 126, 136, 138
economics of supply management 45, 53
evaluating new technology 241, 247

F

forecasting tools 110
forklifts 186, 194–195, 198–199, 201–202, 204–207, 211, 214–215, 246, 251
freight glossary of terms 164
freight management 16, 22, 63, 142, 164, 166–167

freight modes 165, 167–169, 177
freight rates 15, 153, 164, 169–170, 179, 267
future of supply chain 241, 249, 283

G

global sourcing 5, 25, 40, 51–54

H

heuristics 275–276, 278
histogram 38–39
hub and spoke 209–210

I

inbound freight 23, 49, 53, 142, 152–153, 164, 177, 210, 254, 268–269
integration 16, 26, 42, 45, 60, 76, 85, 96–97, 150, 213, 241, 243–244, 252–253, 283–284
inventory 2, 8–11, 14–18, 21–24, 26, 29, 31, 43–48, 52–53, 56, 61, 63, 78, 83, 87, 90, 94–95, 100–101, 113–140, 143, 145–152, 164, 175–177, 180–184, 186–187, 191–193, 207–209, 212–216, 218–220, 222–223, 228, 238–239, 243, 246, 248–249, 251–252, 256–258, 260–261, 263–265, 268–273, 275, 279, 281, 284–287, 289, 292, 294, 299
inventory best practices 133
inventory carrying costs 9, 29, 46–47, 56, 119, 125, 127, 208, 218
inventory drivers 119–120
inventory policy 114, 116, 118, 131, 134–135, 137, 139, 285

inventory stratification 129, 131–132, 135

K

key performance metrics 13, 16, 240, 247–248, 250
key ratios 137, 224, 230

L

levels of technology 241, 244–245, 253
life cycle costing 171, 173, 205
linear regression 99, 102, 104, 106, 109
logistics decision areas 142–143

M

material handling 2, 18, 83, 123, 132, 143, 180–181, 188, 193–195, 198–202, 204, 206–208, 211, 215, 218–220, 229, 232, 245–246, 248–249, 252, 273, 290

N

network planning 256–258, 262–266, 286–288
new product development 32–33, 52–53

O

order entry methods 80–82
order pattern recognition 82, 85
order picking 183, 185, 219
order processing 2, 11, 18, 23–24, 28, 63, 76–82, 87, 89–90, 101, 127, 143, 176, 220, 225, 228, 230, 238, 248, 273
outsourcing 15–16, 23, 52, 57–66, 68, 72–75, 140, 254

P

pallet jacks 186, 194–195, 202–206, 211, 214–215
pareto charts 35
perfect order 10, 77, 85–87, 90, 95, 114, 143, 219, 228
postponement 133–134, 208, 210
private fleet management 2, 63, 142, 170
product development process 32–33, 52
product life cycle logistics 241–242, 253
pull distribution method 149

Q

quality 4–5, 25–26, 28, 30–37, 40, 42–45, 52–57, 59, 62–63, 65, 67–68, 88–89, 91–92, 130, 134, 218, 225–226, 234, 236, 254

R

request for proposal 66, 68
request for quote 68, 169
reverse logistics 2, 16, 18, 30, 78, 88–89, 91–92, 142–143, 175, 177, 218, 242
risk pooling 146, 150–151
role of supply management 26–27
run plot chart 38

S

scatter diagram 37–38
slotting 127, 183, 188, 219
static storage 188
strategic alliances 65–66
strategic planning 19–20, 286
strategic sourcing plan 40–41, 52, 55

supplier decision matrix 43–44
supply chain activities 6–7, 11–12, 69, 93, 95, 225–228, 248
supply chain gap analysis 225, 231, 282–283, 288
supply chain technologies 23, 240–241, 243, 245–247, 249, 253
supply forecasting 98, 100

T

time series modeling 103–105, 109
total cost of ownership 30, 52–53, 205
transshipment 146, 150

W

warehouse layout 136, 190, 192–193, 200
warehouse management system 84, 134, 184, 186, 212, 220

RECOMMENDED READING

Designing and Managing the Supply Chain by Simchi-Levi, Phillip Kaminsky, Edith Simchi-Levi

Supply Management by Burt, Petcavage, and Pinkerton

World Class Supply Management by Burt, Dobler, and Starling

Supply Chain Strategy by Dr. Edward Frazelle

The Supply Chain Handbook by James Thompkins, Ph. D. and Dale Harmelink

www.ingramcontent.com/pod-product-compliance
Lightning Source LLC
LaVergne TN
LVHW061034070526
838201LV00073B/5031